straight
from the
source

straight

from the

source

AN EXPOSÉ FROM THE FORMER EDITOR IN CHIEF

OF THE HIP-HOP BIBLE

KIM OSORIO

NEW YORK   LONDON   TORONTO   SYDNEY

Pocket Books

A Division of Simon & Schuster, Inc.

1230 Avenue of the Americas

New York, NY 10020

First MTV Books/Pocket Books hardcover edition September 2008

POCKET and colophon are registered trademarks of Simon & Schuster, Inc.

For information about special discounts for bulk purchases, please contact Simon & Schuster Special Sales at 1-800-456-6798 or business@simonandschuster.com

Designed by Mary Austin Speaker

Manufactured in the United States of America

10 9 8 7 6 5 4 3 2 1

Library of Congress Cataloging-in-Publication Data is available.

ISBN-13: 978-1-4165-5968-9
ISBN-10:   1-4165-5968-X

This book is dedicated to Kayla and Kiana,
two little girls who will understand one day what it is to be women.

ACKNOWLEDGMENTS

This book wouldn't be possible without my family, who keeps me focused on what's important in life. Kayla and Kiana, and Kino for his neverending motivation, and for pushing me to write this. Mom, Wendy and Ashley (you're in the book!!). To my earliest reader, Tia, for invaluable input chapter after chapter. The prequel coming soon . . . jk. My father and Wela. Greg. The girls, Celena (Angie and the family), Rose (Eric and Dakota too), Minya, Shane. Tyrene and Aya.

Ken Thompson, Michelle Leroux, Doug Wigdor, Scott Gilly and the entire staff at TWG who put in countless hours towards my case for all the right reasons. Thank you to the jurors who sat through a very long trial. Oops, can I say that?

To my extended family. John, Marnie, Linda, Dave and the Domreis family. The Won family: Mingo, Marlene, Bimba, Tony and Magda,

Danny, Looney, Lil' Bimba, Lil' Crissy, Toussaint, Irma, Susie, Pito, Matt, Serena, Jimmy, Crystal, Darryl, Anthony, Bernadette, Danette, Uncle Tuso and the Felix family. Debbie and family, Aaron, Maggie and Joey and family, Philip, Cindy, Junior, Tommy, Jennifer. The entire Childrey family (won't name names 'cuz I'll forget someone), Al Tucker, Royce, Miko Wady.

Thanks to Chaka Zulu for giving me the book name months before I had it, James Cruz, Rhonda Cowan, Torrence (see!! I didn't forget), Carl, Nile, Tricia Newell, Michael Pickrum, Denmark, Diana, Reggie Hudlin, Keith Brown, and everyone at BET. Navarrow Wright, Russell Simmons, Blackspot and everyone at Global Grind. Datwon Thomas, Carlito Rodriguez, Adila Francis, Gotti, Boo, Sandra Guzman, Cara Donatto, Selwyn Hinds, Jon Schecter, Jermaine Hall, Elliott Wilson, Felicia Palmer, Steph Lova, Sibrena Stowe, Tionna Smalls. I'm forgetting people, I know. Biggs, Dame Dash, Angie Martinez, Kevin Liles, Manny Haley, KRS-One, Chuck D, Kanye.

There were people who despite knowing anything about me, took a stand (or the stand) against the injustices with me. Thanks to Joan Morgan, Jeff Chang, Liz Mendes-Berry and everyone who signed the petition. Clover Hope, Jeannine Outlaw, Sabrina Smith, Julia Beverly, Mos Def, Dream Hampton, Ahmir Thompson, Erica Ford.

The Fort Lee Starbucks on Lemoine where I spent countless hours writing. And to Anthony "Intern" Reynolds, who ran there for me whenever I needed a triple shot to keep me awake all night to write.

Last but definitely not least, thank you to my editor Lauren McKenna and everyone at Pocket Books, Jacob Hoye and MTV Books and Marc Gerald, all of whom believed in this story from the beginning. Also, Quinn Heraty, Erica Feldon, Felice Javit, Megan McKeever, and those who helped to make it happen.

And to all the women who have supported me and who go through the same type of stuff everyday. I hope this story will help you in some way.

straight from the source

time's up

Time moves too fast in the mornings. No matter how hard I try to be somewhere on time, I can never seem to get it right. But this morning, driving in New York City in the spring of 2003, it would probably help if I allowed myself more than ten minutes to get from New Jersey to lower Manhattan.

I pressed down on my car horn two times with both hands so that the yellow taxi in front of me got the hint. "Come on. The light is fuckin' green!" My windows are up, and no one is in the car with me. Basically, I am just yelling at myself.

The clock read half past six o'clock, and the radio was tuned to NYC's number one hip-hop radio station. "Hot 97, where hip-hop lives. This is the Renegade Radio," I heard Sway say over the airwaves. I was scheduled to do a live radio interview representing the *Source* magazine.

As the newly appointed editor in chief, the agenda was to promote the new issue, which had just hit newsstands that week.

My friend Miss Info was one of the jocks on the morning show with Sway, and since she and the *Source*'s owners were not exactly fond of each other, she hooked up the interview as a favor to me more than anything else. I typed out to her on my two-way pager, *I am 5 minutes away,* not factoring in the five minutes it would take to park my car and the additional five minutes that I would need to get past the security desk. Altogether, I was fifteen minutes away, which meant any hopes of my getting coffee before I went on the air were pretty much crushed.

I rushed out of the parking lot so fast that I almost forgot my ticket, then I checked in at the front desk. By the time I made it up the elevator, someone was waiting by the back door to take me into the waiting area. "You're going to go on in about two minutes."

Two minutes! *Ugh,* I thought. Not enough time to mentally prepare for an interview I knew could be tough. "Can I borrow this pad?" I asked the guy that walked me in.

"Sure." He offered me a pen to go along with it.

My mind was racing with questions that I anticipated they could ask. So I started to quickly jot down notes on the pad—points that I knew I had to hit and topics I knew I needed to avoid.

Benzino's beef with Eminem not connected to the magazine . . . Stay neutral and don't say anything bad about Eminem . . . or 50 . . . 50! Don't mention knowing 50 personally.

There was so much controversy involving the magazine's rivalry with *XXL*, Benzino's beef with Eminem, and Eminem's record label, Interscope, having pulled their advertising dollars from the magazine that I knew the real reason they'd agreed to have me on the show. This was morning radio. The point was to entertain the listeners by ridiculing the guests. They were not going to ask me anything I wanted to answer. They were not going to help me promote the magazine. That was my job. Their job was to get me to say something that I didn't want to.

"It's time," said the guy, who walked back in the room to take me into the studio. Two minutes had gone by in just one, I swore.

"Okay, I'm ready." I tried to cover up any signs of my nervousness, even though I knew he could see my heart beating through my coat. I'd done live interviews before—sometimes even on politics and shit that I didn't know the way I knew hip-hop or the *Source*—but I was more nervous than usual. And this was not even television, it was radio. Normally, all I had to worry about was not stuttering and making sure I used an SAT word every few sentences so I came off intelligent. But this time was different. I felt like Bill Clinton trying to avoid discussing whether I actually inhaled.

I could handle this, though. *Just stay on topic and never let them see you sweat,* I thought. What was I so nervous about anyway? Sway and I were cool. He would not even go there.

"Kim Osorio, editor in chief of the *Source* magazine, is in the room with us," Sway said, standing in front of the microphone, his long dreads standing behind him.

I sat down, put the headphones on one ear so I could listen to anything that went on in the room, and placed the pad with my notes in front of me. There were so many words on the page, but the number stood out like a sore thumb. The number 50.

Miss Info walked over to me from where she had just finished delivering her "celebrity drama" segment and sat in the chair to my right. She scribbled some notes on my pad, but I couldn't look down to read them because Sway had already started asking me questions.

After a couple of easy ones, I was in my comfort zone and had let go of any paranoid thoughts that I'd come into the room with. Then Sway, out of nowhere, straight violated my whole womanhood.

"You were sucking off 50 Cent?"

"Huh?"

"Didn't Eminem say something about you sucking off 50 Cent?"

"Eminem never said that. No."

"Isn't there a song where Eminem said you were on your knees sucking off 50?"

"No, I think you got that wrong."

"So you were never sucking off 50 Cent?"

"No."

What in the hell??? I started to write down on my notepad to Miss Info. That quickly, I was thrown off. I couldn't look Sway in the face because I didn't want to turn him to stone. I was so angry, Medusa had nothing on me.

Sway cut to a commercial, the on-air light went off, then he walked out of the room to take a break. Miss Info was on her feet. "I'm going to go talk to him."

In truth, it was too late to talk to him because he had already tried to blow up the spot. Did he even know anything about 50? How could I just ignore this now? If my coworkers, or even worse, my superiors, were listening, I was going to be humiliated when I got into the office. I had to calm down and figure out what had just happened.

First off, Sway was way off. I started to work it out in my head like an algebra problem. I've always been good at math, so I knew I could figure out the answer before we went back on the air. *There was an Eminem verse that mentioned my name, but Sway had the lyrics wrong. Wait, maybe this was a new song that he was talking about. Uh-oh. Oh no. No, wait. I know the song he's talking about. Sway's buggin'. That was the song where Eminem was talking about his wife, whose name happens to also be Kim. Damn it, why is her name Kim? "She's probably on her knees somewhere sucking off 50 Cent." He's not talking about me in that song. I should have said that on the air. The song that mentioned my name said something entirely different: "Kim Osorio, you sorry ho . . . drag you through the barrio." Or something like that. Say that on the air. No, duh, don't say that on the air, but clear this up.*

"Hot 97, we're back on the air with Kim Osorio, editor in chief of the *Source* magazine." Sway was back in the room, and the red on-air light was back on. Miss Info was sitting next to me and writing on my pad again. I felt I was in a time warp. This time, I had no choice but to pay attention to her and not him. *He's going to come back to it. Just stay calm. Treat it like they're men in the street whistling at you and you don't turn around so they just automatically call you a bitch. Stay professional.*

"So there is a song where Eminem mentions you, right?" Sway rephrased his question.

I knew that whenever I acted out of emotion it was usually the wrong thing to do. So now I just followed exactly what Miss Info was telling me to do. *Why is her handwriting so damn small?*

"You know what, Sway. It's, like, what's the first thing a man says when he's whistling at you in the street and you're not paying him any attention? He calls you out of your name. That's all that was. I've never even met Eminem."

That damn Eminem, look at all the shit he was about to start.

It's hard to laugh and joke around when you're as mad as I was at the station that day, but I somehow managed to ignore it and forgive Sway. I left the station immediately after the interview and went straight to the office, pretending it didn't all happen, but knowing it was at the top of everyone's mind and on the tip of everyone's tongue. I couldn't let anyone know just how much it bothered me to have been put on the spot like that. When you're in a position of power, you have to dust your shoulders off. You have to learn how to become immune to insults and expect the worst things to be said about you. Throughout my career at the *Source*, mud was slung so many times on my name, both inside and outside the office. Biggie said it best: "Mo' money, mo' problems." For me, though, once I became editor in chief, it was the problems that seemed to come a lot faster.

CHAPTER TWO

south bronx

Before I became editor in chief at the *Source*, I'd like to believe that I was a nice person. I said good morning to the receptionist each day when I got in, and I pretty much talked to everyone on the staff. Sometimes I was bitchy, but it usually only happened every twenty-eighth day. I distinctly remember that I got along well with almost everyone, whether the person signed my checks or answered the phones. I never had a problem with any of my coworkers, and I assumed the feeling was mutual. But while they smiled in my face, some people had ulterior motives.

Number 215 Park Avenue South was home to the *Source* when I began working there in 2000. By the time I had got the job of associate music editor, I had already been writing stories about hip-hop for years.

I'd been a part of the hip-hop community from as early as I could remember, but it wasn't until the nineties that I became a part of the "industry." Back then, in New York, the "industry" was extremely visible. It wasn't as exclusive as it is now. Puffy threw parties for the general community that weren't VIP or guest-list only. Videos were shot in the streets, not on boats or in foreign countries. And artists were more connected to their audience because they did such things as perform on college campuses or hang out at local nightclubs.

I was riding the #2 train downtown one day in 1993 after class at Fordham when I came across an ad in the *Village Voice* that invited me to "work in the Music Industry." It was a $6-an-hour internship to work for the New York sales team at BMG Distribution, the company that distributed record such labels as RCA, Loud, Jive, and Arista. I was so excited that I sent my résumé in the same day and had an interview within a week. I didn't get the job, but the lady in human resources liked me enough to give me some advice and to refer me to another department. She told me "never chew gum on an interview" and that "the national team is looking for someone to intern but they can't pay you."

I accepted the internship and was so excited to spend my own money and work for free just to be able to work in the music industry. But after interning and later temping for a year, I figured out that I was clearly not in the right circle. My passion had always been for hip-hop, and I was surrounded by mostly white industry bigwigs over fifty-five who thought rap was something that you do to Christmas gifts. Though it was great to be able to sit front row at a James Brown concert, I realized that I wasn't making the connections I needed to land the job that I wanted. I got glimpses of hip-hop when I met Method Man after Wu-Tang blew up or lucked out on a pass to A Tribe Called Quest's album-release party for *Midnight Marauders*. So when I realized there wasn't enough to keep me interested in my job, I jumped ship and wound up out at another internship at Profile Records. Only I still wasn't getting paid.

The one thing I remembered about Profile was that no one ever came to work, so while there was much to learn about the industry, I would not be learning it there. I had one assignment to stay on top of, and once the head of publicity explained what I had to do, I don't think I ever saw her again because she went off and had a baby. My job was to go through all of the magazines that came in and collect every piece of writing that mentioned any of their artists. There was quite a bit of negative press about Run-D.M.C.'s comeback album, *Down With the King,* and the staff was salty because they had lost the rap group Onyx to Def Jam, and now that the group had abandoned their dreads and started gun-talking, they were the biggest thing in hip-hop. I started to realize that Profile Records, once a legendary hip-hop label, had fallen off and I had boarded the bus too late. When it came to my job choices, this was my career strike number two.

Back then, I also realized that few minorities held power positions at record labels, and even fewer minority women. I can only remember one minority who worked at Profile, and that was DJ Funkmaster Flex. He had an office in the back, but I never *ever* saw him there. I learned early on that the movers and shakers in hip-hop weren't up in the offices sitting behind desks. They were out in the streets, at the clubs, on the radio, or in the studio making it happen. The common thread about most of the people who are successful in the rap industry is that they make a name for themselves in the streets and then the industry follows. Talib Kweli said it best once: "Artists by nature are followers." But the people behind the scenes are even worse. They usually just find out what's already hot and then latch onto it.

The secret was that you had to already be somebody in order to be somebody. Looking back, I can honestly say that not too many people I know are on top because they sent in their résumé or worked their way up from the bottom of the totem pole. I couldn't go out and get the job I wanted, I had to make the job come to me.

Before becoming a journalist, I always wrote as a hobby. I figured that I'd turn it into a profession and try my hand at that. And if there was one subject that I could write about, it was hip-hop.

Born in the seventies, I grew up in the Castle Hill section of the Bronx. No, not Jenny's block, but Randall Avenue. I moved there from 165th and Grand Concourse when I was about seven. I once went to the local record store when I was around five or six to buy a vinyl record that came in a light blue jacket with the words SUGAR HILL GANG written in big, orange script letters. As embarrassing as it might sound, I learned how to break-dance in the fifth grade off Chaka Khan's "I Feel for You." And though I wasn't very good at it, I could pick up speed in a backspin if it was over a dismantled brown cardboard box and I was wearing a windbreaker. By the time I got to the eleventh grade, I took the dancing thing way too seriously by doing the running man onstage to represent the junior class in a battle against other classes. That was off "Fakin' Da Funk" by Main Source, and I was the only girl onstage. I had my first one-on-one fistfight with someone who mistakenly thought I was going with her boyfriend behind her back, and it happened right around the time that Naughty by Nature decided it was okay to cheat on your girlfriend with "Other People's Property" (aka "O.P.P."). I lost my virginity to the same guy who later punched me and gave me a black eye when the Geto Boys' "My Mind Playin' Tricks on Me" made it cool or "in style" for him to act crazy. By the time I had gotten to the *Source*, rap music had already become the sound track to my entire life.

I believe it's a blessing to work at a job doing something you love. I come from a family of people who all worked hard to make ends meet. My parents met when they were in the fifth grade and stood together until they were married eight years later. My mother got pregnant with my older sister, Wendy, immediately after. Because my father already had a girl when I was born four years later, he always raised me as if I were the son he never had. We were not well-off in the beginning though. My father was a Puerto Rican middle-school dropout who ran numbers on the streets of Harlem for most of his life. He started when he was a teenager and was well liked in the neighborhood, both on the East and West Side. My grandmother once joked that he was the whitest baby born at Harlem Hospital in 1951. There was a time when my mother had to get on welfare to hold us over, but by the early eighties, my father's business starting picking up, and he was doing well enough to move us from the South Bronx to the Castle Hill area, which, for minorities, was like going from Brooklyn to the Hamptons. But after my father's long bout with alcoholism, times started to get hard and my mother had to go to work. She passed the test for the telephone company, a "good-ass job" when I was growing up.

The great thing about working in hip-hop is that you rarely hear people say that they hate what they do. They may actually hate the people they work for or hate what hip-hop has become, but essentially most people who work in hip-hop love it, not in the corny *Brown Sugar* movie sort of way, but in a way where the culture is embedded in their soul. Nowadays, I enjoy going to shows to see certain artists perform just to remember what it was like back then. Whodini, Slick Rick & Doug E. Fresh, KRS-One, LL Cool J, Run-D.M.C., that's the era of hip-hop that I grew up on. And that's the thing I have most in common with everyone else in my generation, from the struggling entrepreneurs to the superstar multimillionaries. All of us have seen hip-hop grow up into the business it has become today. I still get a little starstruck when I see the same artists I used to watch on *Video Music Box* with Ralph McDaniels. Channel 31. How many other girls do you know who can recite the lyrics to "Buggin' " by a group called Whistle? There's only a handful.

It seemed that it took forever just to get my foot in the door at the *Source* for a $45,000-a-year job. A job in either the music or the publishing industry is hard to come by. So trying to get into a music magazine doubles your chances at losing. At the time, the *Source* was the magazine that most hip-hop journalists such as myself aspired to work for. It had been there since the late eighties, '88 to be exact, growing up right alongside hip-hop. It was there throughout the culture's most significant moments—back when A Tribe Called Quest, De La Soul, and other Native Tongues groups turned African medallions into a fashion statement, or when N.W.A. and Ice-T turned the police into rap's biggest enemy, and even when the community turned on itself contributing to the deaths of Biggie and Tupac. If you had followed hip-hop for as long as the *Source* was around, then you had followed the *Source* too.

Me? I had followed the *Source* since its day as a one-page newsletter. And after I started writing professionally, I had hustled my clips enough to get the attention of some of the senior editors at the magazine. My first assignment came courtesy of Elliott Wilson, whom I had come to know from my many internships. We became cool enough that I felt comfortable calling him every month when I saw things worth debating, such as a 4 Mic rating for DMX's album *It's Dark and Hell Is Hot*. Then, after months of my asking for an assignment, Elliott needed a writer to interview Lord Tariq and Peter Gunz, a Bronx-bred rap duo that had blown up because of a hit record called "Déjà Vu." He decided to assign the story to a girl from the Bronx who was overly excited that the borough she'd grown up in was making a much needed comeback.

A few more key articles had proven that my knowledge of the music was worth more than any experience you could get working in the industry or writing for a magazine. Added to that, during an interview with the Roots at a studio in Philadelphia, ?uestlove produced a track on *Things Fall Apart* that he said in the album's liner notes was inspired by me, and I was starting to feel like a borderline celebrity. My writing, described by one *Source* editor as "unlikely for a girl," earned me a spot as a regular contributor to the *Source*. While I hustled my writing skills, I finished college and went on to law school. It is one of those things you do if you can when you don't know what the hell you want to do. If you can figure out a way to pay for it, education is the best excuse for not having a job.

Though I had a law degree that qualified me to take the bar exam and practice law, I was just an aspiring journalist to the *Source* team, one who had held more nonpaid than paid jobs. I had no formal journalism background and was considered a new jack to the writers and editors of my day. Advanced degrees held little weight when it came to hiring at the *Source*. For years, I had been hustling my way into the music industry. Once I decided to pursue hip-hop journalism, working at the *Source* became my ultimate goal. I freelanced and worked for so many different magazines that I confused myself every time I updated my résumé. There were *Billboard*, *Vibe*, *One World*, the *Resident*, *LatinGirl*, *BlackBeat*, *XXL*, and of course the *Source*, which always looked as if it were typed in a bigger font.

Carlito Rodriguez, the editor in chief when I came on board, hired me soon after he took the job. He had the office in the corner with the glass desk, the three big windows, and the holes in the wall that a previous editor in chief had left behind when frustration forced him to throw a chair at it.

My first office was small with no ventilation and a leather recliner that we called the "crack chair," which I inherited from Riggs, whom I replaced at the magazine. Someone in the office told me the story of buying it off a crackhead on the street for $5. It had a few rips on one side, but it served its purpose. Since we usually worked into the wee hours of the morning during closing (the time when the editing of a magazine is done and the pages are being prepared to ship by section to the printer), the crack chair doubled as a bed for me, especially when I was pregnant. These were the type of things that made the *Source*, well, unique.

During my first few months at the *Source*, I got pregnant with my oldest daughter, Kayla, while her father and I were living together in Brooklyn. I feel I didn't find out his government name until we were in a full-blown relationship, but he went by the name Mush. Mush was a hustler on the streets of Fort Greene, Brooklyn, who had missed his calling to be a basketball star. If he were a line in a Biggie record, it would be that he chose to sling rock *instead* of using his wicked jump shot. He is an extremely tall, light-skinned guy who totally got over on girls because of his looks. His money wasn't long by industry standards, but it came fast, and being raised in a household where my father hid thousands of dollars in his white sweat socks under the radiator in our house, I was used to seeing cash flowing in daily.

Mush and I were already having problems when I got pregnant, so I knew two months into the pregnancy that we would break up. But after I found out about a few women he had on the side, my vindictive side forced me to stay in the relationship just so I could turn the tables on him one day. It got to a point where I would answer his cell phone behind his back and take messages just so I could have a girl's name to throw back at him during an argument. *"Who the hell is Keisha?"* One time, I answered the phone and found out about a girl from out of town that he had been seeing longer than he had been seeing me. So she and I arranged to have me show up at the door of their hotel room the next time she came to town. Our dysfunctional relationship made it easier for me to stay at the office and log long hours at work. After a while, I became more comfortable sleeping on the crack chair in my office than I was sleeping next to him.

Kayla was born six years after my mother had my little sister, Ashley, from a second marriage. I lived in Brooklyn at the time, but barely saw Kayla's father. When I wasn't working, I'd take Kayla up to my mom's and stay up in the Bronx. For Kayla, it was fun to be there because Ashley was more like an older sister to her than an auntie. When I wasn't at my mom's, I'd drive two and a half hours to spend the weekend with my best friend, Tia, who had relocated to Delaware. Anything to get away from the drama of my failed relationship.

There's a time in a new mother's life when she learns how to live again, and a year into Kayla's life, I was ready to get my personal life back. I enjoyed my time as a mother and all the new experiences that came with it. But at a certain point, Avent bottles full of Similac and

Baby Einstein DVDs will drive you crazy. I needed an outlet. Work was exciting, but outside of work, I was bored out of my mind. I started hanging out with my friends again, and I started to meet people. Eventually, I started dating.

Dating within the confines of the music industry was not so out-of-the-ordinary to me or anyone else in my immediate circle. That's just how you meet people, especially when you spend most of your day working. Whom else are you going to get with? For men, it's simple. But for women in the industry, it's a little more complicated. Artists, managers, producers, engineers, A&Rs, DJs, they all fit into the same category for me. Men, however, don't necessarily see it that way. "Keep your legs closed" is their mandate to a woman if she wants to be truly successful. If a woman in the industry has a past (and God forbid it includes an artist), then she is typecast as a "groupie" or a "ho." Before I got to the *Source*, I'd already dated a DJ, a producer, an executive, and even a rapper, but because they were all either local or unsuccessful, and I was just a girl from around the way, no one seemed to care. Now, as an editor at the *Source*, my options were about to get a lot more high-profile, and my professional life was about to be compromised because of it.

By the year 2000, the hip-hop industry was comparable to a male football locker room. Most of the top music executives were men, the majority of hip-hop artists were male, as were almost all of the producers, video directors, engineers, and DJs. That basically left video model or personal assistant as the most likely career options for a woman. But as a female, if you were successful and rose to the top of the corporate ladder, your reputation became that much more vulnerable. If you looked halfway decent, then the misconception was that you slept your way to the top. On the contrary, if you were not easy on the eyes, then you must either have been gay or related to someone. As a woman, I knew it would be hard to beat the odds. But because I had put so much time in, I wasn't about to let the odds come between me and what I wanted.

But a woman doesn't only have her résumé to worry about, she's also got her reputation, and when it comes to a woman's reputation in the business of hip-hop, it's almost customary to define her by the men she's been linked to. Pick up any hip-hop magazine and compare the stories done on women to those done on men. I guarantee you'll find out more about the woman's past sex life than you will about the man's. That code doesn't just apply to celebrities, it's the same behind the scenes as well. For me, it was no different. The more successful I became in the industry, the harder it became to keep people out of my personal business.

My days and nights revolved around the magazine and around hip-hop, and my social network was composed of people who were just as obsessed with money, power, and hip-hop as I was. Therefore, the majority of the men that I met along the way had some sort of function in the music industry. But in this particular sect of the industry, known to us as the hip-hop culture, the usual double standard applied to women is administered in much bigger doses. Once Snoop said, "Bitches ain't shit," it was a wrap for us.

CHAPTER THREE

ladies first

By the time I got to the *Source,* I had already either met or known a third of the music industry either through the interviews I'd conducted, the clubs I hung out at, or the conventions that I went to. If it wasn't one of those three, then I knew them through one of my girlfriends. Growing up in New York, I always knew somebody who knew somebody if I didn't know him or her myself. Between my girlfriends in the city, someone had either dated or known someone who had dated pretty much every dude that was making records in the midnineties. We called it the "network," and if you met an industry guy from one of the five boroughs (or occasionally New Jersey and Mt. Vernon), we could send the information through the network and find out whom he'd dated, if he was good or bad in bed, and whether he had a girlfriend or baby mama back home. Six degrees of separation connected everybody on the New

York scene. Trying to come up as a writer, I figured out that the network was good for more than just the girls and our pathways of information. If I could find out information about someone for the benefit of the sisterhood, then that same information was probably good for my own career. I could document the information that I got from the network and make one hell of a story out of it. Where hip-hop was concerned, I had the access to everyone who mattered, and the information from everyone who didn't.

Many of my own girlfriends had their own industry connections. My closest friend, Tia Bowman, went to LaGuardia, the New York City school of the performing arts, otherwise known as the *Fame* school. She knew so many people in the industry by just having gone to high school with them. Tia and I met back when I came in to choreograph a routine for her City College cheerleading team (there goes my dream of being a fly girl actually getting lived out in my history). We got really close when we met up again at the bookstore at New York Law School. During law school, we found a way to balance case studies and legal briefs with impromptu trips to South Beach and frequent appearances at Club New York. From Diddy to Too Short to Jay-Z to members of the Wu-Tang, we hung out with some of hip-hop's most celebrated stars and other notorious street cats—names omitted for obvious reasons. From one week to the next, we were either throwing back shots of vodka, eating at Mr. Chow, or partying with somebody.

Another of my connected friends was Michelle Song [not her real name]. I became really close with her before I got my job at the *Source,* and through her I learned a lot about the magazine, which she had once written for. We met through a mutual friend, Anisa Hull, a Tommy Boy records sales rep, when we all hung out at a Wu-Tang album-release party. It was a hell of a night, especially when my hair had caught on fire after I leaned over a candle. I think the image of me with flames coming out of the left side of my head made Michelle feel bad for me. We kept in contact frequently after that. At the time, she was already the managing editor at *XXL,* the *Source*'s number one competitor, and since I was just a freelance writer trying to land articles in any of the few publications that existed, she looked out and gave me some writing assignments. She eventually wound up at *Vibe* magazine, before becoming a radio personality. She was a haven of information. She always had some random info about someone or something that made you wonder how she got it. That's just how she was. I could be looking into a mirror, poppin' a pimple, and she'd recommend an over-the-counter cream that could banish the zit in an hour.

Through our friendship over the years, I had learned about some of the violence, staff walkouts, and injustices that had made the history of the *Source* an untold story waiting to be made public. But by the time I joined the ranks, the staff had turned over so many times, things appeared to have changed. I believed it could never have been as bad as the rumors of employees getting guns pointed at them or women getting groped in the hallways. Though I do remember when I stumbled on a stripper giving a birthday lap dance to a male employee. The men were cheering her on while the women watched from outside his office door. Then all of us women were told to go back down to our side of the floor so they could proceed with the finale. I can only imagine what happened afterward.

When I first got hired, I saw little of the overtly machismo environment that was rumored folklore. Michelle was an intern during the *Source*'s early days, and she always warned me to "be careful" when dealing with Raymond Scott, otherwise known as Benzino, one of the magazine's co-owners. Ray barely came to the office when I first started working there, so I never really had to worry about the things I'd heard. I reported to Carlito; Nigel, the managing editor; and P-Frank, the executive editor, based on the West Coast; so I had few dealings with Ray and his partner, Dave Mays. There were company picnics when I said hello, and a few friendly conversations in the hallways, but no real interaction. I often saw Carlito stressed when he came out of Dave's office. Still, he balanced dealing with Dave and Ray and being the editor of the magazine pretty well.

In the beginning of my life at the *Source,* my career revolved around album reviews, artist interviews, and internal arguments over why Biggie was the better "MC" and why 2Pac was the better "artist." I was consumed by so much rap music that I wasn't privy to any of the inner office politics. Although I swore he forgot at times, Dave was Jewish, in his midthirties, and had shortened his Jewish-sounding last name to one that would be more acceptable in hip-hop. He had a pointy nose and white skin, but he could still pass for Puerto Rican if he cut his hair in a fade. Even though Dave founded the magazine with Jon Schechter and others, whom they later bought out, Benzino was the true power of the *Source.*

Ray Dog, as Benzino used to be called, was a struggling rapper from Boston who met Dave and became his silent partner back when the *Source* was launched. He was of mixed racial background, half-black and Latino of some sort. Throughout the years, Benzino was in Dave's ear like a bad infection—secretly calling the shots behind the scenes, mostly to the benefit of his own rap career. Most of the time, the decisions he was making weren't the best thing for the magazine, which had become a multimillion-dollar publication and the voice of an entire hip-hop generation. But it only got worse as the years went by. Benzino's influence on the magazine's editorial content was growing fast.

A few months before I was hired, Benzino's group Made Men had received a 4.5 Mic rating in the magazine. It was around the same time that Elliott Wilson had resigned, and I heard that the reason he had quit had everything to do with his being the music editor and disagreeing with the "proposed" rating. Things like that were almost understood in the industry. Anything printed in the *Source* relating to Benzino or any of his groups held little weight. Regardless of how the editors really felt, Benzino was never going to get criticized by the *Source*—not if you planned on working there long. His music was not held to the same standards when it was rated. The Made Men album had earned the same rating as albums such as the Notorious B.I.G.'s *Ready to Die* or Jay-Z's *Reasonable Doubt*. Most albums that received as high as 4.5 were recognized as some of hip-hop's best works. And to put Made Men in the same category as someone like Jay-Z was damn near blasphemy, especially when the album ratings were taken so seriously by the editors, the industry, and more important—the readers.

In 2001, it was quite unusual to get all five of the *Source*'s top editors to listen to one upcoming album to rate it, even when the artist showed up to play it for them. But inside a small room at what was then called Baseline Studios in Manhattan, Jay-Z had the full attention of all of us. He was the most prestigious rap artist at the time. The Almighty Hova. The God MC. One of the few rappers who truly knew how to straddle the line of underground and commercial success. And as a writer who made a business out of being critical, I always held back my pen when it came to saying anything negative about one of my personal favorite MCs, Shawn Carter.

Carlito felt that I should be among the four people to accompany him to hear Jay's highly anticipated fifth album, the *Blueprint*, which would have to be reviewed in one of my sections, known to avid *Source* readers as the "Record Report." It was the most important section of the magazine in that it was home to the coveted 5 Mics, an accolade that many rappers had aspired to achieve.

With Jay's first four albums, he had come close to earning that perfect rating, getting the praise for his quick wit and braggadocio lyrics, but missing the 5 Mic mark by a wack song or two. Many of us in the office, including Carlito, had argued that his debut, *Reasonable Doubt*, was worthy of 5 Mics, but once it had been written in print, there was no going back. We had to respect the minds of the earlier "Mind Squad," as the *Source* editors had always referred to themselves. Now, what we were hearing that hot summer day inside an air-conditioned studio with Jay-Z and his people had all the makings of a classic.

This listening session stood out from the rest. For one, no one was smokin' weed. And unlike most artists, who feel the need to preface each song with an explanation on who did the beat, how they picked the subject matter, and why the music lacked something (e.g., "It still needs to be mixed"), Jay-Z, dressed in a Che Guevara T-shirt complimented by a Nike wristband, said nothing. He played the music with no regard for what we thought. It was that "I don't give a damn about a rap critic but they better give a damn about me" attitude.

We all sat there quietly and attentively, one of my coworkers shut his eyes, listening to the *Blueprint* for the first time. We carefully selected our questions, while Jay briefly explained why he had chosen fairly new names, such as Just Blaze and Kanye West, to produce the bulk of the *Blueprint* CD. He also kept the guest appearances to a minimum. He had Q-Tip, Biz Markie, and Slick Rick delivering the chorus on "Girls, Girls, Girls" and had collaborated with Eminem on a song called "Renegade." We listened to back-to-back tracks from Jay-Z without getting bored or losing interest which was hard because the volume was so loud I could feel the bass underneath my feet. But one track in particular raised our curiosity. For a writer like me who thrives off controversy, this one would pique my interest most:

"Ask Nas, he don't want it with Hov . . . noooooo."

Jay-Z pushed down on one of the 30,000 buttons which temporarily interrupted the music blazing from the speakers. Jay looked around to his cohorts and let out his signature high-pitched giggle, and then, as if on cue, the room laughed with him. "We're gonna save that verse for next time." He tapped my foot, making it clear he remembered me from a previous meeting through a friend a few years prior. "Y'all not allowed to hear it just yet," he said, referring to the second verse of "The Takeover," a song over a beat by Kanye West that was treacherous. All of our expert ears were glued to it.

Skipping the entire second verse, Jay instructed the studio engineer to continue. Everyone in the room was nodding their heads to the rock-influenced track, and Jay had a proud papa look on his face. We didn't know then that the song we had just heard would later spark one of the best battles in hip-hop history. But upon leaving the studio, we were clearly all impressed.

"Yo, that was a 5 Mic album," Carlito said downstairs as we tried to hail a taxi back to the office. It was me, Carlito, senior editor Erik Parker, associate music editor Jermaine Hall, and assistant music editor Johnathan. We were all headed back to the office to wrap up our workday.

"I don't know. I would need to hear the album again," I replied. "And why did he skip a whole verse on that song?" The verse that Jay had actually let us hear was the one where he called Prodigy of Mobb Deep a ballerina and likened his height to just short of money stacks.

"I know why he did that," said Erik Parker. "He knows if he plays that verse, we can put it out there, and then it's fair game for Nas to come back at him before his album even drops." Erik Parker was a college-educated writer from South Jersey who was hired around the same time as I was after coming aboard as an intern for Carlito. Back then, he had a head full of red-colored dreads that were usually half-pinned-up, and he was clear about who he was. He was not a gangster wannabe. He was not an aspiring rapper. He was just a hip-hop journalist, making his way up the ranks.

"Yup, you know how y'all journalists are," I sarcastically added.

As editors, we speculated about Jay's strategy to try to figure out why he didn't let us hear part of the song. But we didn't realize the impact that the song would have because no one believed the verse of "The Takeover," directed at Nas, would be as harsh as it was. It was also not something that we thought would wake Nas out of his slumber. "Nas don't need to respond. He already murdered that mixtape joint we gave the Quotable to," said Johnathan, the assistant music editor.

Being from Queens, Johnnie [not his real name] was always on some Queens shit. He would champion pretty much every artist that came out of the Q-boro, as long as said artist didn't take his shirt off at concerts. Nas was one of Johnnie's favorites, and he wasn't going to let us all count him out. At the time, Johnnie was responsible for picking the Hip-Hop Quotable. The Quotable was another *Source* staple that MCs longed to achieve. Every month, the *Source* would reprint the hottest verse of the month. It could be anywhere from sixteen to twenty-four bars, and the verse had to be good enough to translate onto paper, where the words themselves, not the delivery, were honored for their cleverness and meaning. Johnnie had picked a mixtape verse from Nas a few months before, one where Nas had dissed Jay-Z.

I always stood my ground in this battle, quick to side with Jay. "Nas can't win against Jay-Z. He is on top of the game right now," I said, using my Jay-Z's-biggest-fan voice. "My money is on Jay." It was extremely ironic that I was so adamant in my opinion that Nas's career was basically finished. I didn't know it then, but I was about to switch sides. Before I met Nas, I respected his poetic skill, but was pretty much bored with much of his music after *Illmatic*. But the artist formerly known for his chipped tooth was about to win me over.

By November, Jay-Z had received his 5 Mic rating. Carlito had insisted that he come out of editor mode and write a glowing review that went along with it. For the months following its release, the *Blueprint* was the sound track to our lives inside and outside the office. Good hip-hop music provided an escape to the harsh realities that we had been faced with since first hearing it. With this album dropping on September 11, 2001, it felt good to focus on something besides the thought that a plane could hit 215 Park Avenue South. It was all too close to the ruins that had New York City in panic mode. Our moods had changed drastically because of it.

I remember listening to the radio and hearing "The Takeover" quite often. Everyone was shitting on Nas, including me. *He's finished,* we joked in the office. It was the cool thing to say. I even got phone calls from friends outside the industry asking me for inside details as to why

Jay-Z was dissing Nas so hard on his new song. "Read the magazine," I wanted to tell them. The *Blueprint* was a highly successful album for Jay and was considered the best hip-hop record of its time. He probably wouldn't admit it today—most artists don't—but those 5 Mics helped seal the deal.

A few weeks later, I was in a meeting with Erik and other members of the staff organizing everyone's schedules so that we could all go listen to Nas's new album together. Most of our expectations were low.

Located in the Village downtown on Eight Street, Electric Lady Studios was known for great hip-hop, and the place where I set it up for all of us to hear *Stillmatic*, Nas's fifth album. The studio's history, I later discovered, was much deeper than what I knew. Jimi Hendrix had opened the studio because he wanted his own place to be creative, but he had died soon after. As legend would have it, a black cat is supposedly always there, and some say it houses Hendrix's spirit. I have never seen the cat, but each time I was there, it smelled as if some kind of animal was pushing buttons behind the boards.

When I arrived there, I rang the buzzer to get in, and when it buzzed, I opened the heavy black door. Staring straight at us was what appeared to be a camera, and you had to speak to it the way Dorothy spoke to the great Oz. After a few long minutes, someone finally acknowledged our presence and let us in.

We climbed three flights of stairs before we had any idea whether we were in the right place at the right time. There, we were greeted by Nas's publicist and an engineer.

In my years as a writer for the *Source* and other magazines, I had run into artists all the time. Some of them would hang out backstage at concerts. Some would do the celebrity thing at industry parties. But Nas was much more low-key, as was his listening session.

Though I had met Nas at the Sony offices back in '99 while doing a story on him for *BlackBeat* magazine (where I was humored when he unexpectedly burped in the middle of our interview), we had never really talked. I respected him as an MC, but like most industry folk, I was a fickle fan, believing that artists are only as good as their last album.

After the verbal beatdown that Nas had received on "The Takeover," we pretty much figured that his album was going to be a waste of time on our part. Not to mention, no one in the general population of civilians cared about the release of *Stillmatic* with the *Blueprint* banging so hard out of everyone's car speakers.

After we chowed down on the usual record-label-sponsored catering, Nas's publicist led us into the studio and left us in the dark with the engineer. The room was a big contrast to the crowd and environment we'd experienced hearing Jay's album a few weeks before. "I'm just gonna set you guys up, and I'll be back when it's done," he said. Then he left us alone with just Nas's voice.

When the first song played, I found myself sending two-way messages to my friends about my plans for the weekend, because I didn't expect to hear anything worthwhile. I'd figure I'd assign the album review to one of the guys on staff. That was until I heard two words.

"Fuck Jay-Z!"

I woke up in my chair to something that makes someone like me pay attention. Drama! Beef! Fight!

The first time I heard the song "Ether," Nas's response to "The Takeover," I made my mind up as to who had won the battle between two of rap's greatest MCs. I switched sides like Don King at a boxing match.

As writers, we were all impressed when a rapper went beyond the scope of beats and rhymes. Nas's poetry was what made him a favorite among critics, and even though the rest of the album was playing through the speakers, most of us were still trying to break down the meaning of some of the bars Nas had spit on the best battle song he'd ever written. For me, it was always the simplest lines that had the most impact.

"Yo, did he just say Jay-Z was ugly? That's foul, crazy, and genius all at the same time," I said to the room. "Jay can't let that go. He's gonna have to respond. He just went psychologist on him like he had a complex."

Over the next couple of weeks, I begged Nas's publicist to sneak me an early copy of *Stillmatic*. "Ether" had leaked to radio, and the entire industry was buzzing with the news that Nas had come back with a track more lethal than "The Takeover." Like most publicists, he initially refused to send me an advance, but after we traded a few back-and-forth calls, we started to negotiate.

"I think this is a 5 Mic album, and the only way that's gonna happen is if you give us a copy. Everyone needs to hear it in order to get them on board."

"I have to talk to Nas about it," he said. "I don't think he's going to agree to leak the album to you guys unless he knows for sure that you guys are going to give it 5 Mics."

"You know I can't say that. I'm the music editor, but I can't guarantee 5 Mics. The powers that be need to agree to that, and even though it's good, it still needs to be voted on."

Confident in my ability to argue in favor of what I believed, I convinced him to send us the album advance. So that same day, I received a package with a white-labeled CD that had no writing on it. Record labels act as if an unreleased album is a top-secret government project, even these days when they always seem to make their way onto the internet anyway. I listened over and over until I knew the album like the back of my hand, then I passed it around the office and flaunted my ability to get a copy.

Most of the staff agreed that the genius of "Ether," concepts such as "Rewind," and songs such as "One Mic" had earned Nas another classic rating. There were a few dissenting opinions at first, but in the end, the vote was for 5 Mics, making Nas the only solo artist ever to receive the classic rating twice in his career. Ironically, the first album had been reviewed by a writer who called herself Shorty, a moniker that disguised that the intern who wrote it was actually Michelle, a pint-size Asian female reviewing one of the most talked-about classics in hip-hop history.

Still, Nas's 5 Mic rating had to be approved by Dave Mays. Like all things that meant this much to the magazine, the last step was to get him on board. But when I saw him outside my office bopping his head to the first track on *Stillmatic,* proclaiming, "Hangmen 3 did a track on a 5 Mic album!" I knew it was in the bag. Hangmen 3 was the name for a production trio that produced records for Benzino, so because they had sold one of their tracks to Nas, Dave was not going to object. Once I got the okay to 5-Mic the album, I started writing a review. *This is going to be a good one.*

can i kick it?

"He loves the review you wrote" was all I could make out from Nas's publicist, who was on the other end of my cell phone while I was trying to weave in and out of traffic in my neighborhood in downtown Brooklyn. He had somehow received an early copy of the February '02 issue of the *Source* and shown Nas my review.

With Kayla in the backseat, I was truly multitasking. Between glancing in my rearview to make sure she wasn't choking on the seat belt, flipping the bird to motorist who wouldn't let me merge in front of him, and trying to hold a professional conversation, it was hard to catch most of what he was saying. But when it came to a compliment of my writing, my ego couldn't help but hear that part.

I was on Christmas vacation, and my real agenda for calling was to get me and my "network" of girlfriends into Nas's album-release party, which was taking place at the Hammerstein Ballroom on the West Side of Thirty-fourth Street later that evening. Michelle had already secured her way inside, but we needed more access. It was my job to make sure we got more passes and VIP treatment. "You just wrote a 5 Mic review for him, Kim, you can get us in," Michelle instructed. But when it came to velvet ropes and guest lists, we had to have a plan of attack because there was never a guarantee. Rule number one, we were not waiting on any lines. Rule number two, we were getting into VIP. And rule number three, under no circumstances would we pay for anything. For this party, though, no one we called had any ins.

"I'm sorry. People keep calling me about this party tonight, but it's a paid gig," he said, meaning the label had nothing to do with it.

"Well, who can we call to make sure we're straight?" I asked before skidding a left with one hand. As journalists in hip-hop, it was easy to throw our business cards around and get in anywhere we wanted to, because at the end of the day there was always someone looking for his own press opportunity, whether it was the club promoter, the sidekick, or the brolic-looking security guard standing at the door.

"The only thing I can say is to hit Nas directly. He'll get you in," he continued.

"I don't really know him like that," I said, surprised that Nas's own publicist would offer up his information. For a publicist, it is usually taboo to give out an artist's contact info, especially to a magazine editor. A straight connection to the artist meant that the publicist was cut out of the picture, so most of them usually played middleman for everything. But he was cool, he didn't seem to care.

"He really loves the review you wrote, and he told me to give you his contact information. Call him and ask him. He wants to talk to you."

What could he want? I thought. The review was already written. I took the contact information and paged Nas. I was surprised at how quickly he answered me back.

"Yeah, I know who you are," he responded, before going into

detail about the review I'd written. It always amazed me that artists followed the *Source* so closely. I wrote for the average hip-hop fan, but occasionally I'd pepper my articles with subliminals that only certain people would catch. If rappers could do it in their records, then I could sure as hell do it in my stories. Method Man was the first person who made me see the similarities between an artist and a writer. "I write just like you," he once said. The artists took the articles so personally, and few of them took constructive criticism well.

The hip-hop industry was so tightly knit that if a journalist dissed an artist and then showed up at a party where said artist was, it was a potential problem. As a female, I usually escaped that type of drama. When I saw 50 Cent for the first time after I left the *Source,* he mentioned that his feelings were hurt when I described him as a "greasy convict," but as a girl, I was afforded a pass. Unfortunately, I can't say the same for some male writers who may have got punched in the face by someone in Wu-Tang or had a gun pointed at them by one of the Fugees. For me, however, only one incident with an artist posed a threat. Mase got 2.5 Mics for his sophomore album, *Double Up,* and I was the freelancer who got the chance to break down just how bad the album was. Just as we found out information about artists, they could find someone who knew you too. Mase called me personally to make empty threats. We got into a heated argument, which ended with his telling me he knew where I lived. So when Nas acknowledged that he knew who I was after I formally introduced myself via text message, I wasn't surprised. But I didn't expect our conversation to last as long as it did. My goal was to get us into the party, and I had accomplished that in the first couple of messages. Still, the conversation covered more than the party, as we discussed the review and got a little liberal with the flirting.

Later that night, downtown, I met Tanya Riddick [not her real name], who was Carlito's assistant, and we both parked our unluxurious cars somewhere on the East Side of Manhattan so Michelle could pick us up to floss in a brand-new Ford F-150 truck that she had as a loaner from a car company she was doing something on. Unlike most of us, who knew how to milk our jobs to get advance albums, Michelle was technology-savvy and used her name to get advance cars. Tanya hopped in the front and I took to the backseat.

"Did he hit you back yet?" Michelle asked as soon as I picked up my cell phone. She was still on top of our plan of action.

"Yeah, he said we're straight. He told me to just page him when we're ready to go, and he'll meet us downtown somewhere."

But Michelle's skepticism quickly dismissed his invitation to meet us and get us into his party. "Hit Nas now and see, because I heard it's hectic outside the spot, and we know he's a guaranteed way in."

I started to type out a message: I'M ON 30TH STREET. CAN YOU HELP US GET IN THE PARTY? Nowadays, if you type messages out in all caps, it conveys that you are yelling at that person, but back then on my enormous silver SkyTel two-way pager, which opened up like a laptop, everything was all caps or all lowercase because shifting was just too much work.

Nas quickly responded, SURE. MEET ME OUT FRONT OF MY HOTEL ON 32ND STREET.

If two-way pagers, BlackBerrys, and text phones could talk, so many people in the industry would have their spot blown. Detroit's Mayor Kwame Kilpatrick learned this the hard way, when he got busted cheating on his wife and lying about it. The text was such an addiction: having enough time to type out witty responses, being able to save and document everything that you were told so you could show your friends later, and beaming each other's contact information. Two-way texting was the social-networking tool before MySpace and Facebook existed.

"What did he say?" Michelle asked while aimlessly driving around Thirtieth Street waiting to make an entrance into the party.

"I don't know, my two-way froze."

"Are you kidding me? Maybe if you had a pager that actually worked, we wouldn't be fifteen minutes behind everyone else," Michelle said.

It took me a couple of minutes before my pager rebooted and I saw messages asking me to meet Nas on Thirty-second Street, but by the time we did, he had left, so he instructed me to catch up with him and his crew on Ninth Avenue.

"I bet that was him," said Michelle, pointing out two black SUVs that were screeching down Thirty-fourth Street.

Because of my own paranoia and my delayed messages, I thought he was playing games. "Okay, forget it, he's being an asshole. Let's go straight to the party."

But Michelle drove up to the driver's side of the first black SUV parked on Ninth Avenue anyway and used her driver's door power to roll down my back window. We waited until the SUV's backseat window slowly rolled down and we saw Nas's face hiding behind a pair of dark, don't-notice-me sunglasses. From where I was sitting, I could see everything inside the car. Holding a cane, Nas was reclined in the backseat behind the passenger side wearing a red, black, and green kufi and a matching dashiki. From that moment on, we used the code name Zamunda when referring to him. Zamunda was the fictional country in Africa that Eddie Murphy came from in my favorite movie of all time, *Coming to America*. I let out an unusual cough of laughter that stuck in my throat after seeing what he was wearing. Tanya, whose window was still up, started to make her usual funny comments under her breath.

"Uhuhnohedidn'thelookscrazy," I heard Tanya's one-word sentence coming from the front seat as I stared at him with absolutely nothing to say.

I looked down at Nas's lap and noticed an advance copy of the *Source*. The office hadn't yet received a shipment of advances so I hadn't even seen my own words in print yet. *No fair, he had one.*

"How did you get that? It's not out yet." I said.

Nas rocked his head up and down in slow motion, held up the page where my review was printed, and threw his thumb up in approval. I continued the conversation by blocking out Tanya's run-on jokes and Michelle's under-the-breath orders to "get the passes."

"So you liked the review, right?" I said, making small talk.

Nas responded in his scratchy, whispery voice, "Yeah, yeah. It's cool."

Then an overpowering voice from the front seat of his car scared the shit out of me. "*Yo!* She look Indian or something. Pocahontas."

"Is that Freddie Foxxx?" Michelle said so that only we inside our car could hear. Before I came to know Freddie Foxxx, all I believed of him to be was a bully. Having released a song entitled "Industry Shakedown," in which he verbally assaulted anyone and everyone in rap music, Foxxx was a musclebound, dark-skinned brother who looked as if he could dent a brick wall with his fist and catch a bullet with his teeth.

I put my head down and spoke without moving my lips so that Nas and anyone in his car couldn't hear me. "Yes, shut up before he hears and shoots us."

"So how do we get into this event?" I asked Nas.

"You can come in with us," he said. *Oh, great, there goes our night.*

"Oh, no, we'll never get in," Michelle whispered from the front. We both knew that walking into a party with an artist, especially the guest of honor, almost always ensured getting the wind knocked out of you as you were pushed away at the chest. Somewhere in the pushing and pulling, the chain of held hands gets broken. The artist gets in and you're left behind the velvet rope, claiming, "I'm with them."

Still, I said, "Okay," to him, before he ordered me, "Follow us."

The car sped off and we were left to chase it. During the day, Manhattan is an overcrowded, cramped city where millions of people pass by with no connection to each other whatsoever. But at night, especially on the eve of someone's album release, the city is swarming with tinted-out SUVs, Bentley coupes, and the latest Mercedes-Benz model doing 100 mph, switching lanes on the West Side Highway. One out of every ten cars is hiding some sort of celebrity, whether it's a rapper or a real estate mogul with his own reality show.

"I can't believe he was wearing a kufi. Who does that these days?" Tanya said.

"And a dashiki," I added. "He did not have on a dashiki?"

"Maybe dashikis are in now, and we're going to show up to the party looking very last season with our designer fashions" Michelle said sarcastically.

"What type of material is a dashiki made out of?" I asked. "Is it, like, made of thin fabric? Because it's cold as hell out here."

"It's made up of juices and berries," Tanya said jokingly in an African accent.

"So is Freddie Foxxx Nas's bodyguard?" Michelle said, asking the question that we all had lingering in the back of our heads.

"I hope so," I said.

"Yeah, I guess if I had beef, I'd want Freddie Foxxx to be my bodyguard too," said Michelle.

"Did he call me Indian?" I automatically took offense to any racial characterization that wasn't Puerto Rican, though I was mixed with black and Chinese too. "I knew I shouldn't have let her blow my hair so damn straight."

"So you're Indian today . . . think of it as if it's the new race-specific fetish for rappers. And stop being so racist," Michelle responded.

One of the things that had become customary to us on a night out was the art of jumping from one conversation to the next. We gave each other snappy responses, then abruptly changed the subject. It was a great way to sustain our intellectual stamina.

"Racist? I'm not the one who won't date white boys. That's Tanya."

"Shut up. You won't date white boys either. Name a white boy you've dated," Tanya said.

"Does light-skinned count?"

Michelle interrupted our tennis game of wit with a dose of real world. "Shut up shut up shut up I can't concentrate on driving. We still have to find a place to park this car."

"This is not a car. It is a minihome on wheels. Find a lot," I said.

At that point, we realized that there was no way we could pull up to the venue and throw the car keys at a valet's head, as celebrities do. But we still had the hard tickets from Michelle's man.

"Page him and tell him we'll just meet him inside," she told me.

"I'm so over sweating him to get into this party," I responded. "I feel like a groupie."

"Just do it, groupie!" The car cracked up with laughs, and now that I'd been given my marching orders from the girls, I let my fingers do the talking.

After we parked, we walked right up to the door of the Hammerstein where we were immediately greeted by a familiar industry person who let us right in. After all the drama, no passes or tickets were even needed. We ended up getting wristbands that admitted us to anywhere in the venue: downstairs, upstairs, behind the stage. The odd thing was, although it was nuts outside, the place was kinda empty once you got in. Plus, there was a guy dancing wearing a Toucan Sam–colored Coogi sweater, which I hadn't seen since '97.

"Please tell me we didn't just break our necks to be here and it's wack," said Tanya. "Who are you on your pager with?"

"I'm still talking to Nas. He said he's upstairs. He's telling me to go upstairs. Where's Michelle?"

Michelle was caught up in a networking conversation where some industry has-been tries to get a business card so he can hound you for the next few months and force you to listen to his new artist. She was easily recognizable, and I loved it when I was with her and people didn't know what I did, because it meant I didn't have to be the political one. We rescued her, then went upstairs.

Nas stood on the balcony surrounded by a bunch of dudes from Queens and a cloud of gray smoke. When the smoke parted like the Red Sea, there was Moses, studying the crowd below, which had filled in since our arrival. The music was extremely loud, but when I want to be heard, I make sure of it. "Thank you for taking care of us," I said, even after we had gotten in on our own.

"Of course, of course. I appreciate everything you said in the review," he said. "It was dope."

"Well, I think the album is incredible," I said. "Do you know Michelle?" Though they had met before, I reintroduced them. Tanya had been unlucky enough to run into an old flame, who was pushing up on her once again. Then, as our fear of being seen next to a rapper took over, Michelle gave me the nod that it was time to move away from the chaos. We wouldn't want anyone to see us talking to Nas for too long, because a woman cannot have a lengthy conversation with an artist. It would almost always translate as a groupie move. So even though we were talking about his album, I wrapped up the conversation and kept it moving.

"I can't believe he said, 'I'll see you sooner rather than later.' That is the corniest thing I've ever heard," Michelle said.

After less than an hour at the party, we'd had enough of the loud music, smoke-filled air, and Queensbridge wife-beaters and had made our way to a nearby deli that was still open.

But the SkyTel two-way pager was a dangerous device, and Nas and I had been in contact since the party. Even though our initial conversations were innocent, after a few drinks the tone of our conversation was crossing the line. Nas even invited me and the girls to meet him after the party and hang out. But I backed off the two-way messages and decided to take my ass home instead. I knew that many a fling had come out of what had started as an innocent message, and it was just too soon for all that. But the ball had already been set in motion.

For the next two weeks, Nas and I were in almost daily contact via pager and cell phone. We mostly talked about hip-hop, because it was the thing we had in common. But our conversations were always comprised of or mixed with flirting. Still, despite being interested in him, I was more intrigued by the information I had access to in the midst of his beef with Jay-Z. I was getting the scoop right from the horse's mouth, and it was giving me an edge over everyone else in the magazine world. I couldn't print what he said in our conversations, but I could allude to it. It was the only thing in hip-hop worth talking about at the time, and I had the inside insight.

One day while we were on the phone, Nas invited me to a night of bowling, which I thought was a bit odd, but cute. I accepted and met him somewhere near Roslyn, Long Island, where he lived at the time. Michelle, who was supposed to come with me, had gotten caught up with work and ended up arriving two hours late and meeting us afterward in the parking lot. That left me to bowl on Nas's team against Freddie Foxxx, who was as good at bowling as he was at scaring the shit out of people. His one score beat both Nas's and mine combined. But Foxxx was cool. It just goes to show you that most of what you believe in hip-hop to be true is actually the exact opposite. Freddie Foxx was one of the smartest people I'd ever met in hip-hop, which is not to say he won't still beat the black off someone if he has to. After we finished the game, the four of us sat in Foxxx's car talking hip-hop for damn near two hours. Then, Michelle and I went to grab a bite to eat and contemplated my next move.

"That was a date, you know. You went on a bowling date with him," she said comically. Her laughter made her miss the coffee cup and spill sugar onto the table. After loading up on enough caffeine to keep us awake for the ride back, we both drove home.

Another week went by before the girls and I decided that my two-way talk had crossed the line of platonic. "Are you going to sleep with him?" was the question of the moment. The more we kept in contact, it was something that I knew would eventually happen.

I'd been involved with artists before, only the artists in my past had never made it past a hot verse or an independent label. But to be involved with someone at the height of his career and at the tail end of one of the biggest beefs in hip-hop history, I had to admit, was different. In the past, I was just a girl who had met someone in a club or at an event. And when two random people hook up, it's just two random people hooking up. Past relationships just became coffee-shop conversation with friends who spew, "Ewww! I can't believe you had sex with him." But now, I had a *Source* title, and as my schedule and job would only permit me to have a life through two-way messages, Nas was one of the few people outside the *Source* that I had been in contact with. And because we spent most of our phone conversations talking about hip-hop, it was easy to talk for hours.

The next Friday, I met Nas at a hotel in Long Island after hours. Yes, ready to do the do. When I arrived, Nas had already filled the Jacuzzi with water. He was blasting Power 105.1, a New York radio station that was about to switch its format from classic soul to hip-hop. I could hear Rick James's "Give It to Me Baby" mixed with static playing through what sounded like busted speakers when I knocked on the door. How ironic.

Nas was wearing a long-sleeved thermal and jeans, and was holding an opened bottle of alcohol when he opened the door to let me in. I walked into the empty room and started opening the closets.

Years before Paris Hilton or Kim Kardashian made it the in thing to do and get famous by, sex tapes were every girl's fear. Before I arrived, Tia had called my phone to remind me to voice my disclaimer and search the room, so I rummaged through the closet looking for anything that resembled a video camera. "I do not agree to be photographed or videotaped or anything like that," I said out loud. Just. In. Case.

"You're crazy," Nas said with a laugh. "Now get in this tub."

I spent the next five minutes looking around the room, while Nas smoked a blunt and sat comfortably in the water.

"Oh my God, you're naked," I said jokingly before shutting off the lights so I could take off my clothes. *I may not have found a camera*, I thought, *but there would be nothing visible to tape if the lights were off.*

After a few minutes, I discovered Nas had no condoms. In my experience, providing them was usually the guy's job. So we both got dressed and decided we would drive to the nearest store to get some. It was certainly spoiling the mood.

"You drive a stick shift?" he asked when he got into my five-speed Toyota 4 Runner.

"Yeah," I responded proudly. "Do you know how to drive one?" Most guys I knew didn't know how to drive a stick. I used to push down on the clutch harder just to rub it in their face. In Nas's case, though, he didn't know how to drive, period.

"I don't drive."

"You don't drive?" I asked, pushing the numbers on my CD player until I got to track ten.

"Nah." Nas turned up the volume when he heard the sound of a phone ringing coming through the speakers. "Oh, this is my favorite track on this album," he said of Biggie's "Downfall," which began to play on my car stereo.

"I dreams filthy. My moms and pops mixed it with Jamaican rum and whiskey . . ."

While riding in my car, Nas recited the whole first verse, and I felt as if I were at a free concert with a front-row seat. I never took Nas to be such a big fan of the Notorious B.I.G., especially since Nas was from Queens and Big was from Brooklyn. After KRS-One battled MC Shan, I figured the 5 boros of New York were all against each other. But as he started to break down Big's artistry, I realized that his knowledge of hip-hop was more far-reaching than I gave him credit for.

"Yo, I could listen to him to this day and still be impressed with the shit he's sayin'," Nas said.

Not only was Nas a Biggie fan, but he was a Jay-Z fan as well. Even though he was a lot more fond of Big as a rapper than Jay, he still gave Jay a lot of credit for his craft. I was actually surprised to hear him describe "The Takeover" as a "hot record." *How could someone in the midst of the biggest battle of his career have so much respect and admiration for a song that had dissed him so hard?* Not that he didn't clown Jay-Z when he had the chance, but from the things he told me, he obviously respected him. "He disappointed me with 'Super Ugly,'" he said about Jay's impulsive reaction to "Ether." Then he'd jump back on his own side. It was weird, almost as if he were two-faced to himself.

That night, we had a long conversation about Big that shed some light on how Nas felt about hip-hop. He wasn't as much of the socially conscious rapper as he often got depicted as; he was more of an omniscient hip-hop fan who knew how to accurately critique the art form. He was like a rap critic who could rap, and he seemed to take the criticism that we dished out at the *Source* well.

It's funny how journalists are so confident in our expertise that we feel we can tell an artist how to make his or her music. KRS-One made me really think about it once when he told me, "I wish that I could read articles and then rate them. What if I gave out pens to writers: one pen for a wack story and five pens if it's good? What about that?"

After we got together that night, Nas and I saw each other every once in a while. But as he set out on tour to promote his album, our meetings were usually confined to hotel rooms out of town and, ah, yes, the tour bus. I liked him, but because he was an artist, I never took our relationship seriously, not seriously enough to go anywhere. I saw how they got down, from the way they talked about chicks to the way they treated them. "Treat her like a prostitute" was the mandate from Slick Rick that seemed to resonate with most men in hip-hop. But Nas fit into my hectic schedule perfectly, and I'm sure I fit into his heavy rotation, if he was true to his artistic roots and even had one. In the beginning, we talked every week, but our conversations had dwindled to a quick hello courtesy of Skytel after a while. I always looked at it as if it were over when we last saw each other, and he always looked at it as if it started up again each time he reached out. We kept each other informed of things we felt the other needed to know. Such as the time I told him about Irv Gotti's plans to go public with the news that he was signing Nas to Murder Inc. Nas found it amusing, but would never confirm to me whether it was true. Irv Gotti told me they had met in Miami and that it was a sure thing, so I put it in the magazine, crediting it to Irv. But when it came to giving Nas's side of the story, I didn't use the access that I had to get the information I needed. I felt like that would be wrong. I could have gone to Nas and just asked him if I could print it, but I believed that was overstepping my boundaries. In truth he was not going to sign with Murder Inc., but instead of using my relationship to get inside information, I decided to keep my personal and professional lives separate. It was a double-edged sword, and as luck would have it, news of my discreet relationship with him started to make its way around the industry. It made me extremely careful about where I met him and how I dealt with him in the magazine—if at all. If his name came up in articles, I'd let the other editors handle it. I didn't want favoritism on my conscience, especially not in these modern times when nepotism in hip-hop is a thing of the past. Snicker. Dare I try to have some integrity.

CHAPTER FIVE

strictly business

When I was promoted to music editor, I moved to a window office a few doors away from the corner office, which was occupied by "Cee," as in *C* for "Carlito." Down in the editorial department, we used to refer to the window offices as "condos" and the cubicles as "projects." If you lived in a "condo," you were considered a "top editor." A top editor ran his or her own section in the magazine, which was divided by subject matter into music, culture, and politics. I had always been a music person and rarely dealt with political or cultural content.

The two months following my promotion had become incredibly hectic. For one, I had moved from Clinton Hill in Brooklyn to Fort Lee, New Jersey. The Fort Greene/Clinton Hill section of Brooklyn is the first place you move to when you realize that the only way you can network in the music industry when the entire music industry lives in downtown Brooklyn is to move there yourself. It makes business meetings and going home from industry functions so much easier. The only drawback is that you have to brush your hair and put on makeup just to go to the corner store. Fort Lee is the place you move to after the industry has accepted you, you got enough money to pay the telephone bill on time, and you don't want to run into anyone anymore. In Fort Lee, most of the residents are Korean, and they don't care about the music industry or who you are. Most believe Jay-Z is a subway line.

The *Source* had space on both the seventh and the eleventh floors. The editorial department was located on one side of the eleventh floor with the business and advertising folks on the other. For months, Carlito had preached at staff meetings that he was vacating his position after the 150th issue. I'm not sure whether Dave and Ray knew this, but it didn't surprise me when Cee wrote an editorial letter entitled "The Fat Lady Sings" in the April 2002 issue, which was the 151st. With a few of the other senior staff members resigning for their own personal reasons, that left Erik Parker and me as the highest-ranking editors on the staff.

In addition to my monthly editing duties, I had managed to keep my byline in the magazine in almost every section. My plate was full with editing duties, but as a writer, I wanted my voice to be heard. In our 150th issue, we crowned the Notorious B.I.G. the greatest rapper of all time. Knowing his music, I volunteered to write the story about B.I.G. and what made him the greatest. I had started to become known for some of the more controversial stories, so it wasn't that unusual when Big Pun died for me to cowrite the cover story. I had also developed some strong relationships with artists based on my previous work. When Foxy Brown agreed to do her first *Source* cover, she requested me as the writer.

Because I was editing the music section, I oversaw much of the magazine's music content. In the past, Carlito had trusted my judgment on whom to cover and what writers to assign stories to, especially because I always got it done. But now with his resignation, everyone's decisions were being overanalyzed, and I was ready to prove myself to the new head of the magazine all over again. Then one night, I got an office visit.

I was working after hours when Ray and Dave unexpectedly walked in. "We want to talk to you," said Ray, before quietly shutting the door behind him. Although I hadn't had too many dealings with him, I knew from others that it was wise to let Ray do most of the talking.

"Yo, Dave and I been talking about what's going to happen now that Carlito is gone, and we want you to run this shit. We've been paying attention to your work, and we think you're the right person. You think you can handle it?" Ray was diplomatic with his words. I later learned that he would build you up and give you power, just so that he could exercise his own to show that he was more powerful than you. I wanted to be a powerful woman in hip-hop, so, at the time, nothing I had heard about his disgusting, miserable male-chauvinist ways could stop me from accepting.

"Yes, I know I can handle it," I excitedly answered, still in shock to be hearing this come out of his mouth.

"Don't worry. We're gonna bump up your salary and everything. Dave is gonna take care of that. You'll be the head editor of this, and whoever don't like it, they could go." Ray seemed to be leaving out a lot, but I didn't really ask any questions. I was so happy to be hearing news of a promotion I didn't even know I was up for. I tried to hold back my smile, but I couldn't stop it. The whole time Dave stood next to Ray, listening attentively, as if he was hearing it all for the first time himself.

"Does anyone else know?" I asked.

"Not yet, let's keep this between us for a minute and we'll make the official announcement soon, but we just wanted to make sure you were cool with it first," Ray said, with his heavyweight chain pulling his neck down.

After he broke the news to me, and possibly to Dave as well, Ray left the office with Dave not far behind him. I was so excited, I couldn't bring myself to get back to the story I was editing on the Big Tymers. I immediately picked up the phone and called Tia.

"You'll never guess what just happened."

"What? You got a promotion?" *How does she do that?* She knew right away.

"Yes, I think. No, wait, I don't know." Now I was confused.

"What happened?"

"Ray walked in here with Dave and told me I was getting the editor-in-chief job."

"Congratulations! I knew you'd get it."

"Don't congratulate me yet. You're gonna jinx it. It feels weird. I don't know if I got promoted. He kinda just came in here and told me, but we didn't talk about salary or job duties or anything like that." I had never gotten a promotion this way before, and yet this was about to be the biggest job of my career.

"Well, of course you got the job. I mean, who were they gonna give it to? They're not gonna give that job to Erik."

For the next hour, Tia and I rationalized why Erik would never get the job over me. We came up with a few good reasons, but the bottom line was that Ray did not like him. Ray called Erik a "college" dude who couldn't run the magazine because he didn't know anything about the streets. Since Carlito had left, Erik had stepped up his game. On the hierarchy level, he was the next in line, and much of the staff thought he'd automatically get the job.

A few days later, I was at a loud dinner with the Ying Yang Twins at a restaurant called City Crab, just a few doors down from the *Source* offices, when Tanya called my phone with some information. We were in constant communication at this point, so we skipped the "hello" part of our phone calls. "There's a petition for Erik to get promoted, and everyone signed it," she notified me.

Ying and Yang (I don't know their individual names) were arguing with each other over whether R. Kelly was going to do any time for the child-pornography charges he had recently been brought up on. "Wha iya day wuh yo sista?" The duo were talking so loudly, I could barely hear my call, especially with their annoying *heeeeh* sound, which they used in general conversation even more than they did on their records.

"What do you mean there's a letter?" I asked Tanya. "What does it say? Did they ask you to sign it? Why didn't I know about it?" I had a lot of questions, but she was just finding out the answers herself.

"I don't know who signed it or what it says, but they obviously don't want you to see it. Or me!" Tanya seemed to have received her news from a reliable source, though she wasn't giving that person up. But ironically enough, they hadn't asked her to sign the petition. It also seemed to conveniently pass over my door like the Holy Spirit. This letter had been circulated among the editorial staff for signatures in support of a promotion for Erik Parker to EIC. Word must have gotten out that I was up for the job as well, because everyone purposely forgot to tell me or Tanya about the letter.

Unfortunately for them, those people pretty much wrote their ticket. After some research, we were told that the letter was drawn up by two editors on staff. Though I'd never really had any problems with either of them, I guess they didn't like me too much.

"This isn't a democracy." Dave wasn't big on these types of letters. In 1994, the staff had circulated a letter asking Dave to resign after Dave had inserted an article about Ray's group, the Almighty RSO, at the last minute, without editor approval. As legend would have it, Dave kept a copy of the letter in his top drawer, memorizing each name so as not ever to allow them to work or write for the magazine again. He never stepped down, and as a result the staff walked out.

Dave let me know this new letter would be taken care of. "Don't even worry about this. This is ridiculous. Nobody's gonna tell me what to do." Dave was furious about the letter and was now ready to sign off on my promotion. After that night when he and Ray had spoken to me about the position, Dave followed up by asking me to submit an annual editorial plan for the staff and the magazine. I heard that he also asked

Erik to submit the same thing. I guess he was just going through the motions.

But now, it seemed that the letter had done more harm to Erik than his peers had expected. I never saw the letter, but Tanya snooped around for me and found out whose signatures were on it. So many of the staff had signed it that she would probably have been better off finding out whose signatures were missing.

Before long, the staff heard that their plan had backfired. I got the job over Erik, and everyone panicked. My office door became a revolving one, with people coming in and out claiming they didn't know I was up for the job. Some staff felt they were compelled to sign. I was borderline offended. Still, I didn't want to make any drastic changes right away.

The next day, my promotion was announced. Erik resigned immediately. The first issue was to figure out who was staying now that I had the job. Just as I thought, almost everyone decided to keep his or her job. The only other person to resign at that time was someone who initiated the letter. Because he never came to me or called me about it, I decided that I wasn't going to care even though we had worked together for a while.

After a couple of months, I had three issues of the magazine under my belt, and they were all doing well despite our being understaffed. The June '02 issue featured the rapper Trina in a swimsuit (being poked by a blow-up dolphin right above her . . . uh-oh), a July '02 Nelly cover with him holding up a number one sign, and an August '02 issue featuring Eve. Three big cover artists translated into rising newsstand sales. I was proving myself good at the job.

Even though I thought I was getting money, I really wasn't. The condition was that I'd eventually get the title and the money that went along with being the editor in chief, but first I had to prove myself. I was given the go-ahead to take the corner office, though. With all the publicity, the big office, and a bump in salary, I was content for the moment, despite my doing the job of editor in chief without the title, without a managing editor (she was one of the people who had to go), and without a second-in-command.

But September was going to be even more impressive. I was extremely busy trying to lock down the best cover of my career, and I'd been in and out of the office at meetings and photo shoots to make sure everything was right. Johnnie had been pitching a story for months, but for whatever reason, he hadn't been able to pin the artist down, until now.

"Just bring him up here," I told Johnnie as I was rushing to get to my office one morning. His persistence on doing a story was coming at a bad time for me.

"You sure? 'Cause I don't want them to come all the way up here from Queens and then you forget or something," Johnnie said a bit sarcastically. "So I'm going to have him come up here later today."

"Go ahead and do the story. We'll print it. But he has to talk about getting shot." I could feel my phone vibrating inside my Gucci bag, so I reached in and pulled out my Verizon camera flip phone, which was hiding under a sea of receipts.

"Hello?" My conversation with Johnnie was cut short by a phone call that I'd been waiting for.

"Yo, what's the situation? Are we doing this or not?" I didn't work for Roc-A-Fella CEO Dame Dash, but he was yelling at me through the phone, regardless.

"I'm waiting on an answer from Dave, and as soon as he gives me the okay, we'll be good to go," I said, trying not to be intimidated. Damon seemed to like the sound of his own voice because after that, I couldn't get a word in.

"What the hell am I waiting on him for? We don't need that shit. Y'all called *us* for this cover. This is the same shit they tried to do to us the last time." Dame was waiting on a call back from me to confirm Jay-Z for the September cover. Getting Jay on the cover on the *Source* was a big deal, and I didn't want to lose it. Some underlying drama for years between Jay and the *Source* preceded me. Apparently, Jay had been promised the cover earlier in his career and then the *Source* had reneged and tried to give it to Busta, after doing an interview with Jay bartered on an agreement for the cover. When the *Source* tried to back out of the deal, Damon showed up at the office with a few of his affiliates, the kind that don't care enough to not get involved. Needless to say, Jay-Z wound up getting the cover. But since then, their relationship had soured. So I knew if I made this happen, it would be memorable. I had been pitching Jay for the cover for as long as I could remember working at the *Source*, but the history between them had blocked it. Jay-Z himself had once told me that he didn't mess with the *Source*. And each and every time I brought up his name to Dave, Dave made a "fuck Jay-Z" face. I also heard their drama heightened after something happened between them at the Source Awards one year.

After years of the silent war, I figured that I could somehow make it happen. Roc-A-Fella had a slew of new artists coming, and I convinced Dame to give us Jay in exchange for a lot of coverage of all his new artists, even the ones in State Property. Once Dame agreed, I brought it to Dave, who seemed enthusiastic. But after so much back-and-forth negotiation, Dame Dash had flipped the script. His new condition was that we not only had to do stories on his new artists, he wanted them on the cover with Jay. It made no difference to me if Freeway had to be on there with him, as long as Jay was front and center, but once again I had to get approval from Dave, who, for some reason, wouldn't give me a yes or no.

But Dame wanted an answer, so I tried to give him one when he paused after a sentence to breathe. "I told Dave what you wanted. He has all the information, so now I'm waiting to hear back from him. He's probably busy. He's been out of town." I was running out of excuses as to why we were taking so long to set it up.

"Freeway. Beans. Cam. Bleek. All of us. All of us got to be on the cover or we ain't doing it. Tell Dave I don't like my time wasted. Time is money." Dame was still yelling, but I was so focused on figuring out how to stall that I lost of a lot of what he was saying.

"I know. I'll figure out a concept, but we'll be good. I'll try to get an answer out of him today." Knowing that time my time was running out, both with Dame and with the print deadline, I sent Dave a two-way message while I was still on the phone with Dame to try to pressure him to give the okay.

"Yeah, we need to know, because we have other options." Dame continued, implying that another magazine was offering them a cover as well. I was sure it was *XXL* and especially couldn't let them get the cover first.

No matter how many ideas we threw at Dave for a cover, it took days, sometimes weeks, for him to okay a cover idea. He had this way of answering us, in a stuttered "Uh" that never ended. It was more like "Uhhhhhh," and I later found out that it was his way of saying that he hadn't gotten an answer out of Ray. The two-way was the best way to ask for something, because it forced him to respond comprehensibly. No stutters, no diverting the conversation. Just a direct response to the question. Because we always had to wait on Ray for an answer, we'd wind up pushing decisions so close to the print deadline that it became the hardest part of my job. But Ray and I hadn't yet developed enough of a relationship for me to go directly to him, so in the beginning I had to funnel everything through Dave. On paper, I reported to Dave, even though Ray was calling the shots. The editorial department would plan a cover, come up with a visual concept, then bring it to Dave. It would all seem like a plan until the last minute, when we'd get a call like "Uhhhh, we're changing the cover." It was then my job to rethink everything and make it happen all over again, only with less sand in the hourglass. After a while, I learned how to skip this long, drawn-out process and just go directly to Ray.

I was so tied up that morning running back and forth to see whether Dave had gotten in yet that I didn't realize that I had people waiting to meet with me. As I was walking back to my office, I noticed a bunch of dudes dressed in jeans and the thickest white T-shirts I'd ever seen. It was hot outside, so I could smell the sweat that was leaking through their T-shirts.

"Kim, this is 50, Smurf, and Sha Money," Johnnie said, making the formal introduction. As I approached them, I noticed that they were hiding something underneath their shirts. I could see the shapes of bulletproof vests as I got closer. It was almost as if they'd come to a stickup and not a meeting. But, hey, this is rap. Maybe I was the one who was underdressed.

"It's nice to meet you. Y'all can come in my office now. I'm sorry I was late," I lied, because I didn't even remember that we had a time scheduled. But then again, my new assistant, Tory, was still learning that part of his job. He couldn't seem to get the answering-phones-and-scheduling-my-appointments thing down in between arguing on the phone with his girlfriend. Tory was from downtown Brooklyn, and he looked more like a *Source* reader than my assistant. He always showed up for work, but I usually beat him to the office. Still, I liked that I could get an honest opinion about everything we were working on from someone who actually was still out there in the streets buying magazines off the newsstands.

50 Cent took the seat nearest to the window on the black leather couch in my office. As he started to talk, I sat behind my desk trying to remember what this meeting was supposed to be about. His two associates sat on the couch next to him. I had never met him before, but was familiar with his work. I knew that he was from Queens. I knew he had been signed to Columbia. I knew that he had an album called *Power of the Dollar*, but I didn't know if it had ever come out. I had heard he had punched Ja Rule in the face down in Atlanta somewhere. And I knew that he had been shot nine times and had somehow lived through it. I didn't know, though, that he was about to blow.

"So Johnnie tells me you're ready to talk about everything that happened to you?" I told him.

"It's like this," 50 began. I didn't mean for him to start talking about everything at that moment, but since he was willing to open up, I started to ask specific questions.

"Do you know who shot you?" I got straight to the point.

"Yeah, I know. He's dead now," 50 said, before journeying into his mind and pulling out the longest explanation I'd ever heard. It always amazed me how much information some artists so easily gave up to journalists, and whether or not it was intentional, 50 was giving off the feeling that he had retaliated. He spoke slowly and in run-on sentences. Each sentence fragment seemed disconnected from the next. He would start with something important like "I got shot because . . ." but by the end of his sentence, he'd be offering up words of wisdom such as "the things you go through make you the person who you are." His speech was like one faulty paragraph waiting to be edited. Not all of what he said was important, but certain parts had the promise of one hell of a story. The thing about writing, especially in hip-hop, is that you get to bring these artists to life through your own words, not theirs— thankfully. They just contribute. 50 was certainly one character whose story needed to be told right there at that moment, only he was boring the hell out of me trying to tell me it that day. I was asking important questions and looking for the short answer, and he was giving me the unedited version.

As 50 was talking, my mind was drifting. I couldn't remember the details of his incident, because it had happened so long ago. *Did he get shot in his face,* I thought, *or is that just an awkward place for a dimple?* When he spoke, though, his lips seemed to be struggling to open. His was not an attractive face to me, but something about his smile made me stare at him. Then I heard him say it. "The bullet went through my cheek and knocked out my tooth. There's still a piece of metal in my mouth."

Eww, that must be uncomfortable, I was thinking. "So I want to do the story," I interrupted him. "This is going to be really good. But you've gotta go into detail like you did just now. You're not gonna tell me it's all off-the-record once the tape recorder is on?"

"Nah, I'm gonna talk about everything." Then he paused when Sha Money looked at him. "Well, actually, not the deal. Not that part. I can't go into who we're about to sign to because the paperwork isn't done. Once we close that deal, I'll tell you, but I'm not going to talk about it until the ink is dry."

"Did you get a lot of offers?" I asked.

"Oh, everybody comin' to the table now, especially with the way the mixtape is moving in the streets. But this one, this person is backing up the money truck." He was talking about Eminem and Dr. Dre at the time, but we discovered that later as we were doing the story.

"Aight, so we straight," I said. 50 stood up, then Sha and Smurf rose up off the couch right after him. 50 approached my desk and dropped his mixtape on it. When I looked down at it, there was a photograph of 50, Lloyd Banks, and Tony Yayo all pointing guns at me. "Oh, it's like that. Okay. Don't hurt nobody." I didn't really know if they understood I was trying to be funny. To me, gangster rap went out of style with Snoop Dogg's *Doggystyle* album. Biggie had actually switched things up with his second album, *Life After Death,* when "players" became the thing to be. 50's guns and shoot 'em-up-bang-bang talk was just a little too thuggish for me, and although the music was good, I didn't think the public would eat it up the way they did. His story was interesting, but in the next six months, it would be told a hundred times over. To me, he was like anyone else coming into my office. He'd sell a couple of records and be back to play his second album in a year. I never thought it would turn into the phenomenon that it did. I also never anticipated that things would unfold the way they did.

50 pointed his two-way at mine and held down the send button. I heard the little *Star Trek*–like noise, then I saw the notice that he had beamed his contact information into mine. I hit return and added him to my contacts.

protect ya neck

Memorial Day kicks off the summer for most, but in New York, Summer Jam gets it started. The concert is given annually by Hot 97. The lineup usually features A-list hip-hop celebrities, and a controversial headliner who usually has a media-worthy plan of attack. We were closing our September issue, but I planned to do a story on Summer Jam because I knew something was about to go down.

It had been a year since Jay-Z had posted a childhood picture of Prodigy of Mobb Deep in a dance outfit (it didn't really look like a tutu to me, but that's what everybody said it was) on the big screen during a performance, giving everyone a little preview of "The Takeover" before I heard the verse about Nas. But now the tables had turned, and, of course, everyone was ready to instigate a beef and get it all started back up again.

The rumor mill in the industry had gone nuts with the news that Nas was going to perform a mock lynching of Jay-Z during his 2002 Summer Jam performance. Together, Jay-Z and Nas were like the best of both worlds waiting to happen. Jay had the fame and success that Nas had never had, and Nas had the poetic intellect that Jay-Z lacked. They would, ironically, squash their beef in 2005 when Nas joined Jay-Z onstage at the Powerhouse concert in New Jersey. It was not a Summer Jam concert that brought them together, but if Summer Jam had actually gone down the way it was supposed to back in 2002, things might have turned out differently. Unfortunately for me, my inside access to information had dwindled down.

I had met Nas out of town a couple times while we were seeing each other, but by the time Summer Jam came around, it was getting old for the both of us. I would go see him, we would have sex, and then I would leave. The interesting hip-hop conversations that we'd once had turned into brief dialogues when he would flip through the newest issue of the magazine I always carried with me to show off. I liked to watch him read through the stories to see what kept his interest. Like most *Source* readers, he started at the back, looking at the Mic ratings and the album reviews first, and then paying a lot of attention to the ads for upcoming albums, as if he was studying the competition. "Fabolous. Yeah, yeah, I like him." Then he pointed to Fab's upcoming album title, *Street Dreams,* to make sure I took note that it was a title of an early Nas recording.

I had last seen him when we met up outside L.A. I was out there on business, interviewing a new West Coast editor to fill the void we had on staff. Nas was doing a show in Irvine, a town outside L.A., and when I texted him and told him I was in town, he asked me to meet him at the show and ride back to Phoenix with him. Since I had no friends on the West Coast and nothing to do that evening, I told him I'd meet him out there—even though I was scheduled to fly home the next morning. When I got there, the driver was standing outside on the lookout for me, and the bus was nice and empty. So I headed straight to the back room on the tour bus, shut the door, and intended to stay there until the bus was empty again. Nas was still onstage, so I made myself comfortable in his room and waited. Tia was blowing up my cell phone, but knowing I was dead wrong for deciding at the last minute to go to Phoenix and miss my flight home, I didn't answer.

I was bored as hell, because I had no idea how to turn on the TV, and I wasn't about to emerge from the back room and ask the driver, so I pulled out my laptop and tried to write. Now that I was on the bus, I wanted to go home. I started to contemplate whether the trip was worth it. I had a daughter, a family, and real friends back home, and I was sitting on a bus waiting for a guy whom I barely knew. That was the reason I wasn't picking up Tia's calls. I knew she would read me something awful if I told her that I'd picked up my bags and driven forty-five minutes out to meet Nas and was now sitting on the back of his tour bus. I could just hear her high-pitched voice in my head: *Kim, what's wrong with you? Are you crazy? I can't believe you played yourself.* I picked up the phone to call her and confess my stupidity, but then I heard what sounded like the whole damn Queensbridge board the bus, so I shut my cell phone and decided to wait until tomorrow to call her.

In the morning, as the bus parked outside the Phoenician hotel, we started to gather our luggage to go upstairs. Nas gave me a key to his hotel room. "I'm checked in under the name Justin Case," he said, telling me to meet him upstairs because he had to take care of some business first.

I tried to wait for everyone on the bus to exit before I opened the back door, but my bladder was about to explode. I'd managed to hold it in all night while we watched reruns of the *Good Times* catalog that was sent to him. My plan was to exit the bus when everyone was off, just in case someone knew who I was. But rap chitter-chatter in the front of the bus was holding me up. I could hear the guys talking about the show the night before, and their conversation did not sound as if it was coming to an end.

I couldn't hold my pee any longer, so I threw on my sunglasses, grabbed my suitcase, and convinced myself to walk off the bus. The plan was to go straight through everyone, luggage in tow, look down, and make as discreet an exit as I could. And I almost made it, until I heard someone call my name.

"Kim?"

I didn't recognize the voice, and for a second I contemplated just ignoring it, but that would make my paranoia obvious, so I looked up. *Damn.*

It was Akinyele, a fellow Queens rapper who for this particular tour had become Nas's hypeman. I knew Ak from industry meetings and we had always been cool. But I hated, at that very guilty moment, to have to look into the face of the man who instructed women to "Put It In Your Mouth."

"Hey," I said, looking up in shame. As I walked off the bus, he followed me.

"How are you?" He was talking to me as if we had just seen each other at the supermarket, and not as if he had just found out my big secret.

"I'm good. What's going on with you?" The small talk was killing me, but I held in my pee just because I didn't want to seem shady, even though I was already exposed. So I stood there and talked for a minute, while my bladder held its breath, before I headed up to the room.

"Are you still at the *Source*?" he asked.

"Yeah, I'm there." I opted not to mention that I had just been promoted to executive editor. It was the first time anyone had actually seen me with Nas in a way that it was obvious what I was doing there, and now that I was gunning for the editor-in-chief title, I didn't want to have to deal with this getting back to anyone that I worked with.

I spent that day in Phoenix, ridin' mini-scooters that they had been carrying with them on the tour bus. Even though Nas asked me to stay, I couldn't stomach being there any longer and risking someone at work finding out that I was spending my weekend in Phoenix with "God's Son" which was tattooed on his stomach, imperfectly (the apostrophe and the *s* having to be added after the tattoo artist made a mistake). I decided to catch the red-eye home later that night. Nas arranged to have a car service take me to the airport and gave me just enough cash to buy a ticket out of Phoenix. He was probably wondering what the hell my problem was, because I was acting so weird.

On the way to the airport, I noticed the missed calls from Tia, so I gave in and picked up when she called a third time.

"Where have you been, Kim? I've been calling you for two days?" she yelled.

"I've been out of town. Why are you yelling at me?"

"Because I left you messages and I don't understand why you haven't been picking up your phone. Where are you?"

I felt pressure because I knew the Phoenix thing was out of character for me. "I'm in Phoenix, about to fly home."

"Phoenix? What are you doing in . . . wait, are you with someone?"

"Not right now, but I was."

"Oh, no, you didn't. So you were with him and you weren't picking up the phone for *me* because you were with *him*?" she asked, making me feel as if I were cheating on her. I don't know why I hadn't picked up.

"I'm a private person. Why do I feel like I gotta tell you everything that I do? Like you're my mother or something."

"No. Mm. Mm. You don't have to tell me anything. But if I call, I expect you to call me back. What if something happened?"

Tia and I started arguing until we both hung up and copped an attitude with each other. I boarded the plane, fell asleep, and didn't call anyone until the next day.

At the office, people were starting to notice that I was a little too tied in to what was going to happen before it happened. "Nas is going to hang a Jay-Z doll at Summer Jam," I said a few weeks later, in a meeting with some of the staff.

"What? That is hilarious. What do you mean he's going to hang a doll of Jay-Z?" someone asked.

"It's a life-sized doll of Jay-Z. Like, I imagine it will look like a Muppet character or something." It wasn't Nas who had let me in on his little secret, but someone who knew we had been talking. "We should ask him to do a photo shoot with the doll. Imagine if we put that in this September issue when Jay is on the cover. Okay, I'm getting my hopes up now."

We laughed at the idea, knowing that it would never happen. Then we outlined the page map of the magazine for the September issue, which we were working on in June. Magazines are usually planned three months ahead, and at the *Source,* we worked on three issues at once. You are usually closing one issue, editing and assigning for the one after that, and creatively planning the third. An issue usually came out a month before its on-sale date. So this September issue we had been working on was actually due out in August. And we had just gotten in copies of the August issue, which seemed as if we had finished yesterday.

"Okay, so I'm going to need you to find four pages on the page map for me so I can put in this story about Summer Jam when this happens, because it's going to be big news. Take two pages out of the Jay-Z and Roc-A-Fella story. This means we'll have to cut two pages out of the 50 Cent story too. Cut it down to four," I told Tanya, who was now in charge of the page map. I knew that with her having been both Carlito's assistant and then the editorial coordinator, she had worked closely with the EIC and the managing editor. She was familiar with such things as the closing schedule and the writers' contracts, and she had a great relationship with the production department, so I promoted her to editorial manager. My plan was to train Tanya to eventually become the managing editor, once she learned all the ropes. But I never thought it would be a problem that, technically, two women would be running the editorial department.

Because she didn't have a journalism or a hip-hop background, I always weighed her opinion heavily. She was an R&B head, actually a former singer, and I knew if a story interested her, then it would work for the average reader. I didn't want to dumb down our stories in the magazine, but I also didn't want them to be over everyone's head. Many of my peers in the profession had often been way too critical of my style of writing. One of the things I'd learned in my legal journalism class in law school was to keep it simple. See, me, I'd rather nix all the big words and just give the people what they wanted, the information.

"Oooo, Johnnie gonna be mad," Tanya said about cutting down his 50 Cent story, which was scheduled to run in the hard-hitting September issue featuring Jay-Z on the cover, along with a rundown of Nas's Summer Jam drama. The 50 story hadn't been high on my radar because I was knee-deep in the other two, but after giving it a read, I realized that it was probably the best one in that issue. I came up with a cover line that would play off his getting shot, before every other magazine did: "50 CENT: The Recovered MC Shoots Back."

As Tanya and I continued to discuss the story, Tory opened the door and diddy-bopped into my office. He was adjusting his doorag and chewing on some gum. "Yo, D is looking for you, KO. He said come down to his office."

Still serving in my position as executive editor, I was at Dave's beck and call. If he needed something done, I made sure I took care of it. When his name or number showed up on my caller ID, I picked up, even if I was sleeping. I was trying to earn myself the title I knew I deserved. But while I was trying to be accommodating to my bosses, I was also creating a monster in the process.

I rushed down to Dave's office, at the opposite end of the hallway. His office was huge, and wood flooring instead of carpeting and two black sofas that formed an L-shape opening to the center of his space. Dave kept both of his two doors closed during meetings. You only got to use one door and had to pass through the office of his executive assistant, Dale Johnson. The other door was locked and mostly used by Dave to either rush down to the editorial side or take a shortcut to the bathroom. I'd never seen anyone barge in on Dave through that second door unannounced unless it was Ray.

"Yo, we're about to get rid of Curcurito," said Ray, who was pulling on a blunt and pacing back and forth.

"What? Why?" I was shocked and scared at the same time. I didn't know much about design, and as far as the look of the magazine went, Curcurito, aka Cucs (pronounced "kooks"), was the creative director and controlled most of it.

"He got a fuckin' panther on the cover with Eve. Wasted a whole goddamn gatefold. What kind of shit is that?" Ray was pissed in a way I had never seen him before. The current issue, which featured Eve, had a gatefold, which is an extra page that extends from the cover. Cucs had come up with the idea to have Eve seated by a pool next to a black panther. Crazy shit that didn't make any sense. What a panther would be doing by a pool in L.A., I couldn't tell you. But whereas Cucs was not trying to make sense of hip-hop, the artistic value in his work was intriguing. He would put rappers in the most awkward situations, such as Busta Rhymes drenched in black tar, or Redman cutting open his own head, showing his brains. Most of the time, it never meant anything, and we editors would figure out ways to make sense of it: "Redman is tapping into his own mind" or some shit like that.

Ray hated this Eve cover. To this day, I think if Eve had been in a bathing suit, he may have felt differently. I came up with a different idea for a cover. While planning the Eve cover, I had been invited to a studio session where Eve's first single was being completed. The song was called "Rock with You," produced by Irv Gotti.

Irv and I had developed a good relationship from working together on different stories. Knowing that we were planning an Eve cover, he thought I could get some ideas from hearing the leadoff single, which featured Alicia Keys. Eve had already recorded her verse, and Irv invited me to the Hit Factory so I could hear the record. When I arrived, Alicia Keys was already there in the booth laying down her vocals for the song's chorus, I.G. was punching buttons, Alicia's manager, Jeff Robinson, was watching attentively, and Steve Stoute was talking on a cell phone.

"Jimmy, it's a hit, Jimmy," Steve yelled into the cell phone before passing it around to all parties for confirmation. By the time the phone got to me, Jimmy Iovine was already in midconversation. Steve put the cell phone to my ear. "Talk to Kim, Jimmy," he said.

It didn't matter that Jimmy didn't know who I was. He asked for my opinion anyway. "Kim, do I have a hit on my hands? How does it sound?" I heard a distinctively Caucasian voice in my ear.

It took me a minute to answer because I had barely heard the record before a cell phone was thrust to my earlobe. So I made it a point to agree and then change the conversation and let the head of Interscope Records know that I was a devoted fan of his wife's books. Vicki Iovine was the author of a line of pregnancy and child-rearing books that I had started reading when I was pregnant with Kayla. They were called *The Girlfriends' Guide*, and were some of the few things I had read outside of the music genre in the last couple of years. Jimmy invited me to dinner at his house to meet his wife the next time I was in L.A. But that, of course, would never happen.

Neither would the Eve and Alicia Keys cover that I pitched once we left the studio session. When Keys came out of the booth, I jumped off the couch to tell her my plans. "Alicia, I want you on the cover of this next *Source* we're doing with Eve," I said, before Irv pulled me back. "This isn't *Source* business time, Kim. Get out of editor mode," he said.

"Alicia, I really want to put you on the cover. Will you do it if I can get it done?"

Keys had her hair all head-wrapped into a low-hanging bun. She smiled, probably shocked that someone she had never met was in her session.

"Yeah, I'll do it," she said, smiling, as she walked over to the boards to hear Irv play the track back.

As I think back, it could have been a good use of the gatefold, but it never happened. I was looking for a new approach to an Eve cover, and I thought putting an R&B artist such as Alicia and then doing a bunch of features in our annual "R&B package" in that same issue was a sure winner. But Dave said no, and we still got the post-Grammy Keys to do an interview with us for the issue. Things like that always made me feel that I went the extra mile for the *Source*.

By the time we shot Eve, solo, in Los Angeles for the cover the next week, Curcurito had already ordered a panther as her companion for the shoot. Imagine, we couldn't put Alicia Keys there with her, but a panther fit right in. Whereas I was so new that I'd run every little thing by Dave and risk getting shut down, Curcurito just did what he wanted and dealt with whatever came with it afterward. It was risky, but ultimately he got what he wanted. The idea pissed Ray off so much when he saw it that he decided to fire Cucs. But since I couldn't have my way, which was to put Alicia Keys on the cover with Eve, I found it kinda funny that Ray didn't get his way either. Knowing that Dave saw every cover before it went to press, though, I thought it was suspicious that this was the first time that Ray had heard of the panther. When Ray didn't approve of something that Dave had prior knowledge of, Dave would usually act as if he had just seen a white unicorn instead of owning up to having cosigned it.

"He gotta leave. He gotta get the fuck out today," Ray said about Curcurito while staring at the black panther on the cover.

I was speechless. I got along with Cucs, but wasn't about to go against Ray so early in the game. Three months in and I had already fired three people at Ray and Dave's direction, so I was down for whatever. But Curcurito reported directly to Dave and Ray so it was totally out of my hands.

By the next week, the office formerly belonging to Cucs was now occupied by someone with an extremely long last name. Paul Scirecalibrisotto was the new art director. He had worked under Cucs and, ironically, had signed the anti-me letter. I wasn't holding any grudges, but was always wondering what the art department had to say behind closed doors about my being appointed editor.

Individually, each member of the art department seemed cool, but collectively, a reasonable person could believe that they were out to destroy me. I think they all worked under the guise of "Let's make all these hip-hop artists do weird, funky things so we can win design awards." To them, it was art. But to the rest of us, it was some unnecessary bullshit that didn't always make sense for hip-hop. Our readers wanted to see straight-up, hard-core imagery. They wanted to see artists, dressed in army fatigues or sweat hoodies, mean-mugging the camera like someone had just cut their mama into pieces. They didn't care too much about the light from a window hitting the artist at a thirty-degree angle. A portrait of their favorite artist was fine, and it usually cost less to do and sold more in the end. Sometimes artists even came up with their own theories about what we did to their pictures after a photo shoot. Nas was convinced that the photographer changed his eye color to blue the last time he had graced the cover.

As the editor, I often had to liaise between my art department and the celebrities. It was easy to pitch something to them when I was sold on a concept. But a difference of opinion between the art department and me made it hard to get the work done. When we did come to an agreement, it ended up being one hell of a cover. But when the art department went out on their own and did something that I, Dave, or Ray didn't know about, I usually got blamed for it. That's why I tried to resolve those issues beforehand. But they felt that, as "visual" experts, they knew best. I was responsible for everything in the magazine even though much of it was somehow outside my control.

When we didn't agree, it was like civil war inside the *Source*. Sometimes when the editorial department asked for something, the art department would come up with a way to give us the opposite. In the mainstream, their work may have been considered artistic. And understanding that most of the art department didn't come from a hip-hop background, I couldn't knock their hustle of wanting to eventually land what they would consider a "real job" at a *Vanity Fair* or *Esquire*. But in hip-hop, it was a challenge to come up with ideas that pushed the envelope without being plain ol' cheesy.

"We're gonna have to put all of them on the cover," I said of the September issue. "Jay, Dame, Beanie Sigel, Cam'Ron, Memphis Bleek, even Freeway."

Seated around a large, wobbly conference-room table, the staff tossed ideas around to finish putting together the upcoming September issue, now less one experienced creative director.

"Freeway on the cover of the *Source*? He hasn't even put out an album yet," someone called out.

"It's impossible. I'm not putting all those people on the cover," said Paul. More people on the cover meant more work for the art department, and they usually opposed more than three people on one cover at a time. "There's too many of them and they're gonna be so small you won't be able to see any of them. I thought the whole point was to have Jay-Z on the cover."

"It is. Just put Jay in front and put everyone behind him. What's so hard about that?" I said.

"I don't know. They won't fit. You need to go back and tell them we can't do it," Paul said.

As the head of the department, I just loved it when everyone else told me what we were going to do. But chalk it up to my inexperience. If Dave had told the art department to fit everyone on the cover, it would have been done in a heartbeat. But of course, because I was giving the order, there was always dissension. I suppose it would have been different if there were more bass in my voice. I had to figure out a way to make it work, and to make everyone happy. That was another part of the job. But in the end, someone always had a problem.

After hours of meetings, we decided that the only way to put six people on the cover was to not put six people on one cover, but to put six people on two covers. Of course, Jay-Z would be on both, and since there was a rumor of trouble within their camp, we decided to put Dame Dash on both also. The cover would be what we call a split, the same issue that featured two different covers sold on newsstands. One would feature Jay, Dame, Cam, and Bleek and the other would feature Jay, Dame, Beans, and Freeway. The compromise gave us our Jay-Z cover and gave Dame his Roc-A-Fella cover. We could shoot everybody individually so we didn't run into scheduling issues with the artists, then superimpose all of them together against a New York backdrop. Once we presented the idea to Dave, he finally told us to move forward. I knew that Dave and Ray quietly hated that I had brokered the deal to make it happen. Usually, right before I'd seal the deal on a cover, Dave would step in and say, "Let me call them," and try to use the cover as a bargaining chip for something else he wanted the artist to do. But Jay-Z was never doing a record with Benzino, so I was shocked when the cover made it through.

"There's a black Lincoln Town Car for you outside." Michelle had reserved a car to take us out to the Summer Jam concert. The car had arrived a couple of hours early so that we could get a head start on traffic.

"I'm not ready to go yet. I still have to figure out the cover. And if Dave changes his mind at the last minute, then you should assume I'm not coming to the show," I said.

"Don't make me go alone . . . please." Michelle pleaded. We tried to keep each other company as often as possible at these types of shows so as not to have to talk to people we didn't really like.

"Is it just me and you?" I said.

"I only have passes for us two. But you have to come. Guess what I heard?"

"Uh, someone is going to perform a mock lynching at the show?" I said.

"No. Someone is *not* going to perform a mock lynching at the show."

"Huh. What did I miss?"

"I heard that Jay-Z made a phone call and then they told Nas he couldn't do it."

"Wow. Politics. I love it. I have to go. I'll be right out." According to various sources, Jay-Z had caught wind of what was about to happen and made the power phone call to executives at the radio station to stop it. Word was that if Nas went through with his mock lynching, there would be no relationship between Jay and Hot 97. Because Jay-Z was a bigger industry player, the station told Nas he couldn't do it. Later that night, the information network known as my girls were on top of the scoop while Michelle and I were hanging out backstage at the show. Steph Lova, a friend of mine and the DJ on duty at Power 105, sent me a two-way message as it was all going down.

Nas was going off on anyone and everyone on the air. When he was told he had to change his plan, he decided to detour to the station's competitor Power 105 and pull out of Summer Jam. I communicated with him via two-way that night and he was pissed. But I didn't need to speak to him to know that, because he was on the air dissing everyone at Hot 97. It was a big interview for Power 105, a fairly new station, and it was Nas uncensored. Back at the venue, people in the crowd were booing when they realized Nas wasn't going to show, and I felt that I had somehow missed the story that I could have had the access to.

criminal minded

"Yo, Kim." Antoine stood up from his chair in the large conference room and started to limp in my direction. I was cutting through the conference room just before noon to get to my office. "We should talk," he said with his usual grimy look.

"Yeah, what's up?"

"We're going to be working together real soon."

Most of us liked to cut through the conference room when we got to the office in the morning. But with that shortcut came the risk that you would have to speak to all kinds of people who had parked themselves there. Sometimes, they'd be in there smoking weed. Other times, they'd be in there watching a movie like *Scarface* or *The Usual Suspects*. The worst part was that many times the people in there didn't even work for the magazine. But it had clearly become the inside hangout spot at 215.

Antoine Clarke was a street cat from the Bronx. A brown-skinned dude, he walked with a limp and always talked out of the side of his mouth as if he were making an illegal transaction. Rumor had it that he had been shot in the foot after running away from someone during an altercation. In the late nineties, Antoine had launched his own magazine, called *F.E.D.S.*, which stood for "Finally Every Dimension of the Streets." The magazine did stories on notorious criminals such as Alpo and Nicky Barnes and was known for glorifying the street life. *F.E.D.S.* had not only become popular in the hip-hop community but had also become a favorite of Ray Benzino's. Unfortunately for us, Ray had offered office space to the guys from *F.E.D.S.* and had connected them to the *Source*'s distribution company. Hopes were that the *Source* would one day take over *F.E.D.S.*, but most of us suspected that Antoine and his crew were just juicing Ray and Dave for the free office space and supplies. It became increasingly difficult to deal with Antoine and his staff taking up space when we were already crowded, tripping over boxes in the hallway. They were located on the seventh floor with our accounting department, but as time went by, we started seeing more and more of the *F.E.D.S.* staff upstairs, in the conference room, and roaming the eleventh-floor hallways.

"You know they 'bout to fire you, right?" Antoine didn't waste any time getting straight to the point.

"What? What are you talking about?" I stopped in the conference room to hear what type of information Antoine was dishing out.

"You're too weak. They think that you're weak-minded," Antoine slurred.

"Who said that?" I was annoyed at what I was hearing, but I had to stop and listen.

"Dave and Ray. They want me to have your job."

"Huh?" I said, confused. Over the last couple of months, I had only received praise for the job I was performing, and I had already moved into the corner office. I believed that the title *editor in chief* was attainable, but Antoine was telling me something completely different.

And though things had seemed as if they were okay, he might know something that I didn't.

"I told them to keep you. They were going to just get rid of you. But I said, 'Nah, keep her and we can work as a team. We can be the coeditah." *Coeditor,* which he meant, wasn't a term I had ever heard at the *Source,* but leave it to Antoine to make up a word, then turn what should have been plural into a singular.

"So you're saying that they offered you a job. Wait, not just any job, but the editor-in-chief job?"

"Yeah, they gonna put me on staff. We didn't decide the title, but I would be running things and you could still run them too, with me." I listened to Antoine's incorrect English because it was starting to ring true to me. I started to drift farther away from Antoine as he spoke, walking back to my office worried. From what I observed, he could barely utter a correct sentence, let alone write a paragraph. He consistently used the wrong tense when speaking, so I knew his writing was probably not comprehensible. This couldn't be true. He was either making it up or twisting it around in his favor. But if they were going to bring him on staff, why wouldn't they consult me? Unless . . . unless it *was* true.

As soon as I got settled in my office, I picked up the phone and dialed 1748. Tanya picked up on the first ring. "Tanya, did you hear anything about Antoine coming on staff?"

There was a long pause as Tanya thought about it for a second, then she whispered, "I saw him down there a few times recently. Down in Dave's office, and I figured they were just talking *F.E.D.S.* stuff."

"He is saying that he's about to have my job. That—"

"Uh, Kim, he can't spell."

"I know, but you know how they're always talking about 'the streets' and sweating his little snitch of a magazine."

"Yeah, but . . ." Tanya's dissent started to turn into uncertainty. "Do you think they would do that?"

"I don't know. You know I don't put anything past them."

"Wow. That would be crazy. Wait, does that mean he would be my boss?"

"Girl, he is practically saying that he would be *my* boss. And that would be a hot mess."

After a brief moment of silence, Tanya gave me the prompt I needed to do what I knew I wanted to do. "Ask Dave," she said.

"You think I should?" I didn't really want to do anything that would ruffle anyone's feathers.

But then she gave me another prompt. "Yeah, ask him."

Though I wanted to confront Dave, I figured it was better to wait until the morning. I knew I'd be clearheaded and less emotional about it if I waited, so I decided to keep it moving for the night. I was still in the middle of an issue, trying to lock down all the interviews for our infamous Roc-A-Fella cover. Their publicist had set up a meeting/ interview with CEO Damon Dash for that evening, and I had to pull myself together for it. This September issue was like the one that we just couldn't finish.

I was in a crowded elevator by the time I realized that I was doing an interview. And as so many other times, I didn't have my tape recorder. I always got the best interviews when I wasn't recording them. Subjects are usually more open and up-front when they know there's no proof that they actually said something. Quotes usually turned into paraphrasing and colorful stories about the setting. When the recorder isn't around, I'm much more perceptive about what someone's wearing or what is really going on. It was my way of convincing myself that I was actually working, even though I wouldn't have any hard evidence to back that up.

I noticed that the redheaded white girl in the elevator with us was wearing a Roc-A-Fella chain as a belt about an inch below her navel. "You know who that is, right?" Dame said in his usual I-know-more-than-you tone.

"Am I supposed to?" Sorry, but I didn't recognize random white chicks who wanted to be down with hip-hop.

"Victoria Beckham. Posh Spice. You know, the Spice Girls."

"I know who the Spice Girls are, thank you very much." Though I didn't recognize each of them individually unless it was Eddie Murphy's baby mama, I knew who she was once he said so.

"Her music is gonna be crazy," Dame said to an unconvinced me. I just smiled at her though and acted as if I cared.

"Wait till you hear this M.O.P. music. It's ridiculous," he said.

On a normal day, I would have been excited to hear one of my favorite groups. But this night, on my way up to the studio where they were recording, my mind was preoccupied with the thought that my opinion might not matter in a few days if I got replaced. I knew more than ever that I had to lock down the final piece of the September issue, an interview with Jay.

"So, is Jay gonna do this interview? We need him to do it to finish our story."

Dash got belligerent. "Don't ask me nothing about Jay. Jay does what he does. Ask me about anybody on Roc-A-Fella except Jay. Ask Jay about Jay."

"But I can't because I haven't been able to get at him, and I need to figure this out like now." The elevator doors opened and we all spilled out into the lobby area of the recording studio. Dame conveniently changed the conversation. "So we puttin' M.O.P. on the cover too?"

"You never mentioned M.O.P. I can't do that. It's too late. They'll get a lot of love on the inside."

He laughed, and I breathed a sigh of relief as that brief second had me nervous that my cover would have to be renegotiated all over again. My hip was buzzing.

I opened my two-way and noticed a long message from 50 Cent that I didn't have time to read. I glanced at it and could make out the words *XXL* in his message. Knowing I wasn't about to respond at that moment anyway, I just closed my pager and went on with my meeting.

"What did you think of that?" Damon asked me about an M.O.P. record featuring Posh Spice.

"It was cool." The truth was, I wasn't even paying attention.

It was after midnight by the time I got into my car. The day had passed quickly and I knew by 7 a.m. the next morning, I'd have to do it all over again. I figured I would get a head start on the next day, so I decided to read the message from 50. "*XXL* is going to give me a six-page story if I give my story to them instead." The rest of the message was like Chinese to me because my competitive spirit had me riled up. I immediately responded, SEND NUMBER.

"You sat in my office and gave me your word that you were doing this story, and now you're talking about *XXL*. You must not be a man of your word." I had my professional-snide voice on when I called him back.

"I'm a businessman. I have to do what's best for my career."

"Well, think about this. Is it best for your career to do a longer story with a magazine that sells less or is it best to do a slightly shorter story with a magazine that sells much more. I thought you wanted to be in the *Source*." I knew my September issue wasn't as good without the 50 story, but I was gambling with it because bumping up the page count at this point would shake up my art department.

"I'm gonna give you the story, I just wanted to let you know. That other magazine, they don't like you too much."

"Ha. You know what? And I hate mustard, but people still use it on their hot dogs. You think I care that they don't like me? They wanna be me."

Hate always put me in rare form. 50 wasn't the first to tell me that people at the other magazine had been dragging my name through the mud, but it actually made me feel important. I looked at it, like, I'd rather be talked bad about than not talked about at all.

· · ·

"Kim, pick up the phone." I knew when Tory told me I was getting a phone call from Jay's publicist that something was about to go wrong with my cover.

"Okay, so I need you to fly to the south of France to do the Jay-Z interview." As fabulous as it sounded, I couldn't just pick up and leave. It was hard for people to notice, but I had a little girl waiting for me at home.

"When? I need to have this story in by Monday," I said to her.

"Tomorrow."

"Tomorrow? I can't get out there tomorrow." With no babysitter, picking up and leaving was out of the question.

"I have to call you back to confirm, but you'll have to fly to France, then take a boat to the island where he is."

Seemed like an awful lot of traveling for an interview, but I knew that my new title was riding on this story, so I was ready and willing to go on a scavenger hunt around the world to find the artist that I needed to interview. The magazine issue was completely finished, except for an interview with Jay-Z, and I was now being hit with the news that it couldn't be done in the continental United States.

"We can't call him. We have to wait for him to call in," she said. It was like some *CSI*-type of operation getting this guy on the phone.

"Are you kidding? I'm going to miss my deadline. I need to make this happen. It's already shot, the cover is done, and the story is almost complete."

"There's nothing I can do. Jay is on vacation, but he says he'll do the interview in France. There are things he wants to address."

When it came to my job, I was hungry, and I was willing to do whatever I had to for the benefit of the magazine. Despite the industry flirting, the relationships with artists, and my love for the game, I was truly loyal to only one thing, and that was the black and white ink on the pages that got published every month.

France never happened. It was too close to the deadline and Def Jam was taking way too long to set it up. So Jay finally agreed to do the interview by phone. Although I was supposed to be writing the story, I couldn't get my schedule to match the times he was available to talk on the phone, especially since we were in closing mode and I was in the thick of shipping pages to the printer, so knowing I couldn't do the story justice with my workload, I farmed the interview out to a trusted writer. We decided to insert a question-and-answer section of Jay-Z's interview into the main story at the last minute to allow Jay a fair opportunity to give his side of the story.

Jay didn't seem happy about an announcement that Damon had made while Jay was on vacation. Cam'Ron was the new VP of Roc-A-Fella, and our story was the first real response from him. It was also the first time anyone had talked to him this in depth since "Ether" and the battle with Nas. The cover story was about to be a big one. I started to adopt a familiar Jay-Z motto: I will not lose.

CHAPTER EIGHT

california love

The September issue received a great response. It actually became the bestselling issue of *The Source*, and I had to keep the momentum going, so following it up with a Murder Inc. cover was going to be explosive. The beef between 50 Cent and Ja Rule was heightening ever since Eminem's Shady/Aftermath Records had announced their signing of 50. It was the right time for a Murder Inc. cover, so Ja Rule and his crew could give their side of the story.

We had come up with an idea for the October cover. We would feature the Inc. burning money. Anthony Mandler, an extremely talented photographer who would later win awards for directing music videos, came up with an incredible set that resembled an old warehouse as the backdrop for his dark concept. Murder, kill, dark, blood! The closer we got to a *Godfather* sequel, the happier Irv Gotti became. Everything was set up to take place in Los Angeles.

"Why didn't you take the highway?" I was sitting at a red light somewhere in Queens, trying to block out the sounds of the loud driver's foreign conversation. I knew it wasn't Spanish, French, or Italian, but it sure was annoying.

"Highway is too crowded. This way faster, trust me," said the driver as the words met his spit somewhere outside his mouth.

Rush-hour traffic on a Friday evening is torturous, especially when it's local. At four thirty in the afternoon, I was on my way to JFK Airport trying to catch a 5:45 p.m. flight to Long Beach, California.

"Uuggghhh." I let out a frustrated sigh to let him know I was not happy. Even though I had priority check-in, heightened security at the airport post-9/11 would make it hard for even the president to board a plane. So I knew my chances of making this flight were slim.

As luck would have it, a certain somebody was out in Los Angeles getting his own work done. Curtis Jackson, aka 50 Cent, was almost finished recording his highly anticipated debut album, *Get Rich or Die Tryin'*. The article that we ran on 50 Cent was the first piece that had told such a comprehensive story on him, and we had got really cool since then. A little too cool. 50 had gone to Kinko's and had that story blown up into a laminated photocopy. He had also started calling me.

Right before 50 went out to L.A., we became friends. Industry friends, of course. Then one day, he asked me to be more than that. Initially, I was caught off guard. It happens in the music industry. One minute you are working, then the next minute you are in a full-blown relationship, or at least that's what you think it is until it's over. Our conversations would start off with SoundScan numbers, the recording industry's weekly synopsis of album sales, then end with what he would sound like a song line. I used to hit the speakerphone button while he was talking just so someone in the network could see me mouth the words as he said them because I always knew what he was about to say. Sometimes I would hear words in songs that I swore I'd heard before. "Will you be my best friend," he asked me once during a late night phone call. I think 50's everyday conversation is just constant practice for his next album.

During the time we were talking, there was never a time when I couldn't get ahold of him, until that day when I was on my way to L.A. It took him three hours to return my call, and it made me doubt his intentions. *Now that he knew I was actually coming out to L.A., was he flaking on me?* After talking to Nas for months, it was no longer acceptable to communicate via text messaging which is somehow what our conversation had turned into. 50 was giving me the attention that I needed. His mack game was a joke to me at first, but as with any girl, the more attention they pay you, the more you start to like them.

"Where have you been? I've been calling your phone for three hours!" I said to him when he finally called me back.

"I was at the gym."

"For three hours?" *Who works out for three hours?* I thought. Back then, I didn't believe him. Nowadays, seeing that his physique resembles a professional wrestler, I understand that he was probably telling the truth.

"I'm getting ready for my album-cover shoot. I gotta look right. Wait till you see what the album cover looks like." He went on to explain his concept, and at that moment I realized, whenever it came to our conversations, it was always about him. About his career. About his album. About his projected SoundScan sales (I had heard from him more than once that he was going to sell a million in his first week, although it actually turned out to be 800K). When it came to the business of music, he was like a record industry A&R on steroids. Pun intended.

Never in my whole life had I ever met someone who was so consumed with himself. But then again, that's what my friends had said about me since I had gotten the job of editor in chief. This was going to be my first exercise in bringing myself down a notch. I kept telling myself, *It's not about me*, so whenever I talked to 50 Cent, I let the world revolve around someone else.

"Okay, well, I don't think I'm going to make this flight. I feel like Miss Daisy, that's how slow this car-service driver is going."

"Don't worry, you'll make it," he said, before bringing the conversation back to his favorite topic, himself. "Jimmy thinks my album is going to be the biggest album this year."

"I gotta go." Whenever 50 wasn't talking about the music industry, I sincerely liked him. But he always managed to regroup and make everything we discussed somehow relate back to either what he did or even what I did.

I jumped out of the car when we arrived at the American Airlines terminal at JFK Airport. Luckily for me, I breezed right through security. It's much easier when you're late and you're flying business class than it is when you're a measly peasant sitting in coach.

Flying business class was a perk I had worked out when I negotiated my salary as the executive editor. I had originally asked for 130K to do the job, knowing that the editor in chief's salary was somewhere around there. They had agreed to bump me up to 100K with the condition that if I did a good job as the executive editor, they would promote me to EIC after three months. When three months had passed, I was given a raise to 115K to keep me happy for the moment. Ray always said that the editors at the *Source* were overpaid. Meanwhile, he got paid close to half a million dollars a year. To me, I was right in the salary range I should have been in, with my experience and postgraduate education. I had a JD from an accredited law school, which made my degree higher than Dave's. So what if he had gone to Harvard.

Even though it would totally be justified at any other magazine for the editor to fly business, I became the envy of much of the staff. Major complaints were going around behind my back because I insisted on being upgraded on every single flight. What the staff didn't realize was that this was my condition. It was something I made certain of, just on principle. Men were promoted from the mailroom to music editor, but of course I needed to prove myself first. Dave said the executive editor step was a formality. The magazine's sales were at their best and were increasing with each issue, but apparently it wasn't enough for me to get promoted right away. Damn it, if I couldn't get the title that I deserved, I was at least going to get the perks that came with it. I'll have my mimosa before we take off, please.

It was about 8 p.m. when I touched down in Long Beach, and I had a bunch of two-way messages that had come through. I always flew to Long Beach because it was cheaper for the company. One message was from Dave, instructing me to start setting up a Lil' Kim cover for November. Another was from Tanya, telling me about the party the *Source* was throwing to celebrate the September issue. A message from 50 asked me to page him when I landed. And the last one, surprisingly, was from Nas, who I hadn't heard from in a month. My first priority was always to answer Dave and take care of the magazine. Then I hit 50 back to let him know I had arrived safely and to give him directions to where he should pick me up. I didn't even bother to respond to Nas, who was asking, "Where you been?" Though I had dug him in the beginning, we never addressed his relationship status. Obviously, I understood there were other women, but I had always assumed there was no girlfriend. Then, one day, when he was working on his *God's Son* album in Miami, and I was in town, I met him at Circle House Studios. His phone rang, and he shushed me, with his finger over his mouth, before he picked up the phone and ran out of the room. The last thing I needed was some girl running up on me while I was sleeping, so after that I decided that it was best to leave him alone. *The nerve.*

When I arrived at my hotel in L.A. that night, the concierge told me my reservation wasn't paid for, and since I only had a bank card with a small balance, I couldn't pay for the room. It was just like the *Source*'s travel agent to leave someone stranded out of town on a Friday night. I made some phone calls and told the hotel desk that it would be straightened out by the time I got back. I was staying at the Sunset Marquis, a discreet spot off Alta Loma Road in West Hollywood. The hotel was around the corner from the Mondrian, but because of its location on a side street, I never ran into anyone there. The rooms at the Marquis were all normal-size suites, so there was no chance of getting stuck in a fancy four-by-four room with an art deco sink that would stab me in the stomach if I slipped on a wet floor.

I was exhausted by the time 50 and I sat down at the movies to watch Martin Lawrence's stand-up comedy film *Run Tel Dat* at the Beverly Center. Even though the film wasn't very good, I managed to stay awake. When I looked over, 50's head was bent backward, perpendicular to his neck, and he was snoring. I let him sleep until the movie was over.

When we got back into the rented SUV, 50 popped in a CD and started adjusting the knobs on the car stereo. "I want you to hear something."

Then, with his baseball cap cocked to the side covering his doorag (as if a doorag were a fashion statement), he started nodding his head as the beat started to play. "G-g-g-g-g-Unit." Now he was lip-synching the words to a song called "Back Down." This was a different version from the one that would make the album.

The song dissed everybody. Not just Ja Rule and Murder Inc., but Jay-Z, Cam'Ron, and others. In particular, the lines that stood out were a reference to Ja Rule sounding like the Cookie Monster, a line where 50 called Jay-Z gay, and a dis to Cam'Ron's pink fashion sense, and sudden weight loss. I knew from 50's first album (which never came out) that this was the formula to his success. It was all about putting everyone on blast and talking recklessly on records. But this was song was worse than "How to Rob."

"Are you really going to put that out?"

"I don't care. I'll put it out, but Dre and Em don't want me to," he replied, before quickly switching the subject. "You can stay in my room if you need to."

I let out a big laugh. "I'm not staying in your room. I don't know you like that." I was still undecided about whether I was ever going to sleep with him.

"Listen, I sent Banks and Yayo back to New York, and I'm staying in their room. It's a room at Le Meridien with two beds. I'm not going to try anything. Do you think I really need to do that?"

Unfortunately for me that evening, no one ever responded and fixed my hotel situation. At my sister's request, I had closed all of my credit-card accounts while in law school and had joined a credit-counseling service so that I could pay off my enormous debt. But the *Source* was in a worse position than I was. The magazine had run up an American Express bill into the millions, and therefore no more corporate cards could be issued to anyone on staff. That meant that until the travel agent called the hotel and gave them authorization, I could not check in.

"So what are you going to do?" 50 said as he pulled into the drive-through of a fast-food restaurant called Carl's Jr. on La Cienega, which I decided was a better alternative than trying to find a good place to eat at two in the morning. Plus, it was much more discreet, since you never knew whom you could possibly run into at Fatburger's.

"I'm gonna borrow cash from you and I'm going to check into my hotel," I said.

"I don't have any cash on me." For some reason, I didn't believe him, but I figured if this was his game, who was I to crush his hopes? Plus, I felt comfortable with him and figured we would eventually get together, so why wait three or four more weeks and try to hold out just for argument's sake? One of my male friends always says to me that a woman knows whether she is going to sleep with a man within the first few minutes of their meeting. I disagree with his timing. But I definitely knew after that night. So I hopped out of the truck and went back in to grab my bags from the front desk. "I'll be right back," I said to 50. Then, when I came out, he loaded my bags into the back of the truck. The both of us were so beat when we got upstairs that we just lay down and went to sleep. But we eventually ended up in the same bed.

The next morning, I woke up in a twin-size bed at Le Meridien hotel next to 50 Cent. I hadn't drunk alcohol the night before, but I still felt as if I had a hangover, especially since he may have just had me hung over something a few hours before. I glanced at the time on the clock beside the bed and realized it was 7 a.m., which was normally the time I would have woken up. But since I was on Pacific standard time, 7 a.m. meant that I had slept three hours late. My fatigue made it clear that he was more physically fit than I was.

I slid out of bed to silence my pager, which was continually buzzing. "Why didn't you answer my page yesterday?" The message was from Nas. I hadn't heard from him in a month, and now between last night and today, this was like a movie. My paranoia started to set in again, with me thinking that Nas was paging me only because he knew something. After seeing how much attention I got from 50, I couldn't help but conclude that Nas didn't like me enough for me to respond to him. 50 and I talked every day nonstop, but Nas checked in at his leisure. I was on to the next, and I couldn't keep talking to both of them at the same time.

Men can see as many women as they like. But a woman who decides that she wants to see more than one guy is promiscuous. It worked for the girls on *Sex and the City*, but not for girls in hip-hop. I know women who do it, but I couldn't. And if I was going to start now, these weren't the two individuals to use as lab rats. Maybe part of it was guilt, because I knew there was some issue between the two of them, or maybe I knew that something was inherently wrong with not coming clean with either of them about my relationship with the other.

Both to me and in print, 50 had mentioned more than once that he wasn't happy about Columbia Records' decision to take him off a Jennifer Lopez record and put Nas on it. He had actually opened for Nas on one of his tours, and the two had become seemingly cool. But behind closed doors, 50 felt that Nas had done him dirty. He resented Nas for that, but the interesting thing was that the one time I bought 50 up to Nas before he knew how 50 felt, Nas was supportive of him. Still, I kept the Nas relationship from 50.

Later on that day, 50 and I stopped at the Beverly Center and hit Bloomingdale's. Because I couldn't shop with someone looking over my shoulder, I picked out a pair of 7 jeans and a shirt and threw it on the counter.

"That's all you want?" He seemed surprised I wasn't taking advantage of the shopping spree.

"Yeah, I want to be able to carry my luggage on the plane when I go home, so I don't want a lot of stuff."

50 pulled out a wad of cash and paid for the clothes. It was a nice gesture, but it was starting to seem really awkward to me. He was being way too nice, from the shopping spree to the "baby . . . baby . . . baby" every five minutes. Tia always says my biggest problem when it comes to men is that I don't like the guys who know how to treat me right. But that's because the fairy-tale relationships seem so fake to me. I throw up in my mouth every time I see a couple holding hands in the street. I'm not with the PDA. Plus, when it came to my personal life, I always felt that I had to watch my back. The industry was one big double standard, and as a woman, I knew that this relationship could turn into some ugly gossip that could wind up on the front page of *XXL*. I was not about to get seen at the Beverly Center buying clothes with 50 Cent. That wasn't a scenario I could talk my way out of. If you get caught with someone at dinner, you can always say you were having a business meeting. Even if you're at someone's hotel room, it could be purely professional. I have actually conducted interviews with artists inside their hotel rooms, from Destiny's Child to LL Cool J, so that was something that you could explain too. But being at the mall with someone, there's really no way to get out of that one. "I was doing a story on him and thought the mall would be a great backdrop for our story." It doesn't even sound right.

I remember having dinner with James Cruz, a music executive who worked for 50 Cent's management company at the time, whose advice to me was "Keep your legs closed." I began to wonder how that could be a topic of conversation between two professionals, even though I knew he meant no harm. "As a woman in this industry, you should never get involved with anyone," he told me. Okay, and *who am I supposed to be involved with?* I wanted to ask him. Once you're trapped in the hip-hop industry bubble, there's no getting out. It becomes increasingly harder to meet people that are outside of that bubble. Therefore, the pool of available men for a single woman is slim to none. But knowing the issue was bigger than our conversation, I just responded, "Yeah, I know what you mean." Little did he know, it was too late for that. I had a past, but it wasn't even that bad. These were just two relationships that happened to fall in around the same place on the time line. *C'mon now, I never claimed to be a virgin.*

On our way back from the mall, 50 said he wanted to make a stop. He pulled up to a Bentley dealership on a corner in Los Angeles and started window-shopping. The salesman noticed us standing outside, and that's when we decided to go in.

"How much is this one?" 50 asked.

"This one goes for about 250,000," the salesman answered, looking at 50 Cent as if he were having pipe dreams.

50 opened the door, climbed in, and put his hands around the steering wheel. Then for a moment, he didn't say anything. He got out and we left. Two weeks later, I heard the "Wanksta" record for the first time. Funny, I thought. It was *him* who went to the dealership and didn't cop nothing.

We both couldn't wait to exit the dealership and laugh at that the sales guy's treating us like Oprah at the Hermès store in Paris.

"Did you see the way the sales guy was looking at you?" I asked as we walked out of the store.

"Yeah, he probably though I was about to stick him," 50 said, smiling.

"Ha, it's a good thing you don't know his name or it'd be in your next record."

50 laughed, then held the passenger-side door open for me to climb in. *I know how to open my own door,* I thought. *I can't take much more of this chivalry act.*

Then when he got in the car, 50 continued to run the game. "Wanna go to Tiffany's on Rodeo Drive and look at the jewelry?"

Tempted, I agreed, "Sure, let's go, but I have to warn you, I'm a sucker for gifts that come in a little blue box."

50 put his CD back into the car stereo and I heard the "Back Down" record play again. I only heard that version twice while I was in Los Angeles, but I never heard the same version again. When the album came out, an edited version of the song was on it. It kept the disses to Ja Rule and Murder Inc., of course, and chopped out all the rest. The song is like a pink elephant in hip-hop, because no one will admit that it actually existed. Either way, it was helping to stir the beef with Murder Inc. back up again, and the *Source* was right there to report on it.

murder was the case

I arrived at the Murder Inc. photo shoot in L.A. on Monday, after spending the entire weekend with 50. He caught a flight back to New York that same morning and dropped me off at my hotel, which had finally been taken care of by the travel agent. Ironically, he was fully aware that I would leave him and go straight to the shoot where his number one rival would be featured on the cover. It actually was an interesting end to our weekend. But it was business, and we both knew that he would be one of the biggest topics of the cover story. The controversy was exactly what he wanted for his career, and exactly what I needed for the magazine.

At the shoot, everyone was busy getting dressed up in their 1920s-themed clothing. It all fit into Gotti's recurring gangster theme. And I titled the story, after 50's first album, "Power of the Dollar."

Ashanti and Charli Baltimore had already been in hair and makeup for hours by the time I came in, but we were still waiting on Ja Rule and Irv Gotti. I had no intention of letting anyone within a thousand miles of this photo shoot find out that I had spent the weekend with their archenemy.

Once the major players arrived, my writer started to get his interviews. Gotti kept hinting that there were "spirits" in the room, meaning Tupac. Ja Rule's Tupac references bothered many fans, but at the time you couldn't tell him anything. The story was going to be huge, especially with the things they were saying about 50.

I remember having to fight hard as hell to get Ray and Dave to agree to do a Murder Inc. cover, though it wound up being the second-bestselling cover after the Roc-A-Fella issue. Even after we had photographed it, Dave kept acting as though he were going to change it. This was, of course, before Ja Rule and Benzino became BFFs. But back in August of 2002, Dave paged me with other options for the October cover. "What about Snoop?" he continually suggested.

Snoop had been on the cover numerous times, and we were running out of things to do with him. I fought for the Ja Rule cover because he was hot at this time, with hit songs "Always on Time," "Livin' It Up," and "Down Ass Bitch" on the charts. Forget Bell Biv DeVoe; Rule had become the new definition of hip-hop smoothed out on the R&B tip. And it was working. Ironically, the same formula that early in his career 50 clowned Ja for using would become the formula that 50 himself used. "Ja wants to make gangster records like me, and I want to make pop records like Ja," 50 would say. He was referring to the pop-tinged rap songs with the R&B hooks. Ja may have had some problems with other artists, such as a short-lived back-and-forth thing with DMX, but it was his beef with 50 Cent that was making all the headlines.

50 had gone into detail about his beef with Ja Rule and Murder Inc. numerous times when we talked on the phone. He told me, and every major publication, that it started when Ja had got robbed and then later seen 50 at a club with the person who robbed him. 50 had relived the

story over and over to me in the few weeks before we had met out in L.A. I heard it almost as many times as I'd heard him recite laws from Robert Greene's *48 Laws of Power*. Like any journalist, I went out and bought the book so I could see just how much of it 50 knew by heart. Sometimes artists will cite books just to sound smart, without having even read them. I quickly started to see how 50's moves resembled the laws in the book. *Fascinating. He can actually read,* I thought. But he did more than read that book. He lived by it.

The more I think about it, the more I see how Ja Rule could have saved himself from career suicide if he had just played better chess or got his own copy of the book and anticipated every 50 move. 50 mapped out his plan to destroy Ja's career because he felt that Ja and Murder Inc. had put the stops on his career for so long. He actually kept saying, "I'm going to destroy him completely." And he eventually did. I didn't understand why it was so serious to him. Whenever I brought up Ja Rule or Murder Inc., I always had to hear how 50 punched him in the face down in Atlanta and then somehow ended up with Ja's chain. According to 50, he exchanged the chain for a watch when some street cats from Queens approached him about it. That's how Ja got his chain back, 50 said. I heard that story almost as much as I heard the one about the bullet that hit him in the thumb and came out of his pinkie.

I took a red-eye back to New York that Monday evening and was in the office by 11 a.m. on Tuesday morning. I hadn't seen Kayla in four days so I brought her up to the office with me. I punched in the code to get through the door that separated the reception area from the offices, and the tech guy who was walking by smiled at me deviously and then started singing a familiar 50 Cent mixtape song called "Bad News." *Coincidence,* I thought.

Surprisingly, Tory had beat me to the office that morning and was sitting at his desk. "What's up, K.O.?" His smile was as big as a lottery winner's.

"Hi, Tory. Why are you smiling at me?"

"You'll see."

I was juggling my bag, Kayla's toys, and a cup of Starbucks, so I leaned my back against my office door to push it open. When I turned around, I saw nothing but roses. One hundred of them.

"Tory!" I yelled. *"Come in here."*

Then, as if I could hide a hundred roses from the rest of the staff, I shut the door behind him. "Who sent these?" I asked fearfully.

Tory was still smiling and let out a little giggle. "I don't know. There's a card there."

Up until that day, most flowers were sent to me as thank-yous or as birthday gifts. That day, though, I had a feeling they weren't from my mother. I was nervous to think that they could be from him. And my first thought was *How the heck am I going to get these flowers out of here?* But it was my guilt talking, so I figured it probably looked innocent to everyone else. *I'll just tell them someone has a crush on me.*

I could hear Tanya's voice outside my office. "Did I hear Kayla?"

I saw the doorknob turn and then Tanya walked in. When she saw the flowers, her jaw dropped and she took a deep breath, then said, "Uhhhhh." She was about to yell, but the look on my face interrupted her. My eyes opened wide and I put my finger over my lips. "Sshhhh."

"Kim, who sent these? They're so pretty,"

"I don't know."

"I'm gonna leave y'all alone." Still smiling, Tory walked out and shut the door behind him.

"Is there a card?" she asked.

"Yes, but I haven't looked at it. I'm scared. I think *he* sent those." I paused, then voiced my concern, "I hope he didn't send those."

"Why not? Kim, he likes you."

"He can like me outside the office, but he can not like me here in front of everybody."

Tanya reached into the big bunch of roses on the coffee table and pulled out a small pink envelope.

"Open it," I told her.

Then she read it out loud: "'I have to go out of town.'"

She handed me the card and I noticed the signature first. *50 Cent.*

"Why is it written like that? Look." I flipped the card around so Tanya could see it again. The signature was scratched down into the card so hard that you could feel the words embroidered from the other side. "This is not, like, written by the flower shop. He signed this card himself."

"Maybe he was mad when he wrote it," she joked.

"Maybe he was thinking about Ja Rule. How do you make your *handwriting* look mean?" We both started laughing at the handwriting.

"Don't tell anyone he sent these," I said firmly.

"Uh, please, who am I gonna tell?" Tanya smiled and said in a soft voice, "This is so cute."

"Please stop, Tanya. No one. Don't tell anyone. I do not want anyone to know that 50 sent these flowers."

I went on with my day ignoring all the questions that I got from everyone about the roses. Thinking it was my and Tanya's little secret, I told everyone that it was "nobody" when they asked who sent them. But word had spread like cancer, because little did I know 50 had dropped them off personally.

I looked up from my computer and Johnnie was standing in front of me admiring the flowery decor. "You got the roses from 50, right?"

"Yes. How did you know he sent them?" I asked, not wanting to admit it, but knowing it was probably something I couldn't deny.

"How do you think they got up here? He called me from downstairs, and Tory and I brought them up here."

"He was downstairs?" I asked, though my anger was heightening internally.

"Yeah, he called me real early and asked me to bring them up."

Luckily, Ray didn't come to the office that day because he might have heard who sent them. Dave, on the other hand, had no clue because he walked into my office and just said, "Somebody likes you."

For a few minutes, I tried to rationalize why 50 wouldn't just have the flowers delivered. He had just gotten back into town from L.A. a day ago and was busy finishing his album and apparently getting ready to go back out of town. It was almost as if he wanted people to know. And once I saw how big he was about to become, I knew the editor of the *Source* couldn't afford to let anyone know.

The editor has two jobs. One is to be the editor inside the office, and the other is to be the editor outside the office. Outside the office, however, I had a life that I wanted to keep separate from my job. That's why one of the most important decisions made as the top dawg is to choose the second-in-command. When you are not available to be on television representing the magazine, that person will appear on the show instead of you, and when you are not available in the office, that person should be able to run the editorial department in your absence, keeping you informed and always having your back. Selecting someone to back me up wasn't the hard part; it was getting Dave and Ray to approve of that person.

One of my recommendations for a promotion was Jermaine Hall. Jermaine was a strong editor, still fairly new to the editorial department. Though he had been hired while Carlito was still the editor, I had referred him for the job. Shortly after I was promoted, I bumped Jermaine up in title. But Ray had his reasons for not approving of Jermaine.

"What has he done to get a promotion?" Ray said, standing over both Tanya and me in a back room at his recording studio around Thirteenth Street. His eyes were bloodshot and he was rolling a blunt with his fingers. His hair was in fuzzy cornrows that obviously hadn't been rebraided in weeks.

"He's a really good editor, Ray. He did that industry package we just had, and the baller package." I was not prepared for the conversation, and although Jermaine had a lot of good work under his belt, I was too nervous to think of much at that time or to speak without breaks between my sentences. I remembered a collection of stories that had recently run as part of an annual "industry package" we put together to highlight people working behind the scenes in music, and a package Jermaine had spearheaded crowning artists for making the most money, known as the baller package.

"Industry package? What's an industry package? What was so good about that?" Ray was familiar with most of the things we ran in the magazine, or at least those that pertained to his own career. It might have helped if I had credited Jermaine with some gun-toting photo or a drug-dealing wrap-up, because Ray already had his plans for another top editor, though I didn't know it yet.

"Nah. Jermaine ain't good, Kim. We ain't gonna promote Jermaine. I don't trust him."

"He's good peoples, Ray. He'll be good. The staff likes him too."

"You think I care what *they* want?" The volume of Ray voice's turned up a notch, still controlled enough to remain inside the four walls of the small room. "They didn't want *you* to have the job, remember that, Kim? If I listen to them, then Erik is the new editor."

He had a point.

"Plus, why are you trying so hard to help this guy? What has he done for you?" Ray lit the blunt with his lighter. "Oh, I get it. You're fucking him."

Shocked at the out-of-nowhere accusation, I got defensive. "What? No, I'm not." I was quick to defend myself. I was so pissed off about an accusation like that coming from my boss. But whereas the speed of my answer should have been consistent every time he asked the question in the future, it wasn't. I should never ever have felt that I had to answer him whenever he asked it, which was happening more often than not.

Tanya moved farther back on the couch. "Ray, you're crazy."

"Yes, you're fuckin' him," he continued. "That's why you want to promote him, so you guys can be like the couple at the top. Sorry, but your boyfriend is not getting the promotion. As a matter of fact, I don't like him. He's a hater. Fire him."

Ray was consumed with sex and fucking, and I would later find out that he equated everything to men and women and their carnal pleasures. Accusing me of sleeping with Jermaine wouldn't be the last time Ray linked me to someone on staff. I was so bothered by it, but I knew I had to accept it if I wanted to keep my job. I couldn't tell Ray that I was uncomfortable about it because I was afraid of how he might react.

"I can't believe we have to fire Jermaine," Tanya said to me in her car, which we had ridden in over to the studio after leaving the office earlier that evening.

"We can't fire him. If we fire him, then we will be doubling our workload."

"Well, let's not bring it up to him," Tanya suggested. "I bet Ray will forget about it because he's high right now. Let's see how long we can go without firing him."

Our plan worked up until Jermaine somehow found out his career fate was in the hands of Benzino and quit. He left to go work for his friend Datwon Thomas, the editor in chief at *King* magazine. Ironically, before recommending Jermaine, I had actually offered the *Source* position to Datwon, who turned it down to move forward with the then start-up magazine at Harris Publications, a rival company that also published the *Source*'s main competitor, *XXL*. The irony is that *King* is one of the last surviving urban publications today, and Jermaine Hall is now its editor in chief. Toward the end of my time at the *Source*, Ray tried to get us to be more and more like *King*, with images of women in bikinis on the covers and articles that appealed to mature male readers. But Ray never gave any credit to anyone that left the *Source* (whether people left on their own or not). It didn't matter where you ended up or what you morphed into, he always looked at every former *Source* employee as someone who would not have achieved anything in life were it not for the *Source*. Sounds strangely familiar.

step to the rear

I have this recurring dream that I'm in a plane crash. I can see the mouthpiece attached to a little airbag fall down in front of me, then the plane points downward. Fucked up way to go, it seems. I always wake up before we hit the ground, though. It makes flying a bit troublesome at times. But when you gotta get somewhere, driving just takes too damn long. So I'll take my chances in the sky.

I flew almost twice a month during my time at the *Source*. Cover shoots were often done out of town because we had to get a photographer who cost too much to fly in. I swear the photo editor just wanted to get free trips out of town. One cover was shot by a photographer who did the whole shoot with white powder under his nose. I kept saying to everyone, "He did not just eat a powdered doughnut," but people kept instructing me to be quiet so as to not upset the superstar photographer.

Then there were the free "you gotta hear my album" or "see my show" trips. Def Jam used to be the biggest spender, like we'll fly you halfway around the world just to show you how many Japanese fans Redman really has. And when I got there, I'd just go to a show, watch non-English-speaking Asians mouth the words to "Time 4 Sum Akshun," then turn right around and get back on a plane to go home. That was my life outside the office when I wasn't catching *Dora the Explorer* at Radio City Music Hall. I used to run myself into the ground trying to make up for missed time with Kayla by taking her to the Children's Broadway shows or the zoo, thinking that I was making up for it by being the fun mom, but I would catch myself dozing off sometimes while she was still awake.

When I went away on business trips, I left Kayla with my mother or her other grandmother, Rosa, who would take off work just because she never got to see Kayla. I spent a lot of time in Los Angeles and Atlanta, alone. But, by far, the best trips were the ones that everyone gets to go to. The conventions.

Most of my networking had been done at music conferences. I met tons of people by just flying to Miami on my mother's free buddy passes (she worked part-time at Continental Airlines) and schmoozing my way into the parties. It was part of the hustle. One year, I even lucked out by the pool at the Fontainebleau Hilton and came upon a registration badge belonging to a Jayson Jackson, who worked for Elektra Records. I didn't meet Jayson, who now manages Mos Def, until years later at a spades tournament. I joked with him about it and made sure to thank him for the great access I had in the midnineties at his expense before Miss Info and I went on to beat him and his boy Rob in the spades game and eventually win the tournament. All that practicing against Joe Budden, who is one of the illest spades players, paid off, especially because we beat him too.

A few weeks after the Murder Inc. issue was completed, most of the staff decided to head down to Puerto Rico for the Mixshow Power

Summit, a music conference mainly for DJs where labels showcased their upcoming projects. The Power Summit had officially replaced all the other conferences as the one to be at. It was the Impact, How Can I Be Down, and everything else all rolled up into one big hip-hop gumbo. Everyone from artists to radio DJs to journalists attended, and it was a great place to get ideas for what to cover in the magazine.

I had seen 50 three times since we got back from L.A. The "out of town" note he left with the flowers led to a week of not hearing from him at all for the first time. Sha Money had paged me with a message that 50 was focused on preparing for his album cover but wanted to "check in" with me. But the network and I figured out that he was shacked up somewhere with a wifey. When he resurfaced a week later, he said he had been in the Poconos where there was no phone or SkyTel service. I thought it was funny that he could call Sha Money to get a message to me but couldn't call me directly. That's when things between us started to fade out. Sometimes I think guys just don't care enough to come up with better stories. Either way, I was too paranoid to be played, so I made a pact with myself never to call him again. Ironically, he stopped calling too.

My flight down to Puerto Rico was the soul plane of the Power Summit. And with all the turbulence, I wouldn't have been surprised to find out that Snoop was behind the wheel. A number of DJs, random drug dealers turned hip-hop executives, and artists were on that flight. I was sitting in first class when I heard someone say, "Hi, Kim." Lloyd Banks was already carrying his bags past me. I had noticed that while I was busy getting my orange juice, 50 Cent had just boarded the same American Airlines flight. *I am definitely in a movie,* or even on *Punk'd.* I thought. I don't know whether his label was shitting on him or whether he was just being a team player, but he was seated in coach. I imagined a little devil over my right shoulder, feeling that it was a temporary victory for me. *Ha ha ha* was all I could think, as if a seat on a plane could justify my position in a relationship. *I could be so petty sometimes.* 50 said hi, and I tried to act as if I didn't care that I hadn't heard from him. We briefly spoke, then I picked up my conversation with two business associates who were on my flight.

When the island is filled with hip-hop celebrities such as Lil' Kim, Missy Elliott, Busta Rhymes, and Eminem, an up-and-comer like 50 Cent should fly under the radar without any attention, right? Wrong. You would have thought that 50 Cent was the Dalai Lama by the way the cameras flocked around him every move he made. *How did I get here? This boy doesn't even have an album out, yet he has all the attention. Great, just what I need.*

Because of the attention, I stood far away from 50 Cent that trip, not even conversing when I saw him in the lobby and at a restaurant the first night I was there. I saw him almost as much as I saw Jam Master Jay, who seemed to be in my peripheral vision every five minutes. He was on the elevator with me, at a barbecue, everywhere I looked. I never met him or thought to introduce myself, and then he was murdered a few months later. When I wrote the cover story, I couldn't help but remember how much I had just seen him in Puerto Rico.

Even though I thought it would be a fun-filled trip because Michelle and Tanya were both going, it turned out to be more work than I had anticipated. Most of the staff were there, including Ray and Dave, who took me to dinner with him to talk about the magazine. Ray actually directed him to take me to eat something so Ray could force Tanya to hang out with him at the Casino. Because I was so hell-bent on getting promoted to EIC, I went with Dave so he could talk my ear off about the staff. I took in every direction he gave me, realizing how much sense he made when Ray wasn't around.

At the hotel, I requested a room with two double beds so that Michelle could stay with me since all the rooms were taken by the time she booked her trip. She flew out at the last minute, and since we were together for the entire trip, Ray started to notice that Michelle was a good friend of mine.

"Michelle can't write for us anymore," Tanya told me when we got back to the hotel, after a night of one too many glasses of champagne.

"What? Who said?" I slurred.

"Ray said this to me tonight." Apparently, he had asked Tanya to confirm that Michelle was there with me. Once she told him what he wanted to know, Ray told her to make sure I knew that Michelle couldn't ride in any of the *Source*-sponsored vehicles, and that "she better not be writing for the magazine."

For months, Michelle Song's byline had been in the magazine with no problem. During a brief meeting with Tracii McGregor, the former executive editor turned VP of content, who had been passed over for the job when Carlito was made EIC, she had mentioned that she'd noticed Michelle's name in a previous issue. At the time, I wasn't sure if Tracii was telling me to give me a heads-up or to call me out on it. That was the funny thing about her. Sometimes, she was extra-supportive of me, and other times I felt that she was waiting to stab me in the back so I would bleed to death. Ray used to call her a "weirdo." To me, she appeared to be smart with a mystique about her. She kept herself holed up in her office on the business side, where you could always see the smoke from her incense creeping out from under the door.

"Does Dave know that Michelle Song is writing for the magazine?" she asked me one day while I was sitting in her office. "You should check with him."

I had heard that Dave had a list of writers that were supposedly forbidden from the masthead because they'd signed the 1994 letter. Michelle was on Dave's list. And even though I thought that the ban on the list had expired, Puerto Rico brought it all back up again. When

Michelle became a radio personality, Ray showed just how much he despised her by bad-mouthing her every chance he got. If you worked at the *Source* and succeeded after you left the *Source*, you became what I like to call an ex-man, an ex-*Source* employee who'd managed to break free and use the *Source* as a launching pad to further one's career. And just as editors develop relationships with writers in the small pool of hip-hop journalism, the ex-men always joined forces in their hate for Dave and Ray.

Everyone was pretty much leaving Puerto Rico on the same day, so I caught a ride to the airport with Riggs, who was there to promote Shady's upcoming releases. I actually thought it was funny when he told me not to be late coming downstairs because his car had to take 50 to the airport. Because of that, I took extralong, so Riggs left me.

When I called Riggs on his cell phone, he was already en route to the airport. I asked him to turn around and come back, since I had now forfeited my other ride. His first answer was "Hell no," but then he put me on hold and came back and said, "We're turning back around." *This is a first,* I thought.

I got into a crowded van with Riggs, 50, Banks, Sha Money, and Yayo. Banks moved back one row so I could sit next to 50. His first question to me was whether I had seen his performance the night before, and I told him that I didn't think it was good. He had so much hype around the release of his album that the performance, to me at least, fell short. Although a lot had happened between us by this time, I still wanted him to succeed. I felt the way most of the hip-hop fans did at the time. I was rooting for the underdog. "You moved around the stage, back and forth, back and forth," I said to him, recounting how his stage show had made me dizzy.

"I got a lot of energy when I'm onstage. My adrenaline be going and I gotta keep moving," he said.

"Yes, but when you're moving at the speed of lightning, it often means that you're breathing too hard for anyone to understand your vocals, and your words were slurring. Maybe it's just me." 50 nodded his head in acknowledgment. It was a weird conversation, because even though he had seen my post-pregnancy stretch marks, and I had commented about the indentations in his stomach ("Is this real? Jesus, you're like a black Rambo. I could wash my clothes on this."), I was still the editor whose opinion he respected.

"And there were times where I couldn't tell which person onstage was you, and you should be the one who stands out." As I started to give my rundown of what I thought was wrong, 50 soaked it up like a sponge. Then he put his arm around my waist and told me that he had made Riggs turn the car around and come get me. It made me uncomfortable in front of people, so I quickly figured out a way to maneuver out of that position.

"Let me see your ID." I grabbed his wallet from him as he was about to put it back in his pocket by the check-in counter at the airport. "Ugk. Not-so-nice picture." I laughed. My eyes drifted over to the date. "Hey, you said you were twenty-six, so either you lied or the mean lady at the DMV got it wrong. If I were going to lie about my age, I'd take off more than a year."

50 just smiled. As we started making our way toward security, I noticed the hair from Tony Yayo's back was peeking out from his white T. "Wolfman," 50 whispered to me when he caught me giggling underneath my breath. Then he shouted at Yayo to get his attention, "Wolfman." Everyone around started to giggle. 50 let out his signature "Ha ha ha" as well.

The vibe felt really friendly, so I started fishing for information. "So I heard you ran into Dipset out here and something popped off. You think they heard about the record you did?"

Sha Money overheard our conversation and interrupted, "What record? There's no record."

"The 'Back Down' record I heard in L.A., where he's dissin' Cam."

"He ain't dissin' Cam on that record," Sha interjected.

I was confused. I knew I had heard the dis on the song, but it was like a Jedi mind trick because I started second-guessing what I'd heard. *Did I really hear him mention Cam?* I looked at 50 for validation, but he didn't say anything. Then when Sha turned his back, 50 rolled his eyes back and waved his hand. "I don't care, but he gotta act like that."

"What's the big deal? You already said it."

"They probably gonna take it off." 50 never really seemed fazed about beefing with someone, but everyone around him was walking on pins. But he had this attitude, like, he'd come so close to death before, he knew how to cheat it. Biggie once said in a rhyme, "You're nobody till somebody kills you." Well, the attempt on 50's life already qualified him to be somebody. Now, he was like teasing the drama. *Shoot me again. I know how to live through it.*

"So, anyway, you gonna write about us?" he interrupted my thoughts.

"What? Write about what?" Knowing what he was talking about, I played dumb. This is what I had suspected since the roses. I was the editor of the number one hip-hop magazine, and I realized that 50 had an agenda. Everything he had told me was a part of his plan. That was the reason for the overused media-trained speech during phone conversations, the A&R-type analysis of the music industry, and the retelling of the same stories, especially when it came to the gunshot wounds ("Look, my tooth is gone"). The code of the industry is, like, the "don't ask, don't tell" policy. But he was going to tell. Everybody. I had let my guard down and now it was too late.

He looked at me and said the last words I would allow myself to hear from him in a long time. "About us. I want you to write about it."

Sometime after the trip to Puerto Rico, 50 and I had an unhealthy change of two-way messages. I noticed that he hadn't called in a couple of days so I sent him a text that let him know I wasn't happy.

"I've been busy," he wrote.

I didn't appreciate the short message so I sent him a mean message that mentioned that I remembered the "burgundy booger" van he drove, and how it had no air-conditioning in the summertime. He didn't respond to my message and I chose not to call or text him back anymore that day. As the days followed, there was no communication between us. And the more time that passed, the more I heard about him. He got bigger and bigger, and it became more of a reason for me to keep my distance.

fight the power

There is no such thing as an *industry friend*. I used the term for years, only to later discover that an industry friend is not a friend. A friend is a friend. An enemy is an enemy. But an industry friend is just an enemy in disguise.

An industry friend is someone who will befriend you for his or her own benefit, but will turn on you to get ahead. It's worse when it comes to hip-hop. People are so thirsty to get ahead that they won't just stab you in the back, they'll do it from the front. When people started to realize that I was running things at the *Source*, the number of industry friends I had multiplied like bread on Jesus' table.

October and November of 2002 flew by. The Murder Inc. cover heightened the beef between Ja and 50, just as we knew it would. We shamelessly capitalized off the drama. Never mind the belief that magazines instigate rap beefs between artists, circa Biggie and 'Pac 1996, because the issue sold like the icey man in East Harlem in ninety-degree weather. I always looked at it as that we were just reporting what was going on. We didn't create the problems, we just published them. But sometimes, putting the beef out there put pressure on the artists to deal with it. If someone says something about you behind closed doors, no one calls you a punk if you don't respond, but once it's in print, you've got an image to uphold.

November's issue featured Lil' Kim breaking through pieces of glass on the cover. It was the longest shoot I'd ever been at. I arrived before the Queen Bee, then stayed until she finished in hair and makeup which took close to twenty hours with all the wardrobe changes. It exceeded our budget. Initially, she had actually asked the *Source* for a chinchilla bikini to wear on the cover. Let me repeat that. A chin-chill-a . . . bi-ki-ni. It's an oxymoron. Dave wouldn't approve it because it would have to be custom-made and "we don't buy clothes for artists." But oddly enough, every time artists would ask for something, Dave would just send them back to me so I would look like the one shutting them down. That was the case whenever Dave or Ray didn't want to do something or had made a promise they couldn't keep. They would just make everyone believe that it was my decision. This way, they could make it look as if I had some control so they wouldn't have to be the bad guys when they couldn't give people what they wanted.

When the November issue came out featuring Lil' Kim, I had to deal with calls from Foxy Brown, yelling, "How could you let her talk about me in the magazine!" Having known Inga for years, I tried to explain to Foxy that I couldn't let my personal relationships interfere with business. I didn't write the story, so it would be wrong for me to remove the quotes based on the premise that Foxy and I were "cool." In the end it didn't matter, because the *Source*'s integrity got thrown out of the window and Foxy decided not to talk to me for three years after that, until she called me years later and asked me to write her book.

Our December cover was split between LL Cool and Fabolous, and I had to figure out some way to connect the two. LL had appeared on the cover of the *Source* more than any other artist, and based on the buzz from his new single "Luv U Better," we were planning to do another one. Then we discovered that Dave and Ray had promised a cover to Fabolous, who was gearing up for the release of his sophomore album. It was actually supposed to be Fabolous and DJ Clue together, but then somehow Clue got cut out of the equation. Clue wasn't spinning Benzino's music in regular rotation, and I'm sure that had something to do with it. That's how things happened at the *Source*. A lot of artists thought that having a relationship with Ray helped them get coverage, and it did, at times. But it was better to fly under the radar and never have to meet or deal with Ray. That way, you'd get in the magazine on your own accord and wouldn't have to pay back in Benzino favors.

I wrote two feature stories, in addition to my editorial letter, in the December issue. In retrospect, I should have just delegated those duties, instead of trying to play super-reporter. I was so concerned with making sure everyone on the staff knew I was "working" that I burnt myself out. In my earlier days as the editor, I was on a mission to prove something, not that anyone noticed. It was more important that I answer every call I got from Dave and Ray and manage their expectations. They didn't want an "editor in chief," they wanted yet another glorified assistant. But eight months after I was promoted to executive editor, I was finally officially given the title I wanted in November of 2002. Because I had been the acting EIC all the while, no one noticed when I got promoted with another bump in salary.

December was dubbed the "old school meets the new school" issue, and the cover lines all related to the "school" theme. I interviewed both

KRS-One and LL Cool J and wrote both stories for that issue. One was done in Los Angeles, and the other in New York, but I still made sure I showed up to both cover shoots. I woke up early each morning to drop Kayla off at school and didn't get to bed until after 2 a.m. That's just how my life was. There was no time for anything but the *Source*.

By the time we began to plan the January issue, I was runing on empty. January is special because it's the year-end issue, where we would relive the most significant moments in hip-hop that prior year. It was also the same issue that we compiled the Power 30 list. The Power 30 issue was the ego juice of the hip-hop industry. Once sipping on the juice, you were sure to boost your ego up a few notches. The people in power didn't need the *Source* magazine to validate their status, but when we did, it gave industry heads more reason to inflate their self-worth.

In the corporate-meets-hip-hop world, Steve Stoute was a pretty powerful dude. He was the VP at Interscope Records, but it was his own company that he was caking off of. Stoute was a partner in an advertising agency that linked hip-hop artists to consumer products. In other words, if you saw a Coke can in a Jay-Z video, chances are that he put it there. Once big corporations figured out that hip-hop was a cash cow, they called on people like Stoute to be the conduit. But, to people like me, Stoute was most notable for his famous beef with Puffy. Stoute managed Nas around the time the "Hate Me Now" video—which depicted both Nas and P. Diddy on crosses—was filmed. After Puffy talked to his pastor and decided that he didn't want the video to depict him that way, it still managed to make its way onto MTV. That story ended with Puffy going up to Steve Stoute's office with two cohorts and allegedly beating him with a champagne bottle. People believed Stoute controlled those things behind the scenes. But once the video was out of his hands, he had no power to get it back from MTV. Stoute still took the blame for it. But the incident didn't stop both Puffy and Stoute from doing business with each other a few years later. That's one of the differences I've seen between men and women in this industry. Women tend to hold grudges against each other, while men can have physical fights resulting in hospital bills and then be seen at the strip club together.

Around the time we were planning the Power 30 issue, I called Stoute to fact-check some information, since he was going to be prominently featured. He didn't know, though, that he was going to be number one, so like most of the execs, Stoute tried to get me to give him a clue as to where he ranked.

Over the phone, I made him believe I would tell him what he wanted to know, but in truth we never let that type of information get out. Plus, although Dave and Ray wanted to make him number one, I still knew they might change their minds. So I had no intention of divulging the true number when I started sending random numbers to his pager: 23, 22, 20, 17. I kept sending the numbers, amusing myself, just because I knew he wanted to know: 15, 12, 8, 7. "Buy me lunch and send it over here, and when you do that, I'll two-way you the number," I said. To me, it was a joke, but people really took things like that seriously. Even after lunch arrived, I never revealed the number. I liked that I could make people in powerful positions do things by using the information I had as a bargaining chip.

"Okay, you got me" was the last page Stoute sent after he realized that I was being an asshole, sending him numbers that meant absolutely nothing. He sent over a $90 lunch from Negril anyway, and to a bunch of hungry overworked writers, it was like Thanksgiving. Stoute did turn out to be number one on the list, along with Jimmy Iovine and Interscope Records. They had the top spot and controlled damn near the whole music industry at the time. Most of the hip-hop heavyweights that year belonged to the Interscope roster—Eminem, Dr. Dre, 50 Cent—and giving the big picture to Steve Stoute was Ray's way of overlooking the real head of Interscope, Jimmy Iovine.

Not that they didn't earn their top spot, but the Power 30 was a crock of bullshit. The editorial department would work long and hard for a month, pulling together stats, researching the sales positions of record label rosters, accumulating information on outside hustles, writing the blurbs, then ranking the top thirty people in the music industry by their sales records, income, and overall industry muscle. Then, after it was completed and ready to go to the printer, I would walk into Dave's office with the list and let Ray pick it apart. A number eight could be pushed back to twenty-nine in minutes. Others would be pushed to thirty-one. *Maybe next year.* It was all about what you did for the *Source,* or what you were about to do for the *Source* only you didn't know you were about to be pressured into doing it.

It would make sense that the Power 30 issue would feature someone at the top of the list on the cover, but when Ray was involved in any of our editorial decisions, making sense was out of the question. Ray had made a promise to Brian "Baby" Williams of Cash Money, and January was Ray's promise-fulfillment month. From a business standpoint, Cash Money deserved their props, even years before Lil' Wayne was sellin' a milli a week, but our timing was off. Baby had dropped his solo album months ago, and because we had to squeeze in all of Ray's other favors during that time, he wanted to hurry up and throw Baby on the cover and get it over with. I was happy enough that we had escaped Ray's promissory notes for a couple of months that I did not object to the Birdman cover.

I met Birdman a few months prior to putting him on the cover when we did a feature on the Big Tymers album that he put out with Mannie Fresh. Once I knew him, he was accessible to us at the *Source* whenever we needed anything from Cash Money. A good businessman in hip-hop is one who always picks up his phone and has excellent follow-through. So I got cool with Baby, Cash Money's CEO, because he always made sure I had everything I needed when it came to Cash Money. Of course, he flirted, but that was just part of his image. Birdman threw kisses at me from atop a bird's nest we built for him to sit on at his photo shoot. And even though I've heard that he gives some of the best gifts, I knew that type of flirting is not something you can take seriously, especially when all of your friends say the same thing.

Right before we finished putting the issue together, we received the terrible news that Jam Master Jay had been tragically murdered in Queens. Everyone agreed that a death in hip-hop of this caliber of artist warrants a cover, so all of the editors came together and held a meeting about trumping the Baby cover with a JMJ or Run-D.M.C. tribute cover. Because it was so last-minute, I didn't want to assign the story and risk missing the deadline, so I trusted only myself to write it. But Ray wouldn't allow us to replace the Baby cover. He decided to split the cover, sending the Jam Master Jay cover to subscribers only. Most of us felt we missed out on a big opportunity to sell magazines at the newsstands, because we would have been the only magazine with a Jam Master Jay cover immediately after his death. But that's just how it went. Again, Ray had the final decision.

As noisy as it was one day on a Monday at the *Source* offices, by 7 p.m. it was a ghost town. It only happened immediately after we closed an issue. After spending day and night putting the finishing touches on the magazine, no one really wanted to stay past seven when they could finally get out and have a life for two weeks.

Sometime after the Mixshow Power Summit, Benzino decided that he was ready for a rap battle. His opponent would be none other than the number-one-selling rap artist at the time, Eminem. It came out of nowhere, and the vibe at the office changed drastically because none of us knew why Benzino was going there. To this day, I still wonder whether Ray picked Eminem because he was on top or because he was white and Ray knew that a white boy wasn't going to address his whiteness in a rap battle. Many people believe the latter, especially since the record was all about Eminem being white. How insightful.

In a New York minute, a once happy, fun-filled place where the staff writers and editors would gather in the conference room to watch the latest music video was now a dreadful, don't-say-anything-positive-about-Eminem atmosphere. Ray was setting a tone in the office making sure everyone was on the same page when it came to Eminem.

One day, he walked into my office, which was dressed with gold and platinum plaques, and noticed one in particular. It was a platinum plaque noting Eminem's worldwide sales of over 10 million, with little flags of all the countries where he had sold the most records. I had one addressed to me, as did some other editors at the *Source*.

Benzino: "Is that an Eminem plaque on your wall?"

Me: "Uh, yeah, I guess it is. I forgot that was there, Ray."

Benzino: "Give me that shit. Take it down. I'm sending it back."

Ray snatched the plaque from behind me and put it under his armpit like a newspaper. It was probably the nicest plaque I had, especially because it was one of the few that actually spelled my name right. He walked out of my office and I never saw it again.

At this time, Ray had also somehow become extra tight with Ja Rule, and since Eminem had signed 50 Cent, it was the perfect tag-team match. The Benzino dis song was called "Pull Your Skirt Up," and it was actually a decent rhyme with a halfway important message. Most of the time, artists with semi-wack lyrics can still get by if they have a nice flow, talented delivery, or catchy image. Benzino's lyrics were not as bad as everyone made them out to be, but his delivery and flow were horrendous. Add that to a pretty bad rep, and a hunchback frame, and you've got one not-so-hot rapper.

While the industry clowned Benzino's last attempt at stardom . . . again, the staff sat around frontin' all day. We all became actors, acting as if doing stories on Ray or giving him the Quotable for that issue wasn't making us all sick to our stomachs. And when Dave called us into his office for meetings on the magazine's newest agenda sixty seconds before we were about to head out the door, we pretended as if we cared and didn't have other lives. We watched his sorry videos when Dave played them in his office and nodded our heads to the beat.

The new *Source* motto was to destroy Eminem at all costs and by any means necessary. I'd never really been an Eminem fan, but when Ray took the Eminem plaque from my wall to ship back to Interscope, I thought he was overdoing it. But he hadn't even started to overdo it.

The plan was for the February issue to blow up the beef between Benzino and Eminem. At least, that's what Benzino thought. First, an intellectual analysis of Eminem's existence in hip-hop by seasoned journalist Harry Allen would accompany an illustration of Eminem portrayed as Elvis Presley. It was just a longer way of calling him a culture vulture. The cover would feature a call to action for Eminem on the skyline. Above the *Source*'s logo, the words "Step into the Arena" would be bookended by a picture of both Benzino and Eminem. Then we would include a six-page feature story on Benzino and a poster of him, hair released from fuzzy braids, holding Eminem's ripped head in his hands. Blood dripping from his neck. *Can anyone say overkill?* Then there was my part. I hated that Ray was using the magazine for his personal agenda, but I was still fairly new in my position and didn't want to rock the boat. I knew the beef wasn't as big as Ray was trying to make us believe, but no one would dare tell him. Not to mention, *XXL* was capitalizing off the drama too. They were aligning themselves with every artist who wouldn't fuck with the *Source*. Each month, they were going at us in their editorials, and Ray wanted me to contribute to the madness.

Of course, right as I was about to leave one evening a few days after we closed the Power 30 issue, I was summoned to Dave's office for an impromptu meeting.

"You're not scared, are you?" Ray asked me. He must have been in the middle getting his hair done, because half of his hair was wild and the other was tightly braided. He had a huge Broom Hilda pimple on his nose.

"What do you mean? Scared of what?" I asked.

"I feel like you're scared or something. You're scared to go at him in the magazine. Why aren't you saying anything? He's going at you every month. He's dissing you every month. And you're not saying anything."

Ray was talking about Elliott Wilson, the editor in chief of *XXL*. In the heat of anger, Ray had ordered his Boston crew to accompany him to *XXL* to threaten Elliott and poke him in his forehead a few times. That day, he warned Elliott never again to include Ray's son, little Ray Ray, in the magazine. Most of us felt that Elliott had crossed the line by putting somebody's offspring in a cartoon—even if it was Benzino. As far as I'm concerned, children are off-limits.

Elliott had been taking shots at the *Source* in his monthly editorial letter since he'd taken the job of EIC at *XXL*. And in addition to dissing the *Source*, or more specifically, Ray, he was now making me a target. I had read an interview with him somewhere, and he explained that his gripe with me was that I had been negotiating exclusivity with record labels, meaning if you wanted to be in the *Source*, you couldn't be in *XXL* that same month. To me, it was just a business move to weaken our opponent. Artists and labels still had a choice to pick which magazine they wanted to be in first. Most editors used this tactic when negotiating their covers. I just took it a step further and applied it to feature stories too. Elliott must have thought I wasn't playing fair because he started to say things about me in his editorials.

Now that the beef had jumped off, word on the street was that Eminem was planning on being on the cover of *XXL*, and of course Elliott was loving it. His criticism of me was building with each issue, and now it had become front-page (his editorial, that is) news.

"I'm not going to acknowledge him. Why should I? He just needs to be ignored," I rationalized to Ray. I thought that playing into the drama by responding to Elliott was only giving him what he wanted.

"Ignored?" Ray asked, annoyed. "He's not ignoring you. He's dissin' you! And you're not saying anything. He's dissing us. This is war. You need to say something to this geek. I feel like it's revenge of the nerds out here."

"'Revenge of the nerds.' That's funny. I just think that if I say something to him, it's making him look bigger than he is. Right now, he's just beefing with himself. But if I say something, now I'm playing into it."

"Fuck it. Play into it. Say something. I'm telling you to say something. Stop being scared. I mean, whose side are you on?"

Ray had always questioned everyone's loyalty to the *Source*, and now he was even questioning mine. I looked at the platinum bracelet with the diamond-studded *S* charm on my wrist and realized that this was more than just a job. This was my life. I couldn't go anywhere without being associated with the *Source*, and the *Source*'s enemies had become mine.

bacdafucup

Tension was building within the office as two staff members were asked to leave the building one day after being accused of leaking the poster of Ray holding Eminem's severed head to someone at *XXL*. Dave had the computer-tech guys go through everyone's email, and they discovered that a large unknown file had been sent to someone at Harris Publications. Much of the staff had relationships with editors over at Harris because the industry was so small. But when it went down, it didn't matter to Ray that there was some doubt as to what that file in their email was. It was just the usual "They gotta get the fuck out. *Today*."

It was hard for me to go against Ray when I was now making 130K. In theory, it sounded good, but I always knew in the back of my mind that for eight months I had done the job of the EIC and been shorted.

But my excitement had been compromised when I discovered that Antoine Clarke was going to be appointed executive editor.

I made my way down to Dave's office one night because I had heard the latest Antoine rumor. Dave was standing behind his desk holding his pen, while Ray was seated in a chair getting his beard shaped up by the staff barber. It wasn't a welcoming invitation for a conversation, but I started one anyway: "Is Antoine getting the editor-in-chief job?"

"No, Antoine is coming on staff to help you. You don't have anything to worry about. He can't do what you do." Dave was talking and smiling at the same time. It was interesting how they could find my career fate amusing.

"So what is his title going to be?"

"Don't worry about titles. You'll both be in charge."

I can't believe this, I thought. *All this time, I've been busting my ass for this magazine and they're about to reward Antoine for doing absolutely nothing.*

Antoine roamed the office halls day in and day out talking about his latest issue of *F.E.D.S.* and citing reasons why *F.E.D.S.* was more connected to the streets than the *Source. Unfair* was an understatement.

"I just don't understand what his purpose is. What is he going to do?"

"We need someone with Antoine's perspective," Dave began.

That's when Ray chimed in, "His purpose, Kim, is to give us street credibility. You need someone like Antoine on staff. So when you have things like *this* in the magazine"—Ray held open page 50 of the December issue, which featured a dis to Cam'Ron's use of the color pink—"when you have things like this, someone can stand up to these artists because they're gonna step to you."

"For the Record" was a new small section, no bigger than a quarter of a page, that we had been running in the magazine for the last couple of months. It was a playful way of checking trends in hip-hop that we considered to be out of touch. The first installment had featured Fabolous's larger-than-life earrings. Interestingly, when I met him for the first time, Fab actually acknowledged that he had peeped it and cleverly laughed it off. It made me respect him that much more. This one that Ray was pointing to, however, had a picture of Cam'Ron dressed in pink and it read, "*Pretty in Pink* was a '80s flick, not a fashion statement. The color pink looks better on females."

"Someone like Antoine wouldn't let this get in the magazine, you know. He understands how much of a violation this is," Ray said. "You don't get it. Sometimes, you gotta be a man to understand these things."

There was nothing left to say. I understood that the section was a bit daring, but that's what had made the *Source* what it was. The magazine was built on the integrity of former editors who weren't afraid to be honest. Yes, a few times journalists had been assaulted by artists, but I had never had that problem. Cam'Ron never addressed the column with me, but would later try to scream on me in a club over another cover when we passed on giving it to him. But I had the gift of turning a tense situation into something that made people laugh and look silly for trying to pick a fight with me.

But Ray was telling me that Antoine was being added to the staff because of his perspective—his male perspective. "We need that perspective at the top of the masthead," he said. We had male perspectives on the masthead, but they were all either my own hires or employees that had been hired by former editors. "Stop worrying, yo. You're good. That's word to everything on my arm. I got you."

After Ray's promise, I backed off the conversation and let it go.

Before he resigned, Jermaine Hall had decided to take on the Ja Rule cover story and was pulling together a great piece. Ja Rule and Irv Gotti claimed that 50 Cent had taken out an order of protection after being stabbed by Black Child of Murder Inc. during a fight between all of them that broke out at Sony Studios. Jermaine actually sent the research editor down to the police station to find out whether the order of protection existed, and it did. This was the start of a big issue in the never-ending beef between Ja and 50. Although 50 denied seeking the order, I've now read somewhere that the order of protection was a formality taken out by the police who investigated the stabbing.

Ray requested that his own feature story be written by none other than Antoine Clarke, which meant that our new senior editor, Brett Johnson, whom Tanya had dubbed "the walking encyclopedia," would have to rewrite the piece. Antoine's story was the last thing waiting to be edited.

The Monday after the Thanksgiving holiday was hectic. I had spent most of my holiday on a plane trying to make it to dinner at my sister's house in Portland so I could pretend that I had a family life. Of course, because I didn't know how to take a day off, work had prevented me from leaving until the actual Thanksgiving Thursday, which (duh) is the busiest flying day of the year. Running through Newark airport with Kayla in tow, I wound up missing my flight and detouring to Seattle to catch a prop plane to Portland. Kayla exclaimed, "Whee," throughout the entire flight while I tried to keep my soda in its cup. I missed Thanksgiving dinner, but at least got there before everyone left and went to bed. By the time I got home that weekend, I was dead tired from traveling. Still, I went straight to work when I got off the plane that morning.

It was late Monday afternoon, and I had spent all day reading over pages of the magazine before they went to print. I was searching for the final version of Jermaine's Ja Rule story so I could proofread it one last time. I found it on Tanya's desk in her office, and since she wasn't there, I plopped myself down in her chair to read it again. A few minutes later, she came in, reading over another page before it got to me. She sat on her couch and the two of us sat in each other's presence without talking. That's when Antoine decided to come to work.

"Yo, did Ray call you back?" Antoine's five-foot-ten-inch frame stood in the doorway of Tanya's office, waiting for me to look up from the page.

I didn't even finish reading the sentence I was on as I realized that he was about to make us late to prepress. "What? You didn't meet up with him at the studio this weekend? He was waiting for you to come and do the interview." Dave had paged me several times throughout the holiday with Ray's location and the time for Antoine to show up and conduct the interview. I was supposed to locate Antoine and make sure he showed up there. But Antoine was nowhere to be found that weekend, and when I stopped hearing from Dave, I figured they had located him on their own.

Antoine pulled his head back and frowned. Apparently, Ray had changed the interview and location time more than once. "I wasn't about to spend my holiday chasing him around the city," said 'Toine.

"Chasing him around the city? Jermaine Hall spent his Thanksgiving chasing Ja Rule around the country. You gotta do what you gotta do to get your story in. You're supposed to be the executive editor. I'm not gonna hold your hand through this."

Antoine started walking through the doorway of Tanya's office, coming closer to me. "I ain't gotta do nothing. Who the fuck you think you're talking to?"

My defense mechanism kicked in and I stood up. "Don't curse at me."

Tanya was seated on her couch, looking nervous. "Antoine, why you cursing?" she chimed in.

"You better watch who you're fuckin' talking to," he said to me, his voice getting louder with each word.

"Don't curse at me," I said again, still standing. My heart was beating fast now, the way it did when you were about to fight someone at 3 p.m. in high school.

"I'll knock you upside your fuckin' head. Who do you think you're talking to?" Antoine was invading my space and making threats.

I stood on my two feet and fired back, "Don't threaten me. I'll bring someone up here for you to knock upside their fuckin' head."

Coming from a family of three siblings, all of whom were girls, I never had the luxury of having a brother defend me. Growing up, I always envied the girls who could use the "I'll go get my brother" line in an argument with a man. The only protection I had back then was a Yorkshire terrier who could bite the shit out of your shoelaces, and two friends named Tammy and Lisa, from my crew the Tough Made Girls (TMG), who were known in our neighborhood to never lose a fight. But since I didn't have a brother, my physical altercations with men usually ended in me backing down or getting punched in the eye. In this argument with Antoine, I never had anyone to go and get, but I still had to use something to defend myself in this shouting match. So I threw it out there, and he got even more vexed.

"I'll knock you upside your fuckin' head," he said again as if I couldn't hear him the first time.

Knowing that the entire office might be listening, I wanted Antoine to look like the bad guy. I wanted everyone to know how disloyal he was, and how he'd been portraying the job to me behind closed doors. So I yelled, "Don't you care about your job?"

"No. I don't give a fuck. 'Cause I got *F.E.D.S.*, but you better give a fuck about your job." Once he said that, I realized my plan to expose his disloyalty to the *Source* had backfired, and now the office folklore would be the *Source*'s disloyalty to me.

It was a threat that I had heard more than once from Antoine. And what he had said to me months earlier about coming on staff had proven to be true. *Worry about my job?* I asked myself. *Could he know something that I didn't?*

Laurent, who worked down in the Ad Sales Department, came out of nowhere and grabbed Antoine from behind, put his arms around his neck, and started to pull him out of Tanya's office.

Antoine was yelling from the hallway, "I'll knock her upside her fuckin' head. She better keep fuckin' Nas."

"Kim?" Tanya's jaw dropped. Her mouth stood open in shock.

Standing over Tanya's desk, I was frozen in time. I was too heated to respond to her. With his last comment, Antoine had gone from threatening me to humiliating me in less than a minute.

"Kim?" Tanya said one last time before she jumped up off the couch and slammed the door shut to block out Antoine's screams.

"Tanya, what did he just say?" I asked, to make sure I had heard correctly.

"He just said something about Nas. How does he know that?"

"I have no idea."

I had kept a pretty low profile when it came to my relationship with Nas, but some things you just couldn't escape. Though I had never really thought about it up until then, I knew some sightings had made their way up the rumor mill. I'd met him after a show at the PNC Bank Arts Center in Holmdel, New Jersey. I didn't expect to run into anyone there, but was given suspicious looks when a staff member saw me in the audience. On out-of-town trips such as to Phoenix and Miami, random people had seen me at the same hotel or on the tour bus. In the industry, nosy people have a sick sense for knowing when you're working and when you're not. I know, because I've caught people myself.

However Antoine had found out, he was letting it be known, spreading the rumor about a relationship that had already ended months before.

The next day, I typed out a three-page memo documenting the events that had led up to Antoine's outburst. I sent the memo to Julie Als in Human Resources, to the company's chief operating officer, Jeremy Miller, and to Dave Mays. Jeremy set up a lunch with Dave and me to go through the motions of handling my complaint.

Sushi Samba is a modern-style Japanese restaurant on Park Avenue. It was my choice for lunch the day that I would be told what the company planned to do about the Antoine incident. But what should have been a formal meeting to gather the details of a potential violation of company policy turned into an inquisition of my personal life.

It took a half hour for Dave to open up the conversation that we had come to lunch to have. I was sipping on my usual after-lunch latte when he started to ask me questions. "So we want to know, can you still work with Antoine?"

It felt like a trick question. I could answer either yes or no. But behind the door labeled *yes* would be a smiling Antoine allowed to threaten me every chance he had and make my life at work a living hell. Behind the door marked *no* would be a pink slip with an invitation to hit the road.

"Yes, I can work with him, but—"

Dave interrupted, "No, can *you* work with him?" His voice had a sinister tone, and I started to feel that I was the one that had done something wrong. "None of these complaints about him. Can you work with him because you've got to train him, and this isn't going to work if you don't agree to work with him."

"He can't think it's okay to threaten me or anybody else on the staff. This is supposed to be my job, but I feel like I'm on the streets." I was so upset at the notion that Dave was not ready to instantly get rid of or punish Antoine after his unacceptable behavior. Not to mention, he was not even that good at the job. Waiting on his story, we pushed things so close to our deadline that we almost missed the ship date. And after all the work I'd put in, I couldn't believe that I wasn't worth more.

"We definitely take these things seriously and will be making sure he knows that he can't do this again," Jeremy chimed in, trying to offer the right Human Resources advice.

"Also, I want to talk about some other things." It was just like Dave to finish an important conversation like the one we were having and get to what he really wanted to know. "There have been some concerns about the way you've been conducting yourself outside of the office."

"Excuse me?" Nothing I had ever heard from him had sounded so foreign. *Conducting myself?*

"We have some concerns that your relationships with certain people in the industry could be jeopardizing our business." His choice of words made it sound as if I were running a brothel out of my condo. And although I knew rumors were floating around about Nas, I didn't think my boss would dare bring it up.

"What are you talking about?"

Whenever Dave wanted to be argumentative, he started to speak down to people. In a condescending tone, he would accent every couple of words with a nod of his head. "We, Ray and I"—head shake—"we feel"—head shake—"that you"—head shake—"your relations, are interfering with our business."

Jeremy looked as if he had signed up for the wrong meeting.

"I don't know what you're talking about, Dave." I was shocked at his accusation. Business can be very personal, but my personal life had never come close to compromising any of his business.

"I'm talking"—head shake—"about Nas."

The truth was that I didn't know what he was talking about. What did Nas have to do with any of this? I hadn't seen him since his last video got played on *Rap City*, and that was months ago. And Nas had rarely been featured in the magazine since I met him. I was so upset at what I was hearing that I wasn't going to address it. I knew that would only create problems and a difference of opinion. If I were a man, this wouldn't have even been a conversation, especially since Ray used to brag about the girls in the industry he or any of his boys supposedly "boned." I was not about to volunteer information that I knew would jeopardize my career, so I gave the ambiguous answer that I knew was neither an admission or a denial.

"I don't know what you're talking about, Dave." End of conversation. I wasn't going to say anything else. This was not a conversation about the magazine or anything that I had done wrong at the office. This had nothing to do with his business, because no business had been affected. And at the point where any business would even have come close to being compromised, I would have done everything in my power to make sure it didn't happen. I would have ended any relationship before I ever allowed it to affect my work, unless I valued that relationship more than my job. And in this instance, I didn't.

CHAPTER THIRTEEN

lost ones

Despite the backlash we received from Benzino's beef with Eminem, the Ja Rule issue ended up selling well. But once readers opened it up and saw what was inside, they were instantly turned off. I had never received so many negative letters in all my days at the *Source*. The letters page was usually filled up with positive and negative feedback on the previous issue. But this time, all the comments were negative. So bad, we were told not to print them. Many readers even canceled their subscriptions.

The industry shit on us even more. Every artist associated with Eminem had something negative to say about the *Source*'s position, and me. The only friend I had inside their camp was James Cruz, whom I had connected with right before the beef unfolded. James was part of Violator Management, which managed hip-hop superstars such as Busta Rhymes, Missy Elliott, and 50 Cent. He was a good ally to have in the midst of everything that was going on. James and I maintained our relationship throughout because we both had the "Latinos gotta stick together" mentality. But as much as James and I tried to mend the relationship between our camp and Violator, it was over our heads.

Violator controlled what seemed like half of the hip-hop industry, and coupled with Interscope Records, who controlled the other half it seemed, they amounted to much of the hip-hop that was on top of the charts. The label eventually pulled all of their advertising from the magazine, and Violator stopped dealing with us altogether. The Eminem battle was just plain ol' bad for the business. *And they were concerned with my relationship?* Hmph. Eminem, Dr. Dre, 50 Cent, and G-Unit decided to take a stand against the magazine. In a retaliation of sorts, the three rap mega-superstars appeared on the cover of the next issue of *XXL,* sealing our fate. And it didn't help that all we had to go up against them was a black all-text cover that read "Hip-Hop Under Attack." We were losing.

We had proposed the all-text cover in the past. Actually, Carlito had talked about a "Hip-Hop Is Dead" cover before it really died, but for whatever reason, it never happened. Timing is everything, and as most of us knew, this was not the time to try our luck on a blank cover.

I was driving home after a long day of battling Bill O'Reilly. He was going after Jay-Z for being principal for a day at a school in Detroit, and I was invited on the show to defend him. At this last-minute thing, I represented hip-hop by showing up in a Juicy sweat suit and leaning way back in the chair. Of course, I stood my ground arguing that Jay was doing something positive for the community, while O'Reilly quoted old Jay-Z lyrics to try to make him sound like a misogynist criminal. His hate for hip-hop is so obvious, and when I went on the show, he wasn't trying to hide it. Each time I tried to make my point, in between my nervous stutters of "you know," O'Reilly cut me off. When the cameras went off, he asked me if I knew Jay-Z personally. "You make sure you tell him Bill O'Reilly said hi," he said to me as I was removing the mic from my shirt.

Usually when I did press, I missed out on things that went on at the office. One day out in the field and voilà, there's a new drama unfolding. Tanya called my secret cell phone to deliver some quite comical news. I picked up on the first ring.

"Turn to Hot 97. Turn to Hot 97." She was laughing hysterically.

When I turned the dial, I heard Eminem's DJ, Green Lantern, talking on the radio. He was introducing a new record that had just been leaked to him, an answer record aimed at Benzino. Though I didn't expect him to respond, Eminem had not taken the high road. He was battling, with a song called "Nail in the Coffin." It wasn't "Ether," but it was funny.

"Oh my God. I can't believe he actually answered this idiot back."

"I know, they just played the record. It's hiiiilaaaarrrrious," Tanya said. "He keeps playing it over and over."

"Okay, it's about to come on. I'll call you when it's done." I turned the radio up when I heard the midtempo beat drop. Then the chorus came in with Eminem's singsongy, nasal voice, sounding like he had two pills up his nose:

I don't want to be like this, I don't really want to hurt no feelings
But I'm only bein' real when I say, nobody wants to hear their grandfather rap

The chorus said it all. It was everything that everyone had thought but never had the guts to say. Ray was close to forty years old and was on, like, his thousandth album. There's a time in someone's life when hiding his age can be no more. Ray had reached that time. His skin had started to sag, especially around his cheeks, and he had that old-man kind of look. I always wondered why he chose to pose in pictures and advertisements next to his new group the Untouchables, three kids in their twenties. He looked like their father.

Eminem actually released two dis records in response to Benzino's attack on him, and as corny as it was for the two of them to be battling, at least Eminem could rap. We joked and laughed about it, but inside I knew that it was going to make my job a lot harder. The more Eminem kept playing into this beef, the more Ray would use the magazine against him.

Tanya picked up on the first ring when I called her back. "I just heard the record. It's funny as hell. Does this mean Ray is going to call me tonight and have me write an essay on why Eminem's battle record sucks?"

"I don't know. I hope not. He needs to just leave it alone. Leave it alone, Ray, leave it alone." Tanya and I were saying things to each other that we could never say to Ray. He was supersensitive and couldn't take any criticism. Criticizing him usually cost someone his or her job. So we continually played it off as if his records were decent. "Yeah, sounds good, Ray. Uh-huh. The video looks good too. Yup. Uh-huh. So who produced it?" We would ask questions about the music and act as if we were interested.

Ray never ever, ever left the beef alone. The rest of my career at the *Source* was dedicated to the destruction of Eminem, Interscope, Shady/Aftermath, 50, whatever and whoever were affiliated. If Russell Simmons made a comment in support of Em, the mandate was to bash Russell Simmons. If someone had a problem or beef with 50 or Eminem, they automatically got to be on the cover. Everything was somehow connected to Marshall Mathers thereafter. But Dave knew how to disguise it. After years of dealing with Ray, Dave had acquired a special talent. The art was to take Ray's self-serving agenda and repackage it into a hip-hop emergency that the magazine needed to cover. This time, Dave defined it as destroying "the machine." The machine that had taken hip-hop and turned it into a multibillion-dollar business, forgetting where it came from. The machine that capitalized off 50 Cent's thuggery and was poisoning our culture. The machine is what was keeping Eminem going. *Machine, bad. Eminem, bad. 50, bad. Ja Rule, good. Benzino, good. Russell Simmons, uh, what did he say? He likes Eminem? Bad.*

Hip-hop under attack featured an upside-down microphone behind the text, which was set against a black background. It was a sign of distress, KRS-One told me ("An upside-down microphone! Do you know what that means for hip-hop?"). We tried to hide our real purpose, which was to carry out Benzino's mission. *Save hip-hop. Save it from the machine. Save it from Eminem!* But the readers were too smart to buy it.

Out of the select small crop of celebrities who actually still dealt with us, we did the best with what we could. I would call on friends like Joe Budden or Fabolous to give quotes that we needed from artists. We tried covers with Cam'Ron, P. Diddy, Pharrell, and even OutKast, but sales were so sluggish that no one artist could save us. The magazine's numbers dropped down an average of fifty thousand readers after that Benzino-driven February issue. The steep decline could clearly be attributed to the drama with Eminem. And then it happened.

I was sitting at my desk editing a story one night after everyone else had gone home. My phone was ringing so I picked up. "Kim, did you hear this record?" I didn't even get a chance to say hello before I heard Michelle's voice. It's one of those calls you get when the other person is so concerned with telling you something that the person doesn't even actually realize if it's you on the other end.

"What song?" I asked in my almost dead, after-midnight voice.

Michelle took a deep breath that I could hear through the phone. "Eminem. He's got your name in a song."

My stomach felt the way it did when I rode Freefall at the Six Flags Great Adventure theme park. I so was overcome with fear because I just knew Eminem had blown my spot up about 50.

But Eminem wasn't naming names. Phew. "This record ain't that bad. He's calling me a ho. Didn't he say the same thing about his wife and his mama? I don't really care what Eminem says."

"I know, but this is"—Michelle paused and inhaled another breath of life before she finished—"this is so bad."

It really wasn't that bad. Eminem had a history of mentioning women in his records. Christina Aguilera, Madonna, Britney Spears, Mariah Carey, this was nothing new. And I looked on the bright side, he only mentions famous people, right? I felt famous for a minute.

But Michelle took the fame away. If she were a sideview mirror on a car, then the words across her would read "The things she says appear one hundred times worse than they actually are." So I dragged the cursor on my computer back to the beginning of the MP3 file of "Die Another Day" so I could listen to Em's verse on the song one mo' 'gain.

Kim Osorio, you sorry ho . . . I'll drag you through the barrio.

"He used my entire government name. I should turn this around and find a way to call him a snitch," I said.

"Then you'd be conceding his point."

"Oh. Okay, so that's not gonna work." All out of things to say, I went back to the third grade and used what I knew would discredit his entire being. "He's stupid."

The next morning it was hard to believe that I had gone home the night before because I swear I was sitting in the same exact spot looking at the same exact story. My two-way started ringing with the latest Just Blaze–produced alert when I noticed a message from a not-so-common messenger: "50 is saying he slept with you. Handle that."

It was from Tracii McGregor, and I didn't know whether it was an accusation, a friendly warning, or an order.

I didn't know where, when, or to whom he had said it, but I knew if I sweat trying to get the information, I would look guilty. I thought about what I would say for about five minutes before I typed out my response. "He would say something like that." It was ambiguous enough not to be an admission and honest enough not to be a lie. First, Eminem name-drops me in a record, with some not so flattering comments, I might add. And now 50 was kiss-and-telling, probably to an audience.

A few weeks later, I was at Lil' Kim's video shoot for "Jumpoff," the first single from her album *La Bella Mafia*. Her team was pushing for a 5 Mic rating. It was a solid album, but most of the staff felt it fell short of a classic. The album also, ironically, featured a cameo from 50 Cent on a song called "Magic Stick," which I knew was originally written for Trina. 50 had called me a few weeks after we left Puerto Rico and asked me to listen to a song he'd written.

"Listen to this duet I just wrote. It's real explicit, but I want to put it on my album." I was at a dinner with friends when 50 called, so I could barely hear him singing. *"I got the magic stick . . . I know if I could hit once, I could hit twice . . .* Then the chorus is gonna be me and Trina going back and forth . . . *I am the baddest bitch . . .* You like it? I just wrote it."

"Uh. Yeah, it sounds dope," I said, though I hated hearing anyone rap a cappella. Truth be told, if you wanted my opinion, then it would have been wiser to play the beat, but 50 constantly ran his songs by me right after he wrote them. I was starting to feel like a focus group. Knowing that "baddest bitch" was a moniker for Miami-based rapper Trina, I thought it was odd when I heard Lil' Kim on it a few months later. It was actually a peace offering made by 50 after he dissed Lil' Kim in a verse while performing in Puerto Rico, I read somewhere. But I was starting to understand 50 better. He dissed Kim, but turned right around and did business with her when he needed to. It was business, not personal, and that's when I realized that everything that had happened between us was all business to him too.

At the video shoot, DJ Clue caught me off guard when he asked out of the blue, "You know 50 Cent was talking about you on the radio?"

"Huh? Who?" I tried to pretend that I didn't hear him over the noise, but now I was furious. I took refuge in a quiet corner so I could call the only person inside 50's camp that I knew I could trust.

"James! Why is 50 Cent talking about me on the radio? What is he saying?" I was yelling into James Cruz's cell phone, which he picked up on the first ring.

James gave me the rundown of the news that 50 Cent had gone on a Los Angeles radio station saying that we slept together. I shouted in the phone, hoping that James would go back and convey my anger to 50. Instead, he went into I-told-you-so mode, and I started to block out his voice. I never anticipated that it would get this far. *Locker room talk, I could deal with that. But the radio?! How dare he! Why was he putting me in the middle of this?* In the midst of a battle between my boss and 50's sort-of boss, my past relationship with 50 became a grenade for Eminem and 50 to throw out and blow up in my face. I could no longer stand in the middle of the war zone trying to raise a white flag. I was not about to become a pawn in the game that these men were playing with each other, so I had to strap up.

CHAPTER FOURTEEN

d'evils

Right around the time that the holidays were strolling around, one of the department heads had come up with the idea to do a "Source Employee Awards." It was a mock of the actual Source Hip-Hop Awards, the awards show we hosted each year that had become a staple in hip-hop. The Source Awards were famous for things that had taken place in prior years. It was where Suge Knight had once directed that infamous line toward Puffy: "If you don't want a CEO dancing in your videos . . . come to Death Row." It was also where E-40 and his crew, while sitting in the audience in L.A., had gotten involved in an altercation that shut the show's production down. The Source Awards had so many memorable ghetto moments that it became the butt of all comedians' jokes. Chris Rock even used it as a joke in his stand-up when he hosted the MTV Awards one year.

.

The Source Employee Awards was our internal version of the big awards show. It would be a fun, parody-style event where the staff would nominate each other and then vote for the winners. There were such categories as the Wiseass, Best Dressed, the Porch Award—which honored the person who spent the most time on the back terrace smoking (be it weed or cigarettes)—and even one for Mr. & Mrs. Postal. I only got nominated for one award, Employee of the Year, and I took pride in being nominated for one of the few serious categories they had. Julie Als was also nominated, as the head of Human Resources. On the outside, she was cool with everyone. She was nonconfrontational, and whenever you had a problem, her door was open to talk about it. But I later learned that the problem with that is, as the head of HR, you should be more than just a shoulder to cry on. I had gone into Julie's office more than once to talk about things that I felt made me uncomfortable. For one, I told her about the things that Tanya was going through, and so did Tanya. Tanya told me that she'd confided in Julie many times and told her how uncomfortable Ray made her feel. Ever since Tanya had become the managing editor, I'd seen Ray pursue her heavily. The touching and groping was obvious. He would pull her toward him, hug her, kiss her, and stroke her hair. Then when he looked away, she would make a face as if she just drank a cup of sour milk. She always resisted. But like many women at their jobs, resisting doesn't always mean you tell your boss to fuck off. Sometimes, resisting is just pulling back or gently pushing away. Resisting is never saying yes, even if you never said no.

I also complained to Julie about the Antoine situation and told her how he had disrespected and violated me. I had also, myself, discussed Ray's behavior toward Tanya and how I saw him do things to her in the office. Julie listened, you know, that old sister-girl, sympathetic "I know, girl" response. But both in the case of Antoine and in the case of Tanya, nothing ever happened.

Jeremy had decided that this Source Employee Awards was going to replace the holiday party for that year. The awards would be held in our conference room, and we would just have a party during the day that would be catered. We would also exchange our Kris Kringle gifts at the awards. Early that day, two of Ray's friends went around the office getting footage and interviews with the staff. They called it the "pre-show," and it was likened to a red-carpet type of event. That day, everyone was in good spirits. They caught me in the hallway and I joked around and parodied the way rappers call out their competitors during interviews by calling out Tracii McGregor, who had also been nominated in my category. Remember, I thought we were cool. *Like anyone would look miserable during an office party,* but okay. The tape made the *Source* look like the most exciting and rewarding place to work. Ray, however, was not once seen on the tape—which didn't reveal that he won the award for Mr. Postal.

Ray arrived at the party after the awards ceremony had taken place. He caught me walking out of the conference room and pulled me to the side.

"Kim, come here."

"Oh, hey, Ray, what's up?"

"Guess who I got for my Kris Kringle?"

Tanya was standing not too for from where we were talking.

"I got Tanya," Ray said to me with a devious smile.

"How did you get Tanya?" The great thing about the Secret Santa at the *Source* was that it was far from secret. It was almost a test to see just how fast news could spread internally. I knew Ray didn't originally pick Tanya because Tanya herself had gone around and found out who everyone had. That Ray was now saying he was her Secret Santa was different from what she had found out.

"You had to switch with somebody to pick her name. You can't do that." Rocket science, I figured it out.

"I switched. Now I got Tanya. I'm gonna get her a Jacob watch," Ray said, still smiling.

One thing I love about hip-hop is how things go in and out of style in the blink of an eye. And by this time, Jacob watches were so five minutes ago. But humoring Ray, I went along as if a Jacob watch were the in thing to have.

"You can't get her a Jacob watch, that's over the spending limit. Aren't we only supposed to spend like fifty dollars or something."

"No, don't hate, Kim. You about to get a Gucci bag from Dale."

"Dale has me?"

"Yeah, he switched with someone to get your name. You like Dale?"

"No, I don't like Dale."

"Why not, Kim?"

"Ray, I'm not having this conversation with you. Because I don't."

"You wouldn't get with Dale?"

"No, I wouldn't. I'm not interested, and plus, we work together."

"Aw, so what, Kim? Everybody gets with everybody. That's how this business is. Stop being so stiff and by the book. Lighten up."

The interesting thing about Ray's comment was that there was some truth to it. In the music business, everybody does get with everybody. At the *Source,* I quickly discovered quite a few office romances going on under my nose. I usually found out about these intra-office relationships after the fact. Late nights at the office had brought some employees closer together. Too close. For me, though, I always had this thing about dating someone who worked in the same office. Yuk. Personally, I just couldn't stand to come to work and have to see that person every day. And what happens when you break up and have to face the person at the 10 a.m. staff meeting? Gross. But apparently, romances had started and finished at the *Source.* Dale had asked me out a few times, and I had immediately declined. Not just because he wasn't my type, but because we worked together. He was Dave's executive assistant, and imagine what that would have been like.

"Well, I don't like him then," I said in response to Ray, who was adamant about getting me to go out with Dale.

"You wouldn't give him any?" *Any* in Ray's book meant sleeping with him.

"No."

"Okay, then forget Dale. What about Tanya? Does she like me?"

I was stuck. I knew Tanya was disgusted by Ray, but I didn't want to say anything wrong. "I don't know."

"Yes, you do, Kim. Y'all always together. Tell me, is she feeling me?"

"I don't know, Ray, but it doesn't matter because you're the boss and she's not gonna do that."

"If she was smart, then she would." Ray laughed through his nostrils.

Tanya stood off to the side, but had caught part of the conversation. She was making faces behind his back.

While the party went on, the editorial department was still closing our March issue, the all-text cover. I dipped out for a few hours to pick up Kayla and have dinner with her before heading back to the office to pull an all-nighter.

Because the holidays were in full swing, I was trying to spend a little more time at home with Kayla. She was already two and a half years old, and I was feeling guilty for missing such things as taking her to the movies to see *The Incredibles* or eating dinner with her every night. All the rap drama had robbed me of spending time with her, and people were starting to notice. In particular, my mother was a little antsy because she had retired from her job but picked up another responsibility. Kayla never missed a beat because she loved spending all the extra time with my family, especially my younger sister, Ashley, who is only six years older than her. But for me, it was hard to be away from her for so many hours in the day, and the guilt was wearing on me. That's when things got even busier.

Getting called into Dave's office every evening was torturous. Because Ray didn't usually get into the office until after five, our meetings didn't get started until six or seven at night. I was in the office each morning between 9:30 and 10 a.m. I rarely even had the option to go in later like everyone else. At the *Source,* only two people from editorial were there in the mornings before ten, and that was Tanya and I. We were single mothers who had no choice. Both of our daughters had school, and that meant that we were up before 7 a.m. to have them in school between eight and nine. I dropped Kayla off at her school every morning at 8:30 a.m. She went to Small World Montessori, five minutes from where I lived, and I was adamant about not being the last parent to get her child in, though I often was. Her teacher was strict, and I always felt that I was going to get in trouble if I dropped Kayla off a little late. You were disrupting the class if you were even five minutes behind everyone else. For me, working all hours of the night, I often slipped, making Kayla miss the Pledge of Allegiance and the "God Bless America" song. Shame on me.

Needless to say, I went straight to the office after I dropped her off and only detoured to Starbucks on the way in, so I was there, cup in hand, by 10 a.m. unless someone crashed into the divider on my ride down the FDR Drive. The mornings were nice and quiet. Peaceful, even. And it was a major contrast to the vibe of the office by 5 p.m. In the morning, I had a chance to check my email, breathe, and edit stories. But in the evenings, I was usually pulled away from my duties to sit in Dave's office and hear Ray complain about Eminem.

One evening, as I was sitting at my desk, my phone rang, showing the number 1711, which was Dave.

I immediately picked up. "Hey."

"Hey, come down here. Ray wants to talk to you," Dave said.

Unaware of what idiot campaign he wanted to launch this time, I took the long walk all the way down to the other end of the hall. When I walked in, Dave was seated at his desk, someone I'd never seen before was on the couch, and Ray was standing over the coffee table with the Power 30 issue open to a specific page. I could see the huge picture of our number one executive, Steve Stoute.

"What's up, Ray?"

"Yo, Kim. Did you go on a date with Steve Stoute?" Ray asked, his inner eyebrows pointed to his nose.

"I didn't go on a date with Steve Stoute. We went to a business dinner a few weeks ago." After the Power 30 issue had closed but before it had come out, I opted to accept an invitation to dinner with Stoute, who was still trying to convince me to reveal the order of the Power 30 list. We met at an Italian restaurant in the theater district of Manhattan, the fancy type where the waiters are usually named Francois and get upset if you prefer tap water over sparkling. Stoute was obviously a regular there because the owner kept coming up to talk to him and was opening bottles of wine that I didn't hear anyone order. It was an extremely casual dinner, a late-night one, but it was business.

"Why am I hearing that you went on a date with Steve Stoute?" Ray's tone was bordering angry, and now the skin between his eyes was wrinkling.

"We didn't go on a date. Just because two people go to dinner does not make it a date." *Even if there was a lot of innocent flirting,* the voice in my head finished the thought.

While Ray paced back and forth, Dave continued to stare at his computer screen. I took a seat on the couch's left side.

"Well, Steve's about to catch it." Ray picked up the magazine that was open to Steve's page and studied the words. "Look at this cornball. This is the type of guy who nobody paid attention to in school." Ray backhanded Stoute's picture with his right hand while he was holding the magazine in his left. Then he dropped it back down onto the coffee table. "I can't believe that we actually made him number one in the Power 30. Tsss." Ray rolled his eyes back and looked over to Dave.

The argument can be made that all magazines fudge these types of lists, but when it came to the *Source,* knowing that Ray Benzino was in control of the Power 30 lent extra discredit to it. That year, Ray took one look at the list we submitted and told me to make changes based on what he wanted. I specifically remember him saying things like "Move

Kevin Liles and Lyor Cohen down to the third spot. They don't deserve to be number two. And make Russell Simmons the small picture on the page." He also stated, "Make sure you don't put Tracy Cloherty and Emmis ahead of Clear Channel. Let them be behind them." There were orders to "move Roc-A-Fella down" and "move Sylvia Rhone up" because Ray hated Jay-Z and Sylvia Rhone was the head of his label, Elektra Records. And no matter what kind of year they had, there was always a spot for Suge Knight and J. Prince, so they were on that list too. But the worst was when I was told that we needed to include Dave and Ray themselves, because they had power too. Ugk. In journalism, nothing is worse than doing a story on yourself. And of course that year, there was the ultimate rule, the one that would cost you your job if you violated it. "Do not put Eminem or 50 anywhere on the list!" But I specifically remember, in the case of Steve Stoute, Ray wanted to make him number one.

That day in Dave's office, Ray was spewing insults about Steve Stoute. "Yo, fuck Steve Stoute. We need to write bad shit instead of writing all this good shit we wrote about him in the Power 30." Ray was on a roll, and in typical Benzino fashion, once he started, he would never stop.

"Yeah, D. Yeah, we need to shit on this dude in the magazine," Ray said to Dave, who was nodding his head like a woodpecker, agreeing to everything Ray was saying. I had no idea what Steve Stoute had said to or about Ray in the past thirty days that had made him change his opinion of the music mogul so quickly, but he was now the enemy.

"Kim, I hope you're not scared. 'Cause if you're scared, then you can't do this, and if you can't do this, then maybe you need to think about whether you're built to be the editor in chief of this magazine."

I was at a loss for words. I couldn't say the wrong thing because I would only be diggin' myself deeper in the grave.

"I want a story on Steve Stoute. I want a story exposing him, Nas, and 50 Cent."

I had finally discovered the objective of this meeting, and it was not to tell me that I was doing a good job. Ray had a new agenda. We were all still recovering from the backlash of the Eminem beef, and we had just been forced to run a five-page story on Benzino and a cartoon poster of him holding Eminem's bloody severed head, and now we were right back in "exposé" mode. That was Ray's new thing. He was going to "expose them." Meanwhile, by doing these stories, the only ones truly being exposed were the editors ourselves, demonstrating our lack of control over the content of the magazine.

"Call whoever you gotta call, get some people to give you some dirt on Steve Stoute. Figure it out. I want to see this shit in the next issue. All three. Even Nas. You don't have a problem with that do you?"

At that moment, my nerves were bad. *Did I have a problem?* Yes, I had a problem. I knew it was wrong and I knew I wouldn't be able to find anyone to assist me in my new duties, to expose at all costs. It was easy for writers or editors to tell me that they wanted no part, but I couldn't tell that to Ray. I also wasn't about to let him think that my personal relationships with Nas and 50 prevented me from carrying out his orders, so I had to play it cool. I had to act as if I didn't care.

"Nah, I don't got a problem with it. I'm good."

"You shouldn't have a problem with that. 'Cause Steve talked shit about you too."

"What? What did he say about me?" I was so confused. I never even thought I was that high up on Stoute's radar, but men in the industry have a funny way of gossiping among each other.

"Why don't you ask Nas?"

I knew that I was now skating on thin ice, and I was sticking to my vow to never discuss my personal business in business meetings, especially with Ray.

"Whatever, I don't care what he said," I responded. "I'm fine. I don't have a problem with it." I knew the more I pried for information, the more Ray would pry into my business, so I just let it go. But I was clearly bothered that Stoute had tried to throw me under the bus. It motivated me to want to write the story myself. I knew what Ray was telling me to put in the story, but I had my own intentions now. They wanted him to catch it, and now, because he had put my shit on the line, I wanted it too.

"Aight, good, so we good, then," Ray said to me before taking a seat on the couch, blunt in hand. I got up and walked away like a child who had just stolen a candy bar out of the candy store. You don't really know if the store owner is going to call you out before you get out the door, and you try to walk out of there without looking suspicious. That they suspected Nas and me was enough. And I did not even want to touch the 50 stuff. *Hmph, Steve Stoute doesn't even know me like that,* I thought. *And just wait until I speak to Nas. Let me find out he can't keep a secret either.*

For the next week, I called around to some of my secret sources and asked them to give me dirt on Steve Stoute. I was downright evil with it. Dave periodically checked up, asking, "What did you get? Did you find out anything?" But even though I was coming up with some good stuff, no one would talk on the record for a Steve Stoute story.

As a journalist, you get used to people talking to you "off the record." And sometimes, it even gets insulting when you're having a business conversation and the other party keeps throwing in "this is off the record" every couple of sentences. But there is a benefit to it—that being that anything that isn't said to be "off the record" is clearly "on the record." Some individuals knew when I called that anything they said could be used in a story. But some people spoke freely without knowing that their words would turn up in print. Where Steve Stoute was concerned, most people were shaken enough by his industry prowess that they spoke off the record, anonymously.

"You better not use my name, Kim, I would lose my job," said one source before dishing on Steve Stoute. According to the source, Jay-Z and Steve Stoute had grown rather close over the years. Back then, before Roc-A-Fella records had actually split up, the Jay-Z/Steve Stoute business relationship was a touchy subject at Def Jam.

1711. I could see the number flashing on my phone in my office, but I couldn't choose to let it ring. Even though I knew it meant drama, I had to pick up because Dave always knew whether I was there, and I didn't want him to come marching down to my office mad because I wasn't picking up the line.

"How far did you get with the Steve Stoute story?" said his voice.

"I got some information, but it's not ready yet."

After a brief silence, Dave stuttered, "Uhhh. Okay. Uhhhh. Well, just hold it. Hold that and hold the other ones." His voice was shaking and he seemed unsure of his decision. I wasn't about to ask any questions because, deep down, I knew holding these stories was a good thing. But now that I was halfway through the Stoute piece, a part of me really wanted it to get published—especially after Ray said that Stoute was the one who told him and Dave that I was messing with Nas.

"But I'm halfway done with the Stoute story," I said, "and I have someone working on the Nas piece already. That one's ready to go. They actually had an idea to use his quotes to show his contradictions."

Luckily for me, I had help from a talented writer who knew just what to do when I told him I needed to "expose" Nas. This writer was on staff and opted to take his name off the story when it ran, but he did a good job of showing Nas's inconsistent statements, which weren't too hard to find. The one-page Nas piece ran in the April issue, and although I didn't want any part in putting it together, I felt no guilt in running it. I figured whatever Steve Stoute had said about me had to have come from Nas, and for that, he should catch it too. Nas and I ended up having a not-so-friendly phone conversation about what had happened. He initially called to complain about the piece in the magazine, but in typical Nas fashion, he managed to give us credit for it in the same conversation. "What artist doesn't contradict themselves?" he asked rhetorically. But he could barely get a word in because I was too busy being furious about whatever he had told Stoute.

"When someone asks you about me, you don't know me," I instructed him during our phone call. "You don't know me. This is my job, and what you and your on-again-off-again manager might consider to be small talk can take the food out of my daughter's mouth."

"Well, you should have thought about that before you were clinking wineglasses with Steve Stoute."

It seemed I wasn't the only one with feelings about the whole thing after all. The male ego is a funny thing, and however their conversation had gone down, it had forced the two of them to trade some information about me.

I was relieved that we had made it through the issue with only having to run one of the hate pieces, especially in the wake of the February disaster issue. Sometimes, Dave made decisions that went against what Ray told me to do. Other times, Ray changed his mind and had Dave convey that to me. Either way, it made for confusing direction. One of the best examples of this was the popular Eminem story that would later run in 2004. The story sat for months before it actually ran. Each month, I had to deal with "run the story . . . don't run the story . . . run the story," depending on what Eminem or Interscope had done that day. But this particular month, I was happy to hear "hold the story" in reference to Steve Stoute, even if it only meant that I had bought myself more time to try to figure out a way to convince Ray that we shouldn't do it. But even I was conflicted about it.

Closing the March text-cover issue was still a beast. Dave decided that we should host a roundtable discussion and run that as the cover story. For the "Hip-Hop Under Attack" panel, we would present a number of different issues that the hip-hop community was facing. One of these issues would be Eminem, although none of the panelists knew ahead of time that he would be a topic. I had to pull together a roundtable and invite celebrities to take part. We booked a room at the Soho Grande Hotel and invited press to cover the *Source*'s panel on the "state of emergency in hip-hop." There really was no other emergency other than Benzino's career being on life support. It had never really been alive, but now it was dying a slow death and was taking the magazine with it. For panelists, we invited the usual suspects. Harry Allen was going to moderate, Chuck D. and Talib Kweli were no-brainers as intelligent MCs who always agreed to take part in a discussion about the state of hip-hop. But I had to make the panel relevant and worthy of a cover story. I invited Dame Dash, who didn't, of course, really let anyone else talk, and Fabolous, who didn't, of course, really talk at all. There was Londell McMillan, a prominent entertainment attorney; Eve, the token female, who showed her professionalism by being the first to show up on time; and the break-dancer Crazy Legs, because we had to have someone represent an element of hip-hop other than rap. The biggest surprise was Cash Money's Baby, whom I convinced to be a part of it and had some interesting things to say. But the icing on the cake was that Benzino was on the panel as well. I tried to hide that bit of information whenever someone initially asked me who was going to participate.

Outside of Benzino's rant about Eminem, the panel was successful, and when Dave reviewed the transcript and realized that the other artists were smart enough to avoid the Eminem topic and never once address or dis him by name, he decided that we had to have another panel. *A panel about the panel. Go figure.* The staff had to gather in the conference room and talk about hip-hop's state of emergency for the second time. It was like beating a dead horse, only the dead horse was Benzino, and Eminem was the one doing the beating.

The issue was one of the worst-selling issues ever. It tanked.

the x factor

"I need to see some bitches in here. I'm not seeing any ass or anything like that." Ray was flipping through the pages of the latest issue like a speed reader, disgusted because the women featured had too much clothing on. "Yo, the *Source* is a magazine for niggas in jail. Niggas wanna see ass and titties. They don't care about all this other shit."

The *Source* was a hip-hop magazine, but somewhere along the way Ray decided that the *Source* was going to change its tune. It was going to be more of a men's lifestyle magazine. Men in jail and involved in street activities. It was part of the reason why he became so infatuated with *F.E.D.S.* magazine and hired Antoine—who was not making my job any easier. I had to come to work every day and deal with him after our incident. Fortunately for me, he barely came to work. When he did, however, I pretended as if his being there didn't bother me anymore.

At one point, Ray was inspired to launch a completely new magazine. Originally to be called *Source Style*, it almost made its way onto newsstands. Meetings were conducted, stories were assigned, and a staff was assembled. Everyone was extremely excited about it until all of a sudden Dave called us into his office to inform us that the title for this spin-off had changed. It would now be *ZNO* magazine. For the rest of our days at the *Source*, we would refer to it as *MagaZINO*. Luckily, *MagaZINO* was never released because of budget concerns. But it didn't matter, because the *Source* itself was slowly making its transition into *MagaZINO* anyway.

I was extremely excited when Dave told me that I could give the cover of the April issue to Snoop Dogg. Snoop is one of the *Source*'s most celebrated and high-selling cover subjects, and someone I always wanted to write about. Once I got the okay to move forward, I booked yet another trip to L.A. so that I could talk to Snoop and start coming up with ideas for the cover feature. I was in and out of Cali in a day, which was mostly spent in a car service. The car picked me up from my hotel, then took me to a house where another car service was waiting. I felt like a secret agent on a secret mission. Then I spent an hour and a half in that car driving to a house in a gated community in Diamond Bar, California. It was a modest house in comparison to the others in the community, nothing like the $2 million house he's shown on *MTV Cribs*. When I got there, someone was waiting to escort me to the upstairs living room, where Snoop was sitting, writing in his notepad and listening to beats.

I sat down and waited for the Doggfather to address me. "Hey, *how you doin'*?" Snoop asked in his trademark drawl. His eyelids were so low that it was hard to see whether he was awake or asleep. Still, he was nodding his head on beat and jotting words down in his notepad, pausing the beat on his recording console every few seconds. His wife was trying to get the kids ready for a game, so she walked in the room to hand Snoop a sneaker to lace up for one of his sons.

"I'm good," I responded, before getting down to business. "So you have a lot of things that you want to talk about in this issue I'm told."

Snoop put the pad down and turned off the music. With his wife and kids walking in and out of the room, Snoop talked to me while penning lyrics to a beat with Pharrell singing on the hook. I was trying not to pay too much attention to all the photos of Snoop on the wall while he talked and cursed about Suge and his days at Death Row. Suge still owned part of Snoop's music, and his face got really bunched up when he talked about him, and how he felt that even though his Death Row days were over, he still hadn't broken free.

I could remember a time when I was highly stressed if Ray changed his mind after we had agreed to give someone a cover. That month, I had to split the Snoop cover after I'd already led him to believe that he was going to be the one. After meeting with Snoop and discussing our plans, I looked like an idiot when I had to go back and change everything we had just talked about as if I had wasted everyone's time in the first place. It ruined many of the relationships that I'd had in the business, and with someone like Snoop whom I barely knew, it prevented me from starting new ones.

Post-Eminem, though, I was just happy when we did something that wasn't on Benzino. After closing the March issue, which had a cover story featuring Benzino as a panelist, a spread promoting Benzino's album, a clothing ad with Benzino as the model, and a sure-shot-single review of his song, among other things, it was a relief just not to have to put Ray in the magazine again, or—God forbid—on the cover. Benzino had put himself on the cover, as a four-way split, back in December of 2001. Luckily, I was not the editor at the time. I can remember thinking how Carlito's face looked every time he was forced to address it that month. It was the most disappointed face I had ever seen Carlito make. Right after he would say it, he'd smack his palm to his forehead, as if to punish himself for not being able to stop it from happening. I specifically remember whenever I saw it on newsstands—Ray holding up his three fingers with his hair resembling characters from *Fraggle Rock*—it was waiting for someone to buy it.

Ray called a few days after I'd had my meeting with Snoop to tell me he had decided to do a Cam'Ron/DipSet cover. For Cam, it was his first *Source* cover, and most artists would take it even if they had to share it. Cam would be featured alongside his Dipset cohorts Jim Jones and Juelz Santana. At the time, they were on the come-up. This last-minute decision threw me off completely. I thought about the reasons why Ray allowed us to put them on the cover now and not when Cam had put his album out, and I reasoned that it was their silent beef with 50. Their opinions of each other wouldn't really surface until 2007, when the two would trade sarcastic comments on Angie Martinez's radio show. But at the time, a few industry folks knew that some things were brewing between them. Ray decided that Cam'Ron would be on the newsstands, and Snoop would only go to subscribers, making my job of telling Snoop and his people even harder.

In addition to all his other complaints, Ray had brought up the fashion in the magazine more than once. The then fashion editor, Liza Montoya, had been hired by the former art director, Curcurito. Liza was cool, but her fashion sense was more old school than anything else. More Kangol than Yankee-fitted. Ray had been broadcasting that her run was about to be over. Luckily for me, I had my hands tied, and Tanya handled the termination. Dave told me that we were bringing on Groovy Lew and Misa Hylton-Brim, two celebrity stylists that would replace one fashion editor. I met with Misa at the Coffee Shop, and we hit it off right away, so I had no problems with the two of them coming on board. But I had no parts in the decisions to fire Liza or hire Misa. Neither Misa or Groovy had magazine experience, but I agreed with Dave and Ray that they could quickly learn that part. They had the right fashion sense and that was the point. The art and photo departments, however, felt a lot differently. Because the photo and fashion departments work so closely together, they felt that hiring

Misa and Groovy was creating more work for them and they were not going to teach them the ropes.

One of the things Ray had continually insisted on was a sexy photo shoot of a female, à la *XXL*'s "Eye Candy" section. We had avoided it for months, but with the addition of the new fashion department, Ray insisted that Misa take on the idea as one of her new duties. He came up with the name "Dimepiece" for the two-page column. Misa figured out a way to differentiate it from *XXL*, where they profiled the video chick of the hour. She would get high-profile celebrity females to do it, and since she had all the connections to do so, she started making calls. Misa picked Kimora Lee as the first Dimepiece, and everyone loved it because of her star power. Ray was all for it until he saw the pictures. He was upset to discover that Kimora had not showed enough of her assets. He bitched and moaned about the column being wack because he couldn't see anything.

Around this time, things in hip-hop started heating up, and my new mandate was that we had to keep up with the internet sites. Being a monthly magazine, it was hard to be a leader when it came to breaking news in hip-hop. Irv Gotti's offices had been raided by the Feds, Fabolous had gotten arrested for driving with a suspended license, and Violator's offices were shot up. I was busy trying to follow the real stories in hip-hop until I got sidetracked by a call that put a damper on my work flow.

"Where are the stories on Nas, 50, and Steve Stoute?" Dave yelled through my cell phone one morning, as I waited in my mother's house for a tow truck to pick up my car, which had decided it had enough of the back and forth trips to Manhattan.

"You told me to hold them."

Then, in his sarcastic, demeaning tone, Dave said, "Yeah, I told you to hold them, not to stop working on them. What the fuck is wrong with you? Where are they?"

Considering that I had seen Dave numerous times that week, and he had never once mentioned putting the stories back into the magazine, I was livid. Here he was cursing at me for something he told me to do.

Then I heard Ray's voice magically appear. "Kim, where are the stories, Kim?" It was one of those three-way calls that you can't stand. Not the one where the third party is announced right away, but the one where the third party wants to stay silent just to see what you say before you know he or she is listening.

I could feel my stomach drop, because none of the stories in question were ready, and we were already closing the April issue. I just knew I was about to catch it.

"What's going on with those stories? Do you have those stories?" Ray asked.

"They're not completely done . . . but—"

"They're not completely done?" Ray said, mocking me. "Kim, what does that mean, Kim?"

"When Dave told me to hold them, we stopped working on them."

"Dave, you told her to hold them, Dave?" Ray had a way of starting and finishing a sentence with your name, just in case you didn't already know that he was talking to you.

"I . . . I . . . ," Dave stuttered through the phone.

"Dave, did you tell them to hold the stories, Dave?" Ray was obviously annoyed he hadn't heard this piece to the puzzle.

"I . . . I . . ."

"Well, tell her to run them, now, Dave."

"Uh . . . you can run the stories." Dave sounded like a parrot.

"Why the fuck would you tell her to hold them, Dave? What the fuck are you doing? Are you trying to sabotage this whole shit?" Ray's anger toward me switched and was now directed at Dave. He started cursing uncontrollably on the phone, as I began to climb into the tow truck that would drag my Toyota to the service station to be fixed.

"Tell her you're an idiot. Tell her you're an idiot and that you made a mistake, Dave."

"I . . . I'm an idiot. I made a mistake."

"No, tell her you're a fuckin' idiot."

"I . . . I'm a fuckin' idiot. I shouldn't have told you to hold the stories."

I couldn't believe what I was hearing. It wasn't that I hadn't already known that Ray told Dave what to do, but to hear it word-for-word was a new experience. How pathetic. In those few minutes, I actually felt bad for Dave. The way you feel sorry for your dog when he does something wrong and you have to smack him in the nose with a rolled-up newspaper more than once. Dave was like Ray's pet. After I got over the initial shock of having to revive the hate stories, which at this point I was indifferent about, I called Tanya to joke about the telephone conversation where I had witnessed Dave's verbal beatdown. We both laughed and then felt bad for him. "What does Ray have on Dave to make him act like that?" Tanya asked. I had heard that question before, but never truly found out the answer.

For the first time, I felt Dave and I were equals, and I have to admit, it felt good. It seemed to me that Dave didn't really want the stories to go in, knowing they could further damage the *Source*'s business, so he was doing whatever he could to hold them up without letting Ray know. I always knew I didn't have control, but now to think that Dave didn't either was actually a bit satisfying.

From that moment on, I likened Ray and Dave to Gargamel and Azriel of the Smurfs cartoon. When Gargamel was around, the Smurfs would run for cover and try to avoid him at all costs to save themselves from being swallowed whole. Azriel was Gargamel's pet cat, who performed some of Gargamel's evil duties. When Azriel disobeyed Gargamel though, he was punished. Ray was a real-life version of Gargamel and we were the Smurfs. Dave was now viewed as the lowest man on the totem pole. He was Azriel. At least the Smurfs could be happy when they were at home with no sight of Gargamel, but Azriel was always with Gargamel. That was his home.

The Steve Stoute story was held until the May 2003 issue, the one where we put P. Diddy on the cover. By the time we had actually gotten around to doing it, the anger I had toward Stoute had died down. Not to mention, the story was outdated. It had been five months since the Power 30 issue, and now we were coming back and readdressing his position in the Power 30, as if that were the real reason for doing the story. This type of thing that we printed made it seem we had a self-serving agenda.

The Diddy cover was also one of the most difficult to make happen because we didn't have the money to do anything that Diddy wanted to do. The planning was the most intense ever, with all these phone calls to my cell. I would pick up and a different assistant each time would order me to "Hold for Puff" before I even had a chance to say hello. Even if you're in the middle of something or you can't talk because you are bathing your child, you can say much back to the phone when you're already on hold waiting for Diddy.

"I want to do some real old-school, Harlem shit. You feel me?" He was already in the middle of a conversation when he picked up the phone. It's a character trait I've noticed in only the most wealthy music moguls: Diddy, Russell Simmons, Lyor Cohen. Though you appear to be in a conversation with them, you are not really talking. You are only listening. Only you think you are talking.

"Well, we had an idea also that we wanted to run by you. We want to do something really hot," I said, before he picked up his last thought.

"The Cotton Club. On 125th. You know the Cotton Club on 125th?" he asked, not expecting an answer.

"Yes."

"That's the look I'm going for. Over there by the river. That real Harlem feel."

The art department had been bugging me to get Puff on the phone with their photographer to get all the plans finalized before the shoot, so I was trying to set it up, but I was too busy taking notes to make sure I had Puff's order right. "I want you to have a conversation with our photographer, Anthony Mandler, to discuss these details with him."

"Over there, by the river. That's where we should shoot it," Puff insisted.

"Okay, so are you available to have a conference call with our photographer?"

"My cover gotta be real different. It can't look like everyone else's. If the last cover was done in color, then mine should be in black and white, you feel me?"

"Yes," I answered, putting myself back in my place. *Do you want fries with that?*

"And I'm gonna be in front of a Rolls-Royce. You gotta make sure they can see the whole car, though. I'm trying to do something legendary."

For me, "legendary" translated into dollars and cents because the cover wound up being one of our most expensive shoots ever. When you select a high-profile cover subject, you are left with a high-profile budget. What most of the artists never really understood was that a publishing budget is not near what most budgets in the music industry look like. We tried to keep the cost of our cover shoots under $10,000. We budgeted on average about $1,000 per page, and a cover story was usually a ten-page feature. That $10,000 was flexible, but the P. Diddy shoot was double that amount. After Diddy told me what he wanted, I spent the rest of the week working out how to make it happen with his VP of marketing. We went back and forth and crunched numbers to make sure that Diddy had everything he needed to make it happen, and it almost didn't. No one wanted to pick up the cost. But in the end, I figured out a way to get it done and split costs, without letting Dave and Ray know what Puff was asking for. I knew that would only make them cancel it. And, ironically, it was one of the smoothest shoots that we'd ever done. Diddy was more sophisticated and classy than ghetto and problematic, unlike most of the other artist cover shoots. I was just glad I didn't have to put Benzino on the front page. I had escaped another month.

One of the packages we were planning for the June issue was a feature highlighting women in the industry. We compiled a list of successful industry women to highlight. I suggested Tracey Waples, a female music executive, and Leota Blacknor, who had started her own music-business educational seminar series. Fahiym Ratcliffe, our culture editor, had suggested a few women that had been featured in his section, author Teri Woods, famous for writing *True to the Game,* and one of the few female music-video directors, Nzinga Stewart. Dave had offered the last two women to be featured: Big Pun's wife, Liza Rios, and Lil' Kim's manager, Hillary Weston. I knew that Liza's son was in a rap group with Ray's son, so I figured that was why Dave wanted to include her. And I definitely didn't question Hillary Weston, because I knew exactly who she was. I didn't know that she and Dave were actually dating at the time, although I suspected something when he insisted that we use the picture where she stood front and center. While we were closing the issue, Dale came over, looked at the picture, and spilled the beans. It didn't matter to me that Dave and Hillary were dating, plus, I liked her. She even invited me to her daughter's birthday party that year. But I found it ironic that Dave had tried to accuse me of compromising the magazine's business when he was blatantly letting his relationship interfere with the magazine's content. He decided that we would give Lil' Kim's album 4.5 Mics that year, against the vote of 4 Mics from the music staff. It always amazed me how he voted on Mics when it was convenient for his relationships. Same thing happened with Ja Rule not too long after. Not to say that I didn't like Kim's or Ja's albums, but it was the principle. That was the type of stuff that made the *Source* unreliable, and Dave and Ray were guilty of the one thing they tried to accuse me of.

hey young world

Not that it was a bad idea, but our Pharrell cover was a few months late. Pharrell had produced a song for Snoop called "Beautiful," where he sang the hook that I heard when I met with Snoop at his house in Cali. The song later became one of the biggest records of the year. The video was shot in Brazil, and its success made Brazil the new hot spot among the rap community. I hate how when a rap artist mentions a place on a record or does something there in a video, it becomes the new "in" place to visit. Such as when Puff first talked about St.-Tropez, or when Jay-Z started vacationing in the south of France. All of a sudden everyone has to go or talk about it on his or her record. I wonder if a rapper talked about a third-world country and made it cool to help underprivileged families whether it would change the world, or if Lil Wayne started driving a Prius, would it force hip-hop to be more energy concious. In true follower fashion, Ray felt that the *Source* had to be down with the madness, so he ordered us to shoot Pharrell for the cover in none other than Brazil.

Ray really wanted Pharrell to produce a Benzino record, I later found out. While I was in Brazil, someone in Pharrell's camp told me that Dave had been calling them trying to use the cover as a bargaining chip for a Pharrell track. I don't think Pharrell ever did it, which is actually kind of funny. Good for him. But he did stay on the cover. We were still closing the May issue when I left for Brazil, and Jeremy Miller had issues with the cost of the trip, but when it came to what Ray wanted, no one could object.

I later found out that Jeremy had conversations with some of the staff about my going, and he included it in his June 2003 memo when he decided to write me up because one of the issues was late. Jeremy knew that closings were always held up because Ray and Dave wanted to change things at the last minute. But because of the Brazil trip, which Jeremy felt I didn't need to go on, and my last-minute plans to interview Suge Knight for an exclusive, he went ahead and put it all down on paper. It was the only memo the *Source* would ever have that picked apart my job performance, and it was really just born out of pettiness.

Jeremy and I had an email exchange over my flying to L.A. while the magazine was closing. Although I already had Dave's approval, Jeremy sent me a text message advising me that going out of town while the magazine was closing was a problem. An editor in chief has certain privileges, privileges that I typically wasn't afforded because I was a woman at the *Source*. The editor in chief oversees the editorial direction and content of a publication, but is generally not required to be around for every second of production. It is an unrealistic expectation and almost impossible if you are trying to stay ahead of the game. The managing editor oversees the production and closing schedule.

The production of the "book," as we call each issue of the publication, is finished at "closing." During closing, stories are transferred to the layout, which is designed by the art department, and each page is printed up to what we called a final. Once the pages are printed with the completed text and pictures, they go around from person to person for sign-off. Each page makes its round starting with the art director, who checks to make sure that the words and pictures are properly formatted on the page. Then the photo department would sign off on each photo credit and the picture for any imperfections. After that, photo would walk the pages over to the research editor, then to the copy editor, then to the proper editor in the editorial department, who would read over the story and make any necessary changes. After which, a top editor would read it, then the managing editor, and finally, me. I was the final sign-off on the pages before they were sent back to the art department to be shipped on a disc to be produced onto "proofs," which would come back to me for another sign-off. The book usually shipped in sections so that "forms" could be printed before the book was bound and put onto trucks to go to the wholesaler. During closing, certain people needed to be around to make sure the pages wouldn't be held up before they went to the printer. For me, the "final" stage of closing wouldn't be the first time that I saw the pages. I had the luxury of seeing the pages in Quark, a graphics application where I could see the actual book throughout each stage.

If I had to leave town during closing, I would arrange to see, before they made the rounds, the pages that needed to ship while I was gone. This way, any major change could be made ahead of time. I was around for most closings, but on those occasions when I had to go to Brazil and Los Angeles, some talk went on behind my back blaming me for messing up the schedule. If everyone did his or her job the way it was supposed to be done, then there would be no problem with sticking to the schedule. But whenever someone had a problem, they would use my not being around as an excuse as to why it didn't get done. I'm not saying that I never pushed my deadlines for my own stories, but not the way Jeremy tried to make it sound in his June 2003 memo.

We were incredibly busy after coming back from Brazil, promoting the May issue, closing June, and planning for July. In the middle of my day, Jay-Z sent out a personal message to me and other magazine editors, inviting us up one by one to a studio to listen to his new S. Carter mixtape. Although I had more work to do than a Mexican busboy at a fancy restaurant, I went down to the studio to listen to it. After hearing the mixtape, I told Jay-Z we would review it in our next issue (we didn't review mixtapes in our reviews section, but because Jay-Z was promoting his own stuff, I figured I'd make the exception). I brought along a copy of the May 2003 issue, which was hot off the presses, and when we were finished listening, I gave Jay my only copy.

"Have you seen our new issue yet?" I held up the cover, then handed the magazine to him before pushing the down button to get on the elevator. "It's not on newsstands yet."

Jay rapidly flipped through the pages before stopping at the only story that caught his attention, the Steve Stoute exposé.

"Oh, you might want to read that one," I said to him with a nervous laugh. I knew Jay and Steve were close, and the article mentioned their business dealings with each other, in addition to the drama between Steve and Jay's then partner Dame Dash.

"What's this?" he asked, before skimming the story. As his eyes went from left to right, he read the intro. "That's not cool."

"Oh, well, that's between them," I said before jumping on the elevator. I waved bye, and Jay continued reading as the doors closed. The *Source* was becoming hip-hop's version of *Mean Girls'* "Burn Book," and Stoute was one of the main characters, fighting students in the hallways. No one was exempt from the f'ugliness. Not even the teachers.

That same night, I got a call from Steve Stoute while I was driving to the Bronx to pick up Kayla. I pulled off at the Ninety-sixth Street exit on the FDR Drive when he called because I couldn't drive while I had to concentrate on what I had to say.

"Am I about to be upset when I read this story? Tell me that I'm not going to be mad when I read this." He was asking a lot of questions, and I took that to mean that he hadn't read the story, but had heard about it from somebody.

"What? Are you telling me you didn't know this story was coming out?" I asked.

"If I'm mad when I read this story, I'm telling you, you are going to have a problem on your hands." He didn't seem to know for sure whether the story was malicious or defamatory, but he was trying to scare me into telling him.

"I'm going to have a problem? Are you serious? Do you think I'm responsible?" I expected him to be mad. I expected him to want to do something in retaliation. But I didn't expect him to blame me.

"If I'm mad when I read this story, you won't be speaking to me, you'll be speaking to my lawyer."

After hearing him bark at me for five straight minutes, I finally raised my voice enough to be heard over him. "You know what's funny? All you dudes in your penthouses sit around and play telephone with each other. No one wants to go to the person directly and make all these threats. So instead of calling the person you really want to call and saying what you want to say, you'd rather call me, like I have the power, like I hold the key to this."

In the middle of my own speech, it became clear to me that I had more power than even I knew. I had the power of the pen. To most people, it's just a writing instrument, but to me, it was the power to sway opinion. I was the conduit for certain people in the industry who were too afraid to bring their issues and concerns directly to whoever was in control. Instead of calling someone and telling them how they felt, they called me, had me put it in an article, then waited for all hell to break loose. Many rap artists have picked up the magazine and found out something that other artists have said about them that they probably wouldn't say to their face. Like the time Chingy came to the *Source* to tell us he wasn't in DTP anymore. This was before he had even told DTP. Why would you go up to a magazine and tell the editors something before addressing it with the concerned parties? Artists use the press to manipulate their own situations, but then try to blame the press when they are confronted by that same situation. But in this case, when Benzino was the artist manipulating the situation, there was no balance or quality control. Even though I was the writer in control of what was being written, Benzino's orders had to be carried out. But that didn't matter to the person getting written about.

"Why are you calling me? Why don't you call them?" I said.

"Trust me. Somebody will call them, but right now, I'm calling to tell you that if you don't want to be involved, then keep yourself out of the situation. Don't go around showing people the story like you're proud of it."

After his last statement, I understood why I got the call. Jay must have told him about the story. To this day, I have never spoken to Steve Stoute about it, but the last thing I heard about him was that he told someone I made his mother cry. That was not my intention. But what was his mother doing reading the *Source* anyway?

Steve Stoute might have hated me, but others still wanted to deal with me. No one from Interscope was on that list. In fact, Interscope had pulled their advertising from the book after the Eminem beef. But we still had Def Jam supporting us, and they had a number of significant artists that could fill the pages of the *Source*. Around this time, Ray called a meeting with the department heads to notify us that we would now be running liquor advertisements in the magazine. Chris White, the head of advertising, was devastated. As one of the original employees of the *Source*, C. White was proud that the Source would not run liquor or cigarette ads because they were damaging to the community. It was one of those great things that made the *Source* a true part of hip-hop and its progression. The *Source* cared. But Ray didn't. "We smoke and drink that's what we do," he said, before adding that liquor ads would be saving all our jobs that year.

Though the magazine's last few covers were underwhelming, I was convinced that going in an entirely new direction was a sure win, so when Irv Gotti came up to my office to pitch Ashanti for July 2003, I was all ears.

"Kimmy, this would be some groundbreaking shit." Irv was animated when he spoke that day in my office. He stood up and moved around a lot. It was more like a performance than a meeting.

"Ashanti is the princess of hip-hop/R&B. This is the one. This is the cover that she needs." Ashanti was about to release her sophomore album, after her debut had gone double platinum a couple of years before.

"We don't put R&B artists on the cover of the *Source*. I mean, this is going to be a hard sell to the editorial team here, and I gotta get Ray and Dave to go along with it. You already know that's like selling water to a well," I said, doubtful that anyone would go for it.

"The *Source* did it with Mary J. Blige. Ashanti is not your average R&B artist. I don't make my music for them. The music I make is for hip-hop niggas. Trust me. This will work."

Normally, I'd probably have been against putting Ashanti on the cover. Up until our July 2003 issue, Mary J. had been the only R&B artist on the cover of the *Source*, and that was at the height of her career in the midnineties. I remember seeing a copy of that issue with Mary against a silver-bordered backdrop wearing a hoodied snow bomber jacket. I was working at Muze, a music software company where I entered music information into a database and wrote short reviews on rap and R&B albums.

Getting copies of the magazines and reading them was one of the perks I got at Muze as part of my job. I remember how excited I was to see Mary J. on the cover one year. Mary was the artist who understood how you as a female felt fallin' in love because she had already been there. As a fan of hers, I didn't care too much about all the politics of seeing a female R&B singer on the cover of the *Source*. I just wanted to read it I thought about that during Irv's pitch for an Ashanti cover, and I used it as part of my own argument when I sent Dave an email with the pitch. Ashanti was not the best R&B singer in 2003, but her affiliation with the Inc. coupled with the swimsuit issue made it doable. The cover line read, "Ashanti exposes her private parts." It was one of the better-selling issues that year, but before the numbers came back, everyone on staff was pretty much against it.

With the first half of 2003 being so sluggish after the Eminem and Benzino beef, I was superexcited about getting Ashanti to be on the cover. I knew that the general population wouldn't care about the argument that R&B artists shouldn't be on the cover, and if anything, we would pick up some female readers while we were at it.

I was supportive of Ashanti because I believed that her first two albums were much better than most of the other R&B that was out at the time. Murder Inc. flew me out to interview her before her first album was released, and I wrote the first feature-length story on her in my R&B package that year. The label was really excited about her debut project.

I was pleasantly surprised when Dave gave me a quick answer via two-way: "We are probably going to go with the Ashanti cover for the swimsuit issue."

Phew. I had escaped another possible Benzino cover.

The Ashanti cover was photographed in a warehouse in Miami. It was a great-looking cover for her, and when it finally came out, many of the guys in the office were talking about how good she looked. I was in a meeting in my office with my associate editor Miranda Jane, who had written the story, when Ray rushed in.

"Yo, Kim, what up?" Ray had a copy of the newly released July issue in his hand.

"Hey, what's up, Ray?" I said from behind my computer.

Miranda was sitting in front of my desk, so Ray said hello to her and then, "This is hot. This cover. This is it. I love it."

With all the amazing covers we had done, this might have been the first time that Ray had actually come in to my office to compliment me on a job well done. He usually just called me into Dave's office to pick the issue apart and find things that went against his industry politics, but the Ashanti cover was right up his alley.

"Really? You like it?" I asked.

"Yeah. It's hot. She looks hot." Ray looked down at the cover in his hand and bit his lip. "Mmm. She got a fat pussy."

Miranda's eyes opened in shock. She had never been in a meeting and heard Ray's usually vulgar comments. I was speechless.

"But I can't. That's Irv's piece." Ray threw the magazine onto my coffee table, then rushed out of the office. He was like a tornado. He was in and out, but he managed to do a shitload of damage while he was there.

i got it made

For my twenty-ninth birthday, I decided to have myself a little party. Ten of my closest friends would celebrate it at Mr. Chow, downstairs in the private room. It was not "industry," though, meaning it was for just close friends and family who didn't have to listen to Scarface records for a living. At the same time, my friends decided they would throw me a big party, at a club downtown in the West Village. That, on the contrary, was very industry.

I was getting the venue for free, and my new assistant, Hilary, was helping me out with my guest list. I had asked her to consolidate my list with the list from Kanye West, whose birthday was six days before mine and who was sharing in my "industry" party. Kanye and I had met at Power 105 one evening when I went up to *Roc Radio*, a radio show hosted by Roc-A-Fella Records and Dame Dash, for an interview. I had overcome my fear of radio interviews after that horrible morning with Sway and now felt that I could go on air and face anything. Kanye was being interviewed that same day. And after it was over, we exchanged phone numbers and kept in touch.

Kanye had been the subject of a conversation between Dame, Biggs and me on our way to board a private jet to Philadelphia. "You heard Kanye's shit?" Dame asked me, in a way that made me seem less important if I answered "no." I was about to respond when I realized someone put me on mute. "His shit is incredible, we about to win with him." Dame was nodding his head to the beat like he could see the dollars blowing out the car speakers. Biggs was sitting still and quiet, looking like if I said one wrong thing, he would stab my brain with my nose bone. I listed attentively to Kanye's message, which was much different from what had consumed hip-hop over the last two years. After the commercial success of 50 Cent, and the over-publicized beefs that hip-hop had become, Kanye West was taking the genre in a whole new direction. He was doing feel-good, positive, happy hip-hop, and I had a feeling it was going to be a success. Not to mention, no one could deny the power of his skillful orchestration of production.

"Yo, you didn't tell me that Kim from the *Source* looked good." The signature on the my two-way message said Kanye West, but I was confused, not knowing whether the message was sent to me mistakenly or was just a play by Kanye the day after we met. Rather than be naive, I responded as if it were the latter:

"Haha. You're funny."

"Oh, my bad. I didn't mean to send that to you," he replied, not that I believed him.

Laughing, I responded in a friendly but conversational way, "Things happen. Don't worry, I won't tell anyone."

Not expecting a response, I was surprised when my pager started to ring. I opened it and noticed an invitation to dinner. I felt there was no harm in accepting, so long as we both brought a friend to rule out any public perception of it being a date. Then I called Tanya, who was my first choice, since our being together made the dinner seem more like *Source* business.

"He's taking the mascot thing way too far with the teddy bear Polo sweater," Tanya said in my ear, by the doors at the entrance to Mr. Chow on Fifty-seventh Street in Manhattan, as Kanye checked his jacket at the front.

"Shhh. I don't want him to hear you. Behave yourself," I whispered back.

We sat down to dinner with Kanye and a friend and ordered everything that we could remember on the menu, from green shrimp to orange chicken. Tanya made funny faces to me every time Kanye talked about fashion, which he brought up more than his music. *Is he an artist or a sales rep from Louis Vuitton?* He had an idea for a fashion column, but I just knew that with his unique fashion sense, it wasn't going to fly with Ray. Eventually, he pitched the idea to *Complex* magazine and got it done. There were many missed opportunities like that, because I knew how to judge things based on how Ray would feel about them. I let the Kanye fashion thing slip out of my hands, but at least we got a lot more free dinners.

When it came to Kanye, I could always count on him for a free meal, a night out, or even a nice gift from Louis. When we shared our birthday party at a lounge in the West Village, I figured out a way to make money. Even though I was getting the venue for free based on the prestige and influence of my new title, I told Kanye that I had to pay $5,000 for the spot, and that he should pay half of that because his guest list was giving me and my assistant a headache. After much debate, Kanye wired the money into my account the next day, and after he gave in, I felt guilty. Then I found out that he celebrated his birthday with a party almost every day that week. *Must have cost him a fortune.* I think by sending the money to me he was just being nice and didn't have the energy to oppose my suggestion, knowing that I probably got the place for free. I took the money and went shopping for my own birthday gift.

I had figured out by the summer of 2003 that Eminem had put a major dent in the *Source*'s success. We had lost readers, credibility, and advertisers as a result of his beef with Benzino. And I was starting to see things differently. The failure of the *Source* would result in my own failure as the editor in chief. Somehow, I had allowed Benzino to affect my own career. Despite his controlling efforts in the past with former editors—male editors—this was one of the worst times in the magazine's history. We were running out of cover options and out of time.

The night I took a twenty minute flight to Philly with Dame and Biggs, I even thought about throwing Roc-A-Fella on the cover again. There was so much more to address, especially since that night after the Roc the Mic concert (which I had gone to see), Beanie Sigel surrendered to the authorities. "Something is about to go down but *don't* write this," Damon said sternly, before we packed back into his car. As police cars followed us over the Ben Franklin Bridge, I watched Beans pull over and, once he got out of his car, get handcuffed. Hip-hop was becoming such a soap opera and I had a front row seat. But my interest was fading ever since Eminem had become the focus.

While the *Source* was busy wrapped up in the drama that had put a dent in the magazine's business, the Southern rap scene had become a dominating force in hip-hop. The days of the East-West rivalry were long gone, but so were the days of the East and the West. While people up North were claiming that hip-hop was dead, others were starting to figure out that it had just relocated to the South. And just as I was struggling to find something new to breathe life into the pages of the magazine that had been held hostage by Benzino, the South was right there waiting.

For the *Source*, the Southern market had never been a driving force in sales. Therefore, it was difficult to pitch any Southern artist for a cover. But after the fifteenth-anniversary issue was closed, the presence of the South was undeniable. I started scheduling trips to different cities in the South just to get a taste of what the music scene was like. Of course, Atlanta was the most important city to frequent, but I even flew down to Houston, Kentucky, and Miami just to make sure we were on top of what was going on outside New York. I remember Koch even invited me down to New Orleans to hear Soulja Slim's music. That was an experience in itself. I was ridin' around New Orleans in a small car with him, his publicist, and his boy, and I was petrified because I kept feeling that I was going to get shot up. "Please take me back to the French Quarter where all the tourists and the white people are," I said, as he joked about it and called me "scary." He told me not to worry. A few weeks later, he was shot dead in the head while in front of his grandmother's house in New Orleans. I couldn't believe it, and kept thinking I escaped bullets myself.

No one could deny the dominance of Southern rap, not even Ray. Musically, I started to notice that he was making alliances with a lot of Southern artists, particularly, Lil Jon, who was getting recognized as the hottest producer in Atlanta. He was all of a sudden a friend of Ray's. Ray called and told me he wanted to put Lil Jon, Bone Crusher, and David Banner on the cover of the magazine. The New South, it was called. Every once in a while, he'd come up with a really good idea—even when some ulterior motive was behind his intentions. Everyone loved the idea, only no one wanted to scrap the already photographed OutKast cover that we'd been planning for months. Instead, we suggested that we do OutKast first and then the Southern hip-hop cover. Ray gave a quick "no." He told us we would split the cover and needed to find a way to tie the two together.

OutKast is a well-respected rap group, one of the few that have critical acclaim and hip-hop credibility. They're one of those rap groups that everyone loves. Well, almost everyone. Ray had issues with OutKast that seemed to precede me. OutKast's *Aquemini* album had received 5 Mics in the *Source* from the editorial staff, and whenever an artist had earned a rating rather than bargained for it, it seemed to be an issue when we wanted to give them the royal treatment in the magazine. Ray would call them "weirdos" and come up with reasons why we shouldn't put them on the cover again ("the last cover didn't even do that well").

Ray never factored in cost when he was making his rash decisions. When you split a cover between artists, it costs much more money to produce because you have to pay for two separate photo shoots. The OutKast/New South split meant that the cover story's page count had to be cut down. With the *Source*'s financial situation, it wasn't a smart business idea to keep splitting the covers, but Ray kept insisting so as to fulfill his favors. Throwing a cover away after a shoot meant that we'd be wasting a bunch of money. Still, when Ray wanted something for the *Source* cover, he got it.

The OutKast cover was a well-planned story that started months before their *Speakerboxxx/The Love Below* album was even finished. It was a double-CD release of two separate solo albums from each member of the group. The music was like night and day. Their label flew me to Atlanta to hear Big Boi play his half of the album, then to Los Angeles to hear André 3000 play his. Busy became my middle name. I hated having to make such a big change to the issue after I had spent so much time on it. As I was leaving the studio in L.A., André offered me a ride back to my hotel. I sat in the passenger seat of some old vintage car silently for the entire twenty minutes. André barely spoke. Not a "What did you think of the music?" or anything. I appreciated not having to come up with some politically concocted response so as to not offend said superstar. To me, no one can really absorb someone's album during one listen. I'd already been warned that I didn't nod my head to Busta's last album hard enough for him to ever want to play it for me again.

André 3000 was too much of an artist—not rapper—to doubt his own art and want to hear reinforcing compliments from a journalist like me. I make the distinction between artist and rapper because not all rappers are artists. Artists make creative contributions to their art form for its benefit. Rappers make words rhyme in a verse and crowd the art form with songs and album releases. If I were an artist who made rap music, I'd be pretty upset with all of the garbage that polluted hip-hop these days. It's my rationale as to why André 3000 stopped rappin' for a minute. Who wants to be in the company of such fodder?

Both magazine covers turned out to be amazing-looking pieces of art, but they were so different and too hard to tie together. The OutKast cover shoot had already been done by the time we came with the New South concept (Lil Jon, David Banner, and Bone Crusher burning the Confederate flag), so they looked like two different issues on one newsstand. The sales numbers of that issue were sluggish in comparison to other September issues, the biggest one of the year for advertisers, with the two different covers confusing the audience.

If you ask me, though, we were doing pretty well for a magazine that was blacklisted from the label that controlled most of the genre's artists. The drama between the *Source* and Interscope was dying down a little, and we were tapping into the South to help beef up our content.

I got another call to Dave's office one night to revisit the conversation that we had left off about the exposés that Ray had instructed us to do. Ray was addicted to them now, and it was probably because they had injected me with so much evil that I was doing a good job of executing Ray's stories the way he liked. But this time, given the latest victim he wanted to attack, I knew it would be a problem.

"We're putting 50 Cent on the cover," he said as soon as I walked through the door.

"We are?" I was confused, because we had been planning a Ludacris cover that month. I knew 50 wasn't going to grant us an interview, so I automatically figured this was going to be one of Ray's specialties. But because I was the one who really knew 50, I felt as though anything that was printed in the magazine would be assumed by him as coming from me. Knowing the information that 50 had on me, that he'd been to my house and knew personal things about me, I didn't want to keep the war between us going because he had a bigger platform than I did, and I couldn't risk losing.

"We are going to expose this clown for what he is. He ain't real. The whole 'I got shot nine times.' It's a publicity stunt. He's using that to sell records."

It's not that I didn't agree in part with Ray, knowing how 50 used people and things to get whatever he wanted or needed. But Ray's motive was all wrong.

"Don't you think that's gonna sacrifice our credibility, because of our problems with Eminem?" I asked, genuinely concerned that this move against 50 would destroy any last bit of credibility the magazine had.

"Credibility? Who gives a fuck about credibility? You journalists kill me with this 'credibility' shit. You think Interscope cares about credibility? You think *XXL* cares about credibility? Everyone is pushing their own shit. We the only fuckin' dodos over here concerned with credibility," Ray said.

Dave was sitting at his desk, once again shaking his head in agreement with everything that Ray was saying.

"We need to explain just how fucked-up what he is doing to rap music is." Ray was huffing and puffing as he talked. He was clearly aggravated with 50's success, criticizing 50's influence on hip-hop. 50 had sold over 8 million records with his debut album, *Get Rich or Die Trying*. He had appeared on the cover of our competitor *XXL,* and that issue was the first ever to outsell the *Source.* He had taken stance against the *Source* because of his loyalty to Eminem. He was on the other side of the fence, and I was forced to pick sides.

"Okay, what issue?" I asked, knowing that arguing against it would only prolong an argument that I could not win.

Robotic Dave perked up from his computer. "This issue! Find a writer. Find a good writer. Someone who could handle this story. This story is extremely important. They have to understand what our position is. Don't go getting one of these fucking Eminem followers."

"What about our Ludacris cover?" I asked.

Ray mocked me by repeating my question in an annoying-sounding voice. "*What about our Ludacris cover?* You could still have your little Ludacris cover, just push it to November. This is now, 50 Cent cover gotta be now. Do whatever you gotta do, but make it happen for this month. It can't wait. Tell all the little haters down at the end of the hall if they don't like it, then they gotta get the fuck out."

she's a bitch

Bitch is not a positive word. The term has been used so loosely in hip-hop, though, it's almost become acceptable for a woman to be referred to as such. Oddly enough, the word is most commonly used when referring to women in power, i.e., if you are deemed hard to deal with, then you are considered a bitch. On the other hand, if a man refers to another man as a bitch, then he is soft or being called out on his feminine ways. The term is derogatory because it's gender specific.

I heard the word *bitch* so many times at the *Source*, and I have to admit that it didn't affect me until I myself was called one. It was just something that went along with the territory.

"What a bitch!" Ray slammed the phone down in Jeremy's office after finishing up a conversation with his then label president, Sylvia Rhone. "I hate bitches."

Oddly enough, it was hard to tell that anything had been wrong while he was on the phone, as he had peppered his conversation with "Yes, ma'am" and "I understand." I wasn't sure what their conversation had consisted of, but by the look on Ray's face, I was sure it was one of those "stop this Eminem stuff" calls. Word throughout the office was that Ray was about to get dropped from Elektra Records because his album had come out and done poorly. Surprise, surprise. Plus, I'd also heard that his label was completely against his decision to battle Eminem. The problems with Elektra were troublesome to us because they were just making Ray more and more determined to destroy their crew. It was added fuel to the fire.

After a long, hard two weeks, we were sitting in the art department trying to finish up the 50 Cent story that had taken almost everything out of me. "Performance Thug" was the title, but the byline was a phony one. I had turned myself into Lawrence Beverly, a name that I had picked from two other bylines I skimmed when looking for a pseudonym. Even though I'd assigned the story out to a writer, I had to write it because Dave wasn't satisfied with the direction that the writer had originally taken. Unfortunately, I was the only one who knew exactly how Ray and Dave wanted it to read, and I was the only one who knew enough about 50 Cent.

I was rewriting the story at Paul's computer with Dave over my shoulder. Dave wanted to make sure the 50 Cent story shipped with his approval. Though he had made edits to stories before, this time was different. He picked apart each sentence to make it sound as vicious as it could. But at one point, Dave started to cross the line. Miguel Rivera, another art designer, was in the office helping Dave and me put the finishing touches on the story, which I had been staring at on the screen. Both Miguel and I were exhausted from working that whole night. I couldn't stop yawning, but Robo-Dave was wide-awake.

Dave looked up from a printout of the story that he was reading over. "Where's the chart I asked for?"

He had mentioned a chart before, but sometimes when things were just so ridiculous, we all acted as if we'd never heard of his request. "What chart?"

"The chart. The chart. The chart that lists 50, Eminem, and Jimmy Iovine. We need to show how they make decisions and how it ultimately all points back to Jimmy Iovine!"

Sometime in the past three months, the 50-Eminem rivalry had extended to someone who Dave and Ray believed was the true force behind bringing the *Source* down, Jimmy Iovine. The chairman and CEO of Interscope Records, Iovine was the head of Eminem's label, and the decision maker when it came to pulling all of the label's advertising. Though we all had developed relationships with Interscope employees over the years and could call in our favors to get other artists to be featured in the magazine, it was rumored that the label mandated that no employee deal with the *Source* or any of its employees. Dave wanted both Eminem and Jimmy Iovine to be somehow dissed in the 50 Cent story too, so he came up with an idea to include a chart that showed how Interscope and Jimmy Iovine were using gun violence as a marketing tool and comparing it to the death toll in the 'hood. The problem with Dave's holy cause was that while he was criticizing Jimmy Iovine for it, Dave and Ray were promoting the same things in Benzino's music. Ray just wasn't as successful at it as 50 or Em.

The issue was packed with anti-Interscope stories. There was a story on Big Chuck, a former affiliate of Dr. Dre's, who had defected from Dre's Aftermath Entertainment. There was a story on rappers who need security guards, and although security was becoming the norm in hip-hop, we of course used 50 Cent and Eminem as the examples. And then, the cover story on 50, which I had basically written under Dave's direction. The purpose of the story, as Dave put it, was to show

how 50 "was being used as a puppet by Jimmy Iovine" and the "forces" at Interscope. I took a stab at the cover line numerous times, and we eventually came up with "Inside the Shady World of Curtis Jackson," but ultimately Dave wanted it to somehow use "the destructive machine that's exploiting him," so we tacked that onto the end. Because the readers weren't up on the internal drama, I knew the cover wasn't a win for us. I knew that all journalists were a little biased, but this was extreme. Dave didn't want us to say one positive thing about 50, and it was making us look like sore losers.

Ray had put the battery in Dave's back, and he was not letting us go home. We read the story over and over, until Dave finally decided it was good to go. One thing he wanted to add at the last minute, though, almost caused us some more controversy.

"I want you to say how 50 Cent looks like a monkey," Dave said to Miguel and me while we were about to pack up the last story.

"What? We're not going to say that, Dave." I immediately ignored the request and continued to save the documents in Quark.

This time, even Miguel chimed in, with his Spanish accent. "I don't think you should say that."

"Why not? He looks like a fuckin' gorilla. Print that. Put that in there."

"Dave, you can not say that 50 Cent, a black man, looks like a monkey. *You* can't say that." I'm not sure if Dave knew exactly why I was emphasizing the word *you*. As a white man, Dave didn't always understand that certain things were unacceptable for him to do. Like using the N-word, or calling 50 Cent a monkey.

Dave's phone rang and he walked out of the office. And as soon as he was gone, Miguel commended me on stopping Dave from calling 50 a monkey. "Thank God you told him he couldn't say that."

"I know. I can't believe he would actually put that in. He doesn't get it. Sometimes he really thinks he's not white." Many times throughout my days at the *Source* Dave made references to white people as if he weren't one of them. He spoke about white people in the third person, calling them "they," instead of using the correct pronoun, which would have been *we*.

"Hopefully, he won't say anything else about it. Plus, we need to get out of here. It's after midnight now," Miguel said before burning the stories to a disc to have them shipped out. Then, before Dave could call and tell us to make any more changes, we packed up our things and locked up.

I took a deep breath and sighed. The *Source* had officially become the machine for Ray's twisted agenda, and it had all been done under my watch. Ray had never exercised this type of control over the former editor in chief, all of whom were men. He was destroying the magazine, though, and my career in the process.

A few weeks later, I was in my office when I got a call summoning me back down to Dave's office. When I got there, Ray was there with one of his people flipping through the magazine.

I walked into the room and felt an angry air, and Ray immediately confirmed my suspicion. "Yo, Kim. You didn't go hard enough on him." Ray was pacing back and forth, which meant he had yet another plan to enforce. "You gotta get at the dude."

I quickly defended my position and my story. "We're getting a lot of good feedback on the story. I think people are starting to come around." Feeling that the conversation was going to be lengthy, I sat down in a chair that someone had pulled up next to the couch.

"A lot of good feedback, Kim? What feeeeeedback are you getting?" Ray knew he could get under my skin by mimicking me and questioning my statements. It pissed me off.

"What?" My immediate reaction was to question his question. It was a way of stalling so that I could use the time to get my answer ready in my head. Whenever I answered him, I had to make sure that my answer was long enough to satisfy him, but not say so much that we'd end up in a whole other conversation. "People are getting tired of drinking the 50 Cent Kool-Aid, so they are saying we did a good job with the story."

"So why didn't you put your name on it, Kim?"

Ah, I thought, *the real reason for his anger.* "Because I used part of another story from the original writer." Lie. "And I didn't want them to think this was all coming from me." Mistake. Too much information.

"What does it matter if it's coming from you, Kim? You're the editor, so everything comes from you. If it's not coming from you, then who is it coming from?" Ray's voice was getting louder with each statement, and his pacing got faster and faster. It was almost as if he was itching to say something and wouldn't say it. At this point, my nerves were getting the best of me. I kept reassuring myself that, no matter what came out of this conversation, I was not admitting to any relationship with 50 Cent.

"All I'm sayin' is that I'm not trying to be the one getting lashed back out at . . . in people's records and all that. So I don't need them thinking this is all coming from me."

"Oh, it ain't coming from you?" Ray paused and stood in his place. I could see the lines on the top of his eyebrows frowning inward, so I knew we were really about to get into it. "Whose fuckin' side are you on?"

I started to feel the blood rush to my head. Some question. *Whose side was I on?* was like a trick question. Really, I was on my own side. But in public, I had always been on the side of the *Source. How could he dare question my loyalty at a time like this?* I raised up off the chair to leave the office, thinking if he had to ask me that question, then I didn't belong there. Then I built up my guts to yell back at him, "Don't question my loyalty. I don't like that."

Ray looked at me as if I were crazy. He immediately yelled back at me louder, "Sit the fuck down. What are you gonna do?"

For a second, there was silence while I weighed my options. If I just walked away from everything, that would be it. No more getting yelled at. No more having to join in the Eminem crusade. But that wasn't the right thing to do. I wasn't ready to give it all up. Not over this. Especially not over a 50 Cent story.

Ray stopped pacing, stood in place, then gave me that stare that said *I dare you.* Walk out and leave for good, or sit back down. Those were my options. "G'head. Leave. If you don't like it, you can leave."

I sat down. Ray walked back over to his seat and sighed. "Thank you. Now stop acting like such a bitch all the time."

I couldn't believe he just called me a bitch. I was dumbfounded. With that word, I knew that Ray had no respect for me, and in return, I had lost all respect for him.

CHAPTER NINETEEN

one for all

Knowing the only choice that I had if I was against carrying out Ray's demands was to quit, I decided to stop fighting. To me, it wasn't worth it. It was not as if I were getting recognized by other journalists or the hip-hop community for trying to stand up for what was right. Nor did any of them have another job waiting for me. I was over it. Whatever bit of integrity I had left was easily outweighed by my need to pay bills. I figured I might as well just continue with Ray's evil brand of journalism. I was good at it. I slept a lot easier at night knowing that my job was secure in exchange for a little evilness throughout the day. My new favorite word was *whatever*, and whenever an opportunity arose to trash Em, 50, or anyone affiliated, Ray and Dave no longer had to tell me to do so. If they had a wack record, I took it upon myself to make sure the readers knew.

I had my hands full with carrying out Ray's demands, managing the staff, and writing and editing stories. One of the other effects of the Eminem saga was that we had lost writers for the magazine as well. Some writers were disgusted with our position on Eminem and stopped working for us. Other writers hadn't been paid in months and also called it quits. We were getting busier and busier with the magazine, and the Source Awards were right around the corner. Everyone was heading down to Miami to enjoy some much needed time away from the office. It was also a good time to celebrate. Tracii McGregor was the point person for all things related to the awards. She had been handling the awards show longer than I'd been in my job.

It always amazed me how when the Source Awards came around, the role of the editor in chief diminished. At most magazines, the editor in chief was the face of the publication, but at the *Source,* that face always had to be Dave and Ray. I was relieved that a lot of the pressure and attention were lifted off me and directed toward Tracii. She always looked extra-stressed and bothered at awards time. Because I thought we had a good relationship, I figured I didn't have to worry about getting any access to events at the awards. But conveniently, I could never find her when I needed anything. It seemed a little odd that I wouldn't be able to get into certain parties affiliated with the awards show, or that my tickets to the show were for the general-population area, or that I usually had to upgrade my own hotel room. I later found out that someone was putting my name on the bottom of all the lists to get certain treatment. I used to have to call up my own industry connections and swap tickets with artists to sit up front. And I did that just because I knew that Dave and Ray didn't want me there. That year, I sat right next to Kool Herc, who had received the Hip-Hop Pioneer Award a few years back. Because he is considered the father of hip-hop, everyone thought I was in a special seat. But it was mere coincidence. Initially, I chalked it all up to Tracii just hating, but as with most things, Dave and Ray always knew what was going on.

In the months following the release of 50's album, nothing else in hip-hop was as big. A 50 video was on every music channel I turned to, and his face graced the cover of almost every magazine at every newsstand on my way to the office. It became increasingly difficult to cover hip-hop without being able to do anything with or on "Curtis." Unfortunately, Benzino's beef with Eminem crippled us since 50 had become part of our archenemy's camp. But the *Source* had to recognize his success at the awards that year. 50 Cent, of course, didn't show up, but he won three different awards. Although we hadn't spoken in months, he called me after the show to ask how he could get his trophies. I never mentioned it to Dave or Ray because I didn't want to confirm their suspicions that we had known each other that well. But keeping that information from them was getting increasingly difficult.

COME IN HERE. The message on my two-way from Tanya was in all caps. We were four days into closing the November issue, which featured Ludacris on the cover, and we were in the thick of it. The office was crowded because most of the editors were still hard at work reviewing their final pages. I took a break from reading the cover story to make my way down to Tanya's office to see what the emergency was this time.

When I got to the doorway, I saw Tanya sitting at her desk talking on her office phone, which she was holding between her neck and her shoulder. Her hands were busy writing in her notebook.

"Yes, Ray. Uh-huh. Yes," Tanya said into the phone, gesturing for me to come in and shut the door. "Why are you saying that?"

I could hear Ray yelling through her receiver.

"What is he saying?" I whispered to Tanya. If Ray had an issue with the coverage in the magazine, he'd usually call me to yell about it. But this time, he was calling Tanya so I knew that the problem was with me.

"You don't know that," she said. I leaned over her shoulder to try to hear what he was saying. Then Tanya wrote a number in her notebook that took up half of the page. She circled it.

"50?" I whispered again. "What is he saying?"

Tanya continued to write in her notebook. But he was yelling so fast, her writing could barely keep up with what he was saying. She scribbled, *I know she did. Tell her. She can't do that.*

After Tanya stopped writing, I just waited for her to end the phone call.

"Don't get upset," she said to me.

"Now I'm upset because you just told me to not get upset, so basically I know there's something to be upset about."

"Okay, he's crazy, all I can say is that he's crazy."

"Please, get to it. What did he say?"

"He said you need to go find yourself someone in the background. A producer or someone like that. Not these dudes."

"Find myself. Huh? What? In the background? What does that mean?"

"Yeah, he said he heard that you were dealing with . . . you know."

"50? I haven't spoken to him in months. And what does this have to do with my job? I'm here working and he's calling you about my personal life?"

Tanya raised her eyebrows. "Well, he knows something. Somebody told him something."

"Well, something is not enough." I turned my paranoia toward Tanya. "You didn't say anything, did you?"

"I didn't say yes or no. I didn't say anything. He was yelling the whole time."

Under normal circumstances, for someone to want to know my business that bad, I would just have spilled the beans. But Ray's constant prying made me keep it from him on principle. He didn't have a right to know anything. As my boss, he was making me extremely uncomfortable in the office, so uncomfortable that I wanted to leave. From that day on, things at the *Source* started changing for me. I knew they would try to push me out, but because I loved the job, I didn't want to leave.

Holy. Shit. Kayla's third birthday was less than two weeks away, and I was so wrapped up in my job at the *Source* that I had nothing planned. I was really good with the birthday parties the first two years, complete with characters, decorations, food that my friends and I would cook ourselves, and sending out invitations weeks in advance. But now I was screwed. My neighbor Tyrene usually stopped me to talk when she caught me outside on my way to the office. Tyrene lived in my condo community, and being from Baltimore, she always talked really . . . . really . . . . slow.

"Hi, Kim," she said in her Southern-belle voice. "I know Kayla's birthday is coming up. Are you planning anything?"

"Uh, yeah." *Think fast. You're not a bad mother. Okay, you are, but you won't let her know that.* "I was thinking of doing a party in like Chuck E. Cheese because Kayla loves it and I could just pay for it and let them take care of everything."

"Yeah, that's probably better for you. I know you're busy. Well, you gotta send out invitations soon because isn't it like less than two weeks away?"

"I was going to send out invitations today." Now I had to add invitations to my list of things to do.

"If you need any help, just let me know."

I always found it hard to accept other people's help because I didn't want to feel that I was indebted to them. But my pool of help had been really slim since my mother had moved to the Poconos and Tia relocated to Miami.

"Thanks, Tyrene. I think I'll manage, though." Sometimes for me, it's good to tell people things because it forces me to honor my own commitment. Now, in addition to everything I had to do at work and with Kayla, I now had to transform into Parties R Us.

"Tell your assistant to do it," Tia said, her high-pitched voice piercing my eardrum as it left the phone.

"I can't tell her to do that. That's not her job. Besides, she hates that stuff," I said about Hilary. She was the new Tory, who had moved over to the music department in my attempt to get organized. Michelle had sent Hilary my way from MTV ("She's an overachiever. But she's really good. She'll force you to get organized"). Hilary Crosley was an aspiring writer who'd interviewed for the position of my assistant. Tanya told me that the day Hilary started, she went into Tanya's office and asked, "How long do I have to be Kim's assistant before I can get promoted?"

Tia continued her lecture. "What do you think you have an assistant for? What do you think all these men out here do? These assistants get their lunch. They pick up their dry cleaning. They do all that. That. Is. Their. Job." Tia had a point. But I had a problem asking my assistant to carry out certain tasks. I did it and eventually got criticized for it. Usually, when a man in a position of power has an assistant, that assistant seems to have no problem doing what the boss asks. People thought I was a diva about having an assistant, but I was too intimidated by my own reputation for being "extra" to ask my assistant to do anything outside of getting coffee or lunch. I mean, it's not as if I asked her to paint my toenails, which was rumored that another female editor at a magazine had done to her assistant, sending her home crying one day.

"Ooh, hold on, Dave is calling me on the other line." I clicked over from my conversation with Tia to answer Dave's call. "Hello."

"Uhhhh. Uhhhh. Umm." I knew whatever Dave was about to say was coming from Ray, because Dave was stuttering trying to make sure he said it the right way.

I thought I would save him from the embarrassment. "Hey, Dave, what's up?"

"Uh. December. Uhhh. You can go ahead with the Lox and Westside Connection split . . . uh . . . for December." The staff had come up with the idea to split the cover in an attempt to win back the streets on both coasts. But Dave had waited until the last minute to give me the okay, probably because he couldn't get approval from Ray.

"Cool. Okay. I thought the Lox's album got pushed . . ."

Dave wasn't listening to what I was saying. Instead, he was answering the questions he was asking himself in his head. "Yeah. Fuckin' Interscope. They're trying to shut it down. They don't want the Lox to do it. So fuck 'em. Yeah."

At times when I talked to Dave, he was just a regular, smart, articulate, educated Jewish man who knew how to hold a conversation with upstanding business professionals. And then at times he made absolutely no sense at all. He was Dr. Jekyll and Mr. Hyde. When he was Dr. Jekyll, I understood him. But when he went the other way, he would say things over and over out loud, as if he was trying to convince himself of something Ray had made him say but he didn't understand. And he would throw a lot of *fuck*s in his sentences, using the word as a verb, an adjective, a pronoun, or whatever.

"Fuck Interscope. Fuck Jimmy. Fuck those fucks. I've been doing this shit for fuckin' years. When Eminem is done, the *Source* will still be fucking around." Dave showed glimpses of his whiteness when he pronounced the *g* in *fucking*.

I never really knew how to get out of those conversations and transition into normalcy. "So, I'm gonna call the art department and let them know we can start moving on this."

"Uh . . . yeah. Good. Cool." Dave hung up, and I looked at my cell phone to see if Tia had held on, which she hadn't. Back then, I didn't usually have the time to call back, so I figured I'd call her later.

Tia called me back that night and told me she had got engaged. It was bad enough that I forgot to plan my daughter's birthday, but now I was finding out that my best friend had been in a serious relationship for the past few months. I was crying both out of happiness for her and regret for myself.

"How did all this time pass by? Where was I?"

"You were working," she responded.

And I was. I was always working. In the last year, I had been at the *Source* around the clock. Nothing outside the magazine existed. I almost neglected my daughter's birthday and hadn't even called my real friends to see how they were doing. Everything was about the magazine or the music industry. When I went out, I was the editor of the *Source*. I remember a line from the film *The Devil Wears Prada*, where the art director tells Andy, "Let me know when your life falls apart, then we know it's time for a promotion." I realized there would never be a promotion for me, because there was nothing to get promoted to. I was at the top. My job was my life. And my personal life was nonexistent.

it★s a demo

Fahiym came into my office one afternoon and told me that he had spoken to some guy who claimed to have a tape of Eminem making "racist" comments. Both of us were doubtful that someone would have such a tape. Eminem's story had played out over and over in the pages of the magazine, then ultimately in his movie, *8 Mile*. I had seen the movie while in Puerto Rico at the Mixshow Power Summit the year before. I didn't truly watch it at the screening that day because my friends and I couldn't get past the part where Mekhi Phifer comes out sporting a wig of dreads. From that moment on, no one could focus on anything besides that ridiculous wig. Anyway, I did eventually get through the movie when I couldn't help but catch it on VH1, where it played continually after it was released on DVD. But the story in *8 Mile* was somewhat different from the story I discovered once we found this particular tape. To this day, I have never ever met Eminem. Our paths have never crossed, and if they did, I wouldn't really have much to say. What's done is done. I owed him no loyalty, so when the tape made its way to our office, I simply did my job.

It's probably not correct to say we found the tape, but rather that the tape found us. As I was passing by Fahiym's office on my way out to lunch, only a day after the phone call he had received, Fahiym pulled me in to hear it.

"Yo, KO," said Fahiym, as he stepped out of his office into the hallway to talk to me.

"Hey, Fahiym. Big meeting, huh?" I sarcastically said to him, noticing the three non-industry-looking individuals sitting in his office.

"Those are the guys that called in yesterday."

"Really?" I took a step back to get a good look at the three people sitting in his office. I noticed they were all white and looked extremely low-budget and as if they hadn't showered in days. One of them was vertically challenged. "Do they have the tape?"

"Yeah, I just heard it. You gotta come in here and hear this."

I glanced at my watch and realized that it was past 2 p.m. I was running behind for a lunch meeting. "Okay, but I'm already late for lunch, so we gotta hurry."

Fahiym and I walked back into his office, and I stood at the doorway so I could quickly exit when the song was over.

"This is our editor in chief, Kim Osorio," said Fahiym. "Kim, this is Warren [not his real name], and his two friends. They drove ten hours from Detroit last night to let us hear this tape."

I was anxious to just hear the music, but Warren felt the need to explain himself.

"Yeah, we've been sitting on this tape, and we know that you guys need to hear it." He went on, but I blocked most of it out because I was doubtful that the tape was going to be something we could use. Even if it was Eminem on the tape, how would we prove it was him?

"Well, let's hear the tape," I interrupted, so we could get to the heart of the matter. "Fahiym, can you play it?"

Fahiym picked up his remote control and began to rewind the cassette tape that was playing in his stereo. He pressed play and we listened attentively as Eminem speed-rapped a few verses. At the time, I wasn't sure that it was Eminem, but the vocals, which definitely sounded both like a white boy and an amateur, closely resembled those of a pre-platinum Eminem.

As I was listening, Warren shouted out, "There, right there. Did you hear it?"

I missed it, so I asked them to rewind it again. Once they did, Eminem was using the N-word.

"What did he say?" I asked. "I didn't hear it."

"He said the N-word," Warren replied.

"But how did he say it?"

"It doesn't matter how he said it. He shouldn't be saying it." Then Warren turned toward Fahiym and pointed to the tape deck. "Play her the other one. The one about the black girls."

Fahiym searched the tape for a couple of minutes. It was a full cassette tape of different Eminem verses, most of them freestyles.

"Here it is," said Fahiym as he pressed the play button.

". . . 'cause black girls are bitches."

"Whoa. Rewind that," I said.

Fahiym played the cut again so I could hear what Eminem was saying, and he went on for an entire verse, talking specifically about black girls, calling them "bitches."

"Fahiym, let me talk to you for a second in my office," I said.

Fahiym and I quickly made it back down to my office, and even though I was now twenty minutes late for my meeting, I knew this was a bigger priority.

"Fahiym, do you really believe that's Eminem on the tape?" I asked as I sat down at my desk.

"Yeah, I do."

"So do I. "It kinda sounds like him. But even if it is, how do we prove it?"

"I don't know how we're going to do that, but if this is truly him, then our readers need to know. Despite all the controversy that's surrounded us with this whole Benzino thing, we still have a responsibility to our readers. If none of that would have happened, and we stumbled on this, it would be a no-brainer, but now we're sitting here second-guessing ourselves because of that."

"You're right." I knew that if we didn't report this, someone else would. "I have to tell Dave. Ugk."

Up until we had heard the tape, the rule in the office was to limit all conversation with Ray or Dave to just necessary answers. Any extraneous words could wind up as part of a conversation that you never meant to have. And in your answers, it was wise to steer clear of such words as *white*, *beef*, or *shady*, words that would conjure up any thoughts of Eminem in Ray's head. But I knew if someone else reported the tape, and it came back that we had had an opportunity to do so first, then my job would be a wrap. I couldn't hold something this big from Dave and Ray.

Both Fahiym and I shook our heads over what we knew was about to happen.

"I have to tell him," I said again, waiting for Fahiym to give me his approval.

"Go ahead."

I started to type out a message to Dave on my two-way, backspacing every three letters to make sure the message was right.

"Fahiym just found . . ." Backspace. "Fahiym ju . . ." Backspace. "Fahiym got a tape . . ." Erase. "There's a tape of Eminem using the N-word and calling black girls bitches, and the guys who have it are here in Fahiym's office."

Within seconds, Dave paged me back and asked me to bring the guys down to his office, which I did. I introduced them to Dave, then he told them to wait a few minutes because he had just phoned Ray and was waiting for him to call back.

Dave asked the three of them if they wanted anything to eat and was scurrying around the office waiting for the moment he would tell Ray. Then the phone rang and it was Ray.

"I knew it. I knew it, yo. I knew this dude was a racist." I could hear the excitement in Ray's voice through the speakerphone. He was talking so much, no one could get a word in. "All this time. Things like this. I can sense it. I got a sick sense. I knew it."

I was waiting in Dave's office, listening to Ray, waiting for his directions as if he were Charlie and Dave and I were two of his angels.

"Where's Kim?" Ray asked.

"I'm right here, Ray."

"Get ready. This is a big one. You're gonna have to get everybody on the same page. We gotta expose this dude. He needs to go down. He's going down with this one. He's finished. We're making this the cover."

Once I heard the excitement in Ray's voice, I started to regret ever sending that two-way message. Did I believe it was Eminem on the tape? Yes. Did I think we needed to go forward with the exposé of all exposés? No. I knew the effect that the last Eminem exposé had had on the magazine, and I quickly remembered what my life was like whenever Ray had gotten pumped up about Eminem, but I knew this one was the killer. I was never getting to my lunch or going home.

Ray's voice was amped. He was starting to shout out orders like a drill sergeant. "Dave, we need a press conference. We need to get this out there. "Kim, you listening? I need you to do this story. It's gotta come from you."

This was going to seal my fate as a permanent enemy of Eminem's. But the funny thing is, I can't say I cared. I thought back to his mention of me on his record and figured that he had it coming. This time, there weren't going to be any regrets on my part, especially because I didn't know him personally.

"I'll do it. Ha ha. He should have never mentioned my name," I said.

For months, I had quietly protested the decisions that Ray had made in the magazine. His self-serving agenda had worn me thin, and it was eating away at the magazine's credibility. But my distaste for what he was doing had blinded me to some of my own mistakes. I'd been guilty of some of what had driven Ray to his madness too. The way I so easily gave in to the hatchet job we'd done on 50's image, the vindictiveness that had led me to dig into Steve Stoute. I was trained in investigative journalism, but only the kind of investigation that is motivated by malice. After two years of following orders and doing things out of fear for my job security, I had become immune to these type of stories. And I was damn good at them. And while Ray and Dave were the ones coming up with the hare brained schemes to try to destroy people's careers, I was the one carrying them out, like an assassin. I was now guilty of the same things I had criticized them for. And I had become what I had despised most. One of them.

CHAPTER TWENTY-ONE

eye for an eye

Being evil was becoming fun. Not fun in an evil way, but fun in a laughable way. Especially when it was directed at Eminem. Remember, he was the only artist to ever truly shout me out on a record, and although I had been thanked in the album credits of Kanye West, Nas, and Foxy Brown, there's no fame like that you receive when an artist as big as Eminem decides you are important enough to call "ho" in one of his verses. I especially appreciated it when my uncle in Puerto Rico mentioned that he had heard it. *Thanks, Marshall. That was a great look.*

Vindictive is probably a better word to use than *evil*. Evil is inherent in one's soul, but *vindictive* is an adjective that you can make an excuse for. Almost like when you get in trouble in school for talking in the classroom, and you tell the teacher that the boy who pulled your hair daily was talking to you first. Therefore, if you hadn't been provoked, you wouldn't have done it at all. That's how I felt about the Eminem situation. He started it. It's not my fault his tape of racially insensitive comments made its way to our office. Oh, well.

While I was planning the story lineup for the anti-Eminem issue, Dave was carrying out Ray's orders and planning a press conference. Dave had decided to put Warren and his crew up in a hotel while Dave made his plans to get possession of the tape. Warren had originally asked for $50,000 in exchange for the tape, although I'm not sure how much the *Source* ended up paying for it. I know for sure, though, that there was a dollar amount because I remember seeing the paperwork. Ray had given Dave the okay to cough up the money, but Dave did some negotiating. Of course, Dave being Dave . . . he decided to have contracts drawn up for the legal transfer of the tape. He would pay the money only if they transferred ownership to the *Source*. It was probably the quickest payday that kid ever had. But even when we obtained the tapes, there was no tangible proof that it was actually Eminem, and that's where I came in.

Ray directed me to go to Detroit, along with Antoine Clarke, to gather information about Eminem and try to get some of his former affiliates to spill the beans about the rapper's true persona. Being that I was not about to travel with Antoine, I booked a flight for the next Saturday morning, while Antoine decided he would drive through Friday night. To me, the only reason someone would drive ten hours instead of flying was either because he was scared to fly or he wasn't allowed to leave the state, so I had my suspicions. Nevertheless, I agreed to work with Antoine on the story, knowing that anything else would make me look as if I couldn't get over our other issues.

Antoine said he'd already been in contact with Champtown, a guy who claimed to have been there in the earlier days of Eminem's career. So though we agreed to collaborate on the story (which ultimately meant I would be doing the writing), he had a leg up because his first interview was with the one person who would provide a bulk of the history. I found out that Eminem's former bodyguard Big Naz had already tried to blast Eminem in a book for using the N-word, so I immediately set out to find him. But it ended up taking a minute to track him down, so I started calling my own connections to see who could help me.

Kino, who managed Royce da 5'9", had told me to reach out to them whenever I needed anything in the D, so I called him when I got to Detroit and asked for a car to drive me around to anywhere I needed to go. Antoine kept stressing me about whether I had scheduled Royce for an interview, but Kino kept saying that if I was doing a story on Eminem, then I couldn't do an interview with Royce. Because Royce and Eminem had fallen out, Antoine and I figured we could get Royce to shed some light on Eminem's past. Royce was actually signed to a solo deal on Columbia with Eminem serving as his executive producer. He had also worked as a ghostwriter for Dr. Dre's second *Chronic* album. The two MCs fell out not too long after that. My intention was to get to Royce to get some of the story about the early Eminem recordings. If this tape was really true, then I thought that Royce would have to know something about it. But even after I convinced Kino to let me talk to Royce for a few minutes, I still couldn't find what I was looking for. Royce said he'd never heard Eminem use the N-word or degrade black women, and it turned out that the tape was recorded before they met.

By this time, I was so preoccupied with Eminem that I just ignored that I couldn't stand working with Antoine. Plus, there wasn't much I could do about Antoine, who was staying at the *Source* whether I liked it or not. Between the two of us, we were running *Source* enterprises out of the Atheneum Suites hotel. The anti-Eminem division. We had a number of people come to our hotel so that we could conduct interviews with them and start gathering information. While Antoine was filming his interview with Champtown, who was proving to be the best source we had, I decided that I would scout locations with a photographer. Since we couldn't photograph Eminem, I came up with the idea to show pictures of different locations to help tell the story. I conducted interviews, then made my way around all the Miles, 7 Mile, 8 Mile, 9 Mile, but I couldn't really find anything but Coney Island and White Castle restaurants.

Later that night, Kino convinced me to hit a club in Detroit, and I went under the guise that I might find some Eminem haters there to divulge information. The party turned out to be a dud, in the sense that I didn't know anyone and no one knew me, so I sat on a couch all night and joked about some guy wearing an 8-ball jacket trying to get into VIP. Kino was proving to be helpful, though, in that he was paying for everything and trying to woo me. At first, I wasn't interested. For one, he was smart, regular smart, and I was used to dealing with guys who were street-smart. Street-smart is just another way of saying someone is an overall dumb ass, but could think on his toes when it came time to hide the stash. Kino didn't look like a street dude, and my dating past had consisted of everything from petty thugs to aspiring rappers to Grammy winners, but they all had the similar young, hat-down-low, sagging-pants look. Kino dressed like a regular guy and often wore suits. He spoke in complete sentences and could use a three-syllable word in the proper context before it made its way into a rap song by Jay-Z (note: how many people in the hip-hop community cared about a *double entendre* before Jay said it?). Kino just wasn't my type.

When it came to men, I had actually been on strike for two months. I didn't have the time. In between work and home, I found some time to entertain a brief relationship with an extramasculine, gun-toting man that I'd met at a photo shoot. He was extremely nice and attentive to me, but when I asked if he was sleeping with anybody else, he said, "I'm not going to say that I'm not." A double negative equals yes. It was probably my pride more than anything else, but I decided that

I couldn't waste any more time in relationships that weren't going anywhere. So I politely told him that our relationship needed to end—or maybe I never really told him but just stopped answering calls. After him, I decided that it was time to focus on me. So I invested in a few more AA batteries to keep me satisfied until the right person came along.

I had no idea if Kino was going to turn into the right person, and especially not after he joked to me about his infidelities in his last relationship. Before we headed out to the club that night, I requested that we stop for dinner at Mongolian Barbecue. I remembered how good the food was because Jaydee took me there when I came to Detroit for the first time to interview Slum Village. At dinner, Kino and his two friends gave me a descriptive version of how men cheat on their girls. It was like a super-advance screening of Chris Rock's film *I Think I Love My Wife*. All the things you know about men that they never admit.

"Men are liars. I guess I could hang it up now, because I can't deal with a cheating man. I caught my daughter's father in a relationship more than once. And it took me a while to get over it."

"Things happen. I broke up with my last girlfriend because of a similar situation, I just didn't think we would stay broken up," said Kino.

"Oh, so that must be another man secret. Breakups aren't really real."

"Oh, yeah. Men don't really break up. We just take breaks."

"You're funny."

Kino's two friends joined in with their own stories and agreed with the consensus that most men have cheated. I laughed and joked about things that closely resembled my own devastating heartache in the past. After Kino got a couple extra shots of his gin and tonic at the club, he forgot about his limits and started to try to convince me that we would make a good couple. I laughed at him and left the party early because I was tired and ready to leave.

The next morning I had an afternoon flight out, so I had another interview meet me in the lobby of the hotel, but that proved unsuccessful also. For the most part, all the interviewees were telling me that they felt Eminem wasn't helping them get out of the hood. But as disloyal as Eminem was proving to be, nothing was supporting the idea that he was racist. The only person whose word that we had to go on was Champtown. He was giving Antoine some really good history on Eminem for the story, but one person's word wasn't enough.

Em's former bodyguard Big Naz hadn't called back by the a.m., and with Kayla home waiting for me, I couldn't stay in Detroit any longer. Because I knew that Antoine's interviews would only be good for additional reporting, my competitive spirit was kicking in. I couldn't let Antoine come away from the Detroit trip with more information than me. He had done two interviews, and I had done five for this story, but he was coming back with someone who was authenticating this tape. Champ identified Eminem as the rapper and said that he had heard Eminem refer to blacks as "spear chuckers," "porch monkeys," and "moon crickets." All I had was a bunch of rappers from Detroit who were pissed with Eminem for their own reasons. Champ managed Eminem's original four-man group, a group of white boys called Bassmint Productions. And Champ claimed to have introduced Eminem to the black hip-hop community.

Champtown led Antoine to Chaos Kid, one the guys in the original group. Chaos Kid provided us with some old pictures of Eminem and some more background information. The foul thing was, when Antoine approached Chaos Kid, he told him he was doing a documentary for HBO, so as I was writing, I had to set up my own phone interview with Chaos Kid so that he knew he was being interviewed for the *Source*. Though he later said his quotes were taken out of context, there was nothing in the story that he didn't say. Someone told me Eminem contacted him and that's why he changed his tune, but I don't know whether that's true. The important thing about Chaos Kid was that he validated the tapes, although he seemed nervous when asked about them.

According to Chaos Kid, Eminem's rant about black people came out of something called the "Racist Rap Hour," which was a satirical racist rap that Em would record as a joke. Chaos Kid said he never participated in it because he didn't want to be a part of something like that. Though we only had one of the tapes, there were supposed to be others. The public never knew which tape we had, but when Champtown was quoted in the magazine saying that he'd heard the tape on which Em was calling black people "porch monkeys" and "spear chuckers," everyone assumed that the *Source* had those tapes too. We didn't. We never even heard those directly, we just heard about them.

When I got back to New York, I continued my research on the Eminem story, and I finally heard back from his former bodyguard Big Naz. Big Naz overnighted a copy of his book to me two days after I got back from Detroit. I read the short book in one night. Titled *Shady Bizness*, it told the story of Eminem from his former bodyguard's perspective. At the end of the book, Naz is fired and the two get into a heated argument, which triggers Eminem's calling him "nigger." With the *er*, not the *a*. At least that's how it was written. I got in touch with Big Naz the next day and told him that I needed to meet with him. I had to interview him to find out whether Eminem had really used the term in a derogatory way or if it was just a slip of the tongue of someone trying to be down.

I always thought Eminem could rap, but I was never really interested in his story. But the more I researched it, the better it got. *Who is he really?* I thought. *Is there a possibility that he actually is a racist? Oh, no, would this make Ray right at something?* I was so confused that I had to find out the truth. I was about to put my name on this story, and this time I wasn't about to say anything just because Ray wanted me to say it.

By the end of the week, others had caught wind that I was in town working on this story. I got in contact with a guy named Strike, who played the rival in *8 Mile*, and I'd heard that he was willing to talk too. I scheduled another trip to Detroit for the following weekend to find the rest of my sources and finish up my interviews.

CHAPTER TWENTY-TWO

victory

Detroit is depressing. I grew up in the Bronx, with the first seven years of my life spent living on Grand Concourse and 165th Street. But the Detroit that I saw when I did the Eminem story made my Yankee Stadium neighborhood look like Beverly Hills. When I arrived there the following weekend, it didn't take long for me to start acting paranoid. I was all alone in a city where I didn't really know anyone, and I was about to check in at the hotel where I'd conducted my interviews the weekend before. Strangely, I found myself looking over my shoulder every five minutes on the way there. I checked into the hotel under an alias and called Kino to ask if he would provide the same tinted-out, black Suburban for yet another weekend. The industry had started buzzing that we were snooping around Detroit looking for information about Eminem, and I didn't want to get caught by Eminem while on 8

Mile snooping around. Up until that point, I'd flaunted my bravery by telling people I was investigating the true history of Marshall Mathers. But somewhere along the line, I realized that even though I was doing the dirty work of the *Source,* I wasn't the one walking around with a bodyguard.

After my interviews were done, I called Kino to thank him for having his people play chauffeur while I was in town, and he invited me to hang out and go to dinner with him and his crew. At dinner, he was still trying to convince me that he could make me his girl if he really wanted. "All women want is a little attention, so that's all I would need to do to make you like me," he said. After a few drinks, I started to think his lame game was kinda cute. When I got back to New York, we were calling each other back and forth. I was still in denial and using the story as an excuse to keep in touch.

I was fully entrenched in Eminem's world, but the director of photography, quickly reminded me that we had a cover shoot scheduled with Nelly in Las Vegas for the 2004 January issue. It was normal for us to be working on something so high priority, then to be fronting to the rest of the world as if we were actually working on something else. Nelly had agreed to be on the cover, but unbeknownst to me, that was conditioned on Murphy Lee's being on the cover with him. This was the type of stuff that I hated to find out after the fact.

With the magazine suffering from all the negative attention associated with Benzino, I was open to the idea. Putting Murphy Lee on the cover with Nelly had been talked about in passing, but no one was really for or against it. The plan was that we would go out to Las Vegas and shoot some still shots of Nelly with Murphy Lee and of Nelly alone. We were never told that the cover had to feature both artists, but rather that we should get as many options as possible.

The shoot was scheduled around an awards show that was being taped in Las Vegas. I remember getting there a day early just so I could watch Beyoncé hang from a rope and then dance onstage in the middle of what looked like the California wildfires. There is no limit to the lengths she will go to outdo everyone else. Anyway, we scheduled the shoot for the day after the awards, and the idea was to photograph Nelly in the desert, with Murphy Lee and other members of the St. Lunatics. It didn't have anything to do with anything, but the photo department thought the desert was nice scenery for a background. For the cover, Paul mocked up a picture of Nelly by himself. Katie made her case why the shots of Nelly and Murphy Lee together didn't make a good cover. I brought the cover and showed it to Dave, who signed off on it. He had no problems with leaving Murphy Lee off. Then of course, when Nelly's people got pissed, Dave blamed it on me.

Our fashion editor Misa also came out to Vegas to style Nelly. It was one of the few cover shoots where I actually had someone from my own staff that I could talk to. Normally, the photo department kept their distance at cover shoots, and it forced me to make friends with the artists and their crews. Surprisingly, given how successful he was, Nelly was one of the more humble artists. For a rapper who had sold as many records as Nelly, he was not as boisterous and overconfident as the rest of them. Unfortunately for him during that trip, his jewelry was stolen from his hotel room, but I was impressed that he still showed up to our photo shoot and did what he had to do. That's why I hated taking the blame when the cover turned out to be something different from what he'd expected. Everyone at the *Source* and at his label made it seem as if I deliberately screwed them, and then this was turned around and used against me.

Dave called me in Vegas and told me not to mention that we were holding the Nelly cover so that we could run the exposé on Eminem. At dinner, Nelly's publicist said that she had heard we were doing an Eminem cover instead. When she asked me specifically about it, I had to play it off as if we weren't going to push the Nelly cover. It turned out that we did run Nelly first, but not because that was the plan. The Eminem cover was like a stop-and-go, on-and-off-again story, for a few reasons. One reason was that Ray and Dave were trying to leverage some sort of deal with Interscope Records for a Benzino album.

Another on-and-off-again thing that I had to deal with was the press conference. And it was on again. When the day in November of 2003 finally came, Ray summoned me back into the holding cell that was temporarily known as Dave's office to let me know what my role would be.

"Are you coming to the press conference tomorrow?" he asked me, in a way that was telling more than asking. Let's see, if he was going, and Dave was going, and so was everybody else that was supporting them, then my answer would probably be . . .

"Of course I am. I'll be there." I had always planned on going to the press conference, particularly because all my friends in the press would be there. Journalists in the industry have to attend press conferences to hear first whatever news is being announced, and as the editor in chief I couldn't just be absent. Plus, press conferences are mingling events for journalists. They go so that they can be seen among their peers. It's a way for us to prove our relevance or importance in the industry. It's like "Look at me, I am here reporting, therefore I still have a job."

The press conference would be the first public announcement that we would make about the Eminem tapes. We usually held press conferences to announce some big initiative by the *Source*. The last couple of press conferences we had were to announce the all-text "Hip-Hop Under Attack" cover and the nominations for the Source Awards, but this one was going to be interesting. No matter how hard we tried to disguise our intentions to bash the MC at other *Source* functions, this was a blatant "Eminem, we got you" event.

"So what are you going to say?" Ray asked.

"You want me to speak?" I asked, buying time.

"Yeah, you have to say something. Dave's gonna talk, I'm gonna talk, and you, you should talk too. You should say how this makes you feel. As a woman."

Huh! As if Ray really cared about how I felt "as a woman." More and more of our conversations were about men and women. I definitely felt that Eminem was disrespecting women in this early recording, but I didn't know how to feel. We didn't have all the facts yet. We didn't know when the song was recorded, and we still didn't know if it was really him. But Ray was so passionate about the upcoming press conference that I wasn't signing up to be the one dissenting.

"Um. Okay, I'll talk. I don't know what I'm gonna say, but—"

"What do you mean, you don't know what you're going to say? Say how fucked-up this is. You know what to say." Ray had a weird way of making you do something you didn't want to do. The Eminem press conference was not a make-or-break thing to me. It wasn't something worth going against Ray for. I could remain publicly silent on the issue, but then I would have to deal with the *Source* questioning my loyalty. I'd heard the tapes. I was writing the story. I could talk at the press conference too. I wanted to avoid a four-hour conversation with Ray where he questioned my intentions until I ultimately gave in.

It took three SUVs to transport Ray and Dave to the venue in midtown where the press conference was being held. I managed to get downstairs early enough to reserve myself a seat in one of them. While I waited for everyone else to pile into the cars, I started to craft my ever so important speech on the back of a press release that I had grabbed on my way out of the office. "Excuse me, can you pull up the windows? It's freezing," I said to the driver, who was jittering his fingers waiting for the rest of us to make it downstairs. The car had been waiting for over an hour.

I jotted my thoughts in sloppy script so that anyone sitting next to me wouldn't be able to make out what I was about to say. "These are racist remarks by someone who has the ability to influence millions of minds," I wrote. It seemed powerful enough to get quoted, but short enough to memorize just in case I lost the paper on the way inside.

One behind the other, we walked into a room packed with cameras, tape recorders, notepads, and writers. I was behind Ray. Because I had come with Ray and Dave, I forfeited my mingling time with any friends in the room. I went from reporting the news to being the news in the blink of an eye. We all stood on the stage, and Ray motioned to someone with the tape deck. Then a tape of a young Eminem started to play from the speakers.

Ray was standing on my right side, and Dave was waiting by the podium for the song to finish. The plan was to play the song for the press to hear. Afterward, Dave would speak first, then I would speak, then Ray would give his "closing argument." No time would be dedicated to a question-and-answer period.

As Eminem's young voice was playing through the room's speakers, Dave started bobbing his head.

"Blacks and whites, they sometimes mix / but black girls only want your money 'cause they dumb chicks."

Ray walked in front of me and leaned toward Dave. "You like this music?" Ray said under his breath. The wrinkles in his forehead doubled. Dave looked up and shook his head from left to right to indicate no.

"Then why are you bobbin' your head?" Ray's voice got louder, but still quiet enough not to be heard by the audience. For a brief second, the two of them locked eyes, then Dave looked as if his father had just told him to sit still at a restaurant. Ray stared at Dave, then let out an intimidating laugh. Dave immediately stopped moving his head in any direction.

The Eminem song continued to play.

"All the girls I like to bone have big butts / No, they don't 'cause I don't like that n—ger shit."

I looked out into the seats in front of me, and the press were attentively listening. They seemed confused, though. None were talking among themselves, but everyone was scribbling down lyrics in notebooks. After the song finished, Dave stepped to the podium and gave his lengthy speech about the damage that Eminem had done to the hip-hop community. When he was done, he stepped down, and I knew it was my turn to talk. I noticed all the familiar faces looking at me, then I lowered the microphone so I could talk into it. I couldn't bear to look anyone in the face, so I stared directly into the camera that was staring back at me. Then I forgot my lines. I took a deep breath, looked down, and started reading off the paper that I had written my mini-speech on. As the editor in chief, I had done much public speaking, but speaking with Ray standing over my shoulder was scary. I didn't want to go back to the office and get chewed out for not being hard enough on Eminem. Michelle sent me a text message after I spoke saying that I looked as if someone had held a gun to my head.

After I spoke, Ray approached the podium and gave his quick two cents: "Don't make this right now a double standard. We gotta treat this the same way you treat Mike Tyson. Like you treat Kobe Bryant. Like you treat R. Kelly. Like you treat O. J. Simpson."

I remember when Ray finished speaking, he quickly walked away as if he were the president of the United States and the press were about to ask questions about the war in Iraq. The Boston crew that had come with him followed him out like ants, and so did I.

Everyone squished back into the trucks with their leather jackets, and Dave was the last person to jump in. He was overly excited and was smacking his hands together to show his joy. I hated how every time Dave thought he won something, he started acting like a little kid, rubbing his hands together as if he had just masterminded some Pinky-and-the-Brain-type scheme.

After all the detours and stops at the store, we finally got back to the office just in time for dinner. It was as if our workday consisted of two shifts, of which I had to work both. I sat in Dave's office with a bunch of Ray's people while Dave sat at his computer trying to look at all the internet sites to see if they'd posted anything about the press conference.

"He just released a statement," Dave said while reading his computer. We all anxiously waited to hear what Eminem had said. "MTV.com has a statement from him." Dave read the statement from Eminem out loud:

Ray Benzino, Dave Mays, and the Source have had a vendetta against me, Shady Records and our artists for a long time. The tape they played today was something I made out of anger, stupidity, and frustration when I was a teenager. I'd just broken up with my girlfriend, who was African-American, and I reacted like the angry, stupid kid I was. I hope people will take it for the foolishness that it was, not for what somebody is trying to make it into today.

"Those fucks," Ray exclaimed loudly. "He runs to MTV and they're supporting him. I'm telling you D, MTV and Jimmy, they got something going on with each other. They're tied into each other."

I was astonished that Eminem had released a statement so quickly, without gathering the facts of what we had first. "He just said it was him?" I asked.

"Of course he did. What's he gonna say? He has to admit it, Kim." Ray was happier than ever that he had won this little battle, not that he would ever win the war. So he stood up in the room and started pacing back and forth, directing Dave to find more stuff on the internet.

His excuse about the black girl-record was that he had been dating a black girl and she'd broken up with him right before he recorded it. It was comparable to when white people get accused of being racist and mention that they have a friend who is black. I was conflicted now. I was glad that he admitted it, but I knew this would only further feed into Ray's ego and his justification for doing the story.

Ray spent a lot of time surfing the Web, and I found it ironic that he constantly criticized journalists for "sitting behind the computer all day." I walked in on him with his eyes glued to the computer many times, reading pages and pages of comments that users had posted about him.

That was one of the few days that the *Source* chalked up a victory on the board. There was even free food to celebrate. Good food. After a while, I dismissed myself and made my way home. It was late. I was tired. And Kayla was at home waiting.

ain't no half-steppin'

My desk was messier than it had ever been, with Eminem memorabilia spread across it. I had his albums, though I hated listening to any of them all the way through except for the *Marshall Mathers LP.* I had a little rainbow of sticky papers, each with the name and number of some Detroit resident scribbled on it. These people represented my sources, and I had more than ever. I had empty, flipped-over, horizontal Starbucks cups covering mountains of research. And there were little audiotapes of recorded interviews, a VHS of Chaos Kid talking to (ahem) HBO, and scattered magazine pages that I needed to read before the story went to print.

Despite all the time I spent in the office with my coworkers and staff, most of the memories I have from 215 Park Avenue South are of me in the office alone. I'm not trying to make it seem that I was the only one who worked long hours. That isn't true. So many of the employees put in ridiculous hours. It was standard practice to order dinner together, and sometimes we weren't eating until 10 p.m. But in truth, I couldn't work unless everyone was gone, because if I was in the office, then someone always had a problem, and I had to deal with that during daytime hours. So I used the late hours to get the work done.

Some days I would just up and leave the office in the middle of the afternoon, to pick up Kayla from school at three just so I could see her before she went to bed. I wouldn't come back to the office until 7 p.m., and I would stay there until after three in the morning. On the other side of the office, Tracii would be working late as well, but we never really knew if the other was there. One night, I didn't check before I left and ended up locking her in. She told me she had to let herself out by sticking her hand through the gate and using her key to unlock it. Sometimes I even came in at the crack of dawn to finish up last-minute things before anyone else got in. One morning I got there before 7 a.m. and caught Tracii on her way home. Thinking back, I'd say I was pretty pathetic for devoting so much of myself to the *Source*. But Tracii was worse than me.

Right before we were about to send the Eminem issue to print, Dave got news that Eminem was taking legal action and trying to prevent the magazine from including the CD in the issue. The rationale for a lawsuit would be, if the *Source* included a CD of Eminem's recordings in the magazine, and the magazine was being sold (and this time it was to be sold for $1 more), then the *Source* would be selling Eminem CDs and infringing his copyright.

"We gotta hold the Eminem story," Ray said one night. "Let's go with Nelly and we'll come back with Eminem for February, when we straighten all this legal shit out."

Dave was seated in a chair getting his hair cut. "You have the Nelly story ready, right?"

I'm thinking, *Uh, no, because I've been working on Eminem.* "We've already told everybody that we're doing Eminem. Don't you think that people are expecting us to release this now?" I was trying to hide my frustration. The Eminem issue was near done, complete with exposés and quotes from other artists, and now we were going to hold it. It would be old news in another month. My work had to begin all over again. Plus, I never understood why we held a press conference to tell the world we had the tape. It should have come as we were about to release the magazine, but of course Ray didn't really care about what made sense for the business. It was all about him getting credit for something. He couldn't wait to let everyone know he had something on Eminem. It seems that the magazine could really have made history with sales numbers through the roof if no one knew about the tapes, and then, boom, here it is. *Racist Eminem tapes! Read what he said in early recordings.* No; instead, we told everybody about it first, then had to figure out a way to write about what we had already told everyone in a way that would make people want to read it. *Extra, extra, read all about the same Eminem tapes we already told you about at our press conference!* It was even more of a problem because we didn't have an interview inside. Dumb move.

I dusted off the Nelly story.

A month later, I was in the same spot at my desk, pushing the space bar on my computer trying to stop it from going into screen-saver mode. Finishing up the Eminem story had taken longer than I thought. It went through rounds and rounds of editing by Dave, who added what seemed like an entire paragraph about corporate responsibility in the beginning of my story. The type of sentences I used to skip over when I read stories in the *Source* before I worked there.

Dave called me on my cell to tell me the good news for them, bad news for me: "Okay, we are probably not going to run the Eminem story."

"What?" It was all I could say after almost three months of torture, including showing up in court to support Dave when Eminem got an injunction to stop him from putting the CD in the magazine. I had an overall sense of accomplishment that I had been able to turn this story around, even if it was born out of evilness.

"Jimmy Iovine flew out here last night, and he met with Ray and I," Dave began. I couldn't believe it. After all that shit they'd talked about Jimmy Iovine, Eminem, Dr. Dre, and Interscope, they were such suckers.

"What did he say?" I acted as if I cared at that point.

"He's talking a lot of good stuff. He wants to work with us. You see, they're scared. They don't want this Eminem CD to come out. They know how important the *Source* is." Dave's excitement could be heard through the phone.

"So what are we going to put on the cover now?" I asked seriously. For a brief second, the thought of Ray's Afro spread out over the *Source* logo holding a championship belt that said VICTORY crossed my mind. But the way a child wakes up from a nightmare, I shook it off.

"We'll figure something out, but this is a good thing for us. We've got to wait a day because Jimmy is supposed to call us later and work out all the details, but he's talking about giving us a label"—*a label???*—"and he wants to do things for the community like provide computers for youth centers that the *Source* foundation would start. We had an extremely in-depth conversation about the steps we're going to take from here to resolve our issues."

"So no Eminem cover? Don't ship it?" I usually had to ask Dave specific questions so that I was absolutely positively sure that *he* was absolutely positively sure that he knew what he was telling me to do or not to do.

"No, not yet," he said with a confident snicker.

"But we're already late with this issue." The more excited that Dave was getting while he spoke, the less excitement I had.

"Let's talk when I get in the office. I'll talk to Jeremy and let him know that this issue is going to be late." It was almost February, and the February issue wasn't at the printer yet. Usually, an issue will hit newsstands three weeks before its on-sale date. This issue was held up for numerous reasons, but it was mainly because of the CD that was going to be included with it. I was in court when the injunction was lifted and the court ruled that we could use a portion of the music (not the whole song) on the CD to go out with the magazine because it was being used for news purposes. But now, we were about to be even later with the issue, especially if we had to change it.

Dave's and Ray's good moods lasted for about a day before they went back to acting miserable. No one ever heard back from Jimmy Iovine, so we shipped the Eminem cover, an image of him sticking up his middle finger, after all.

CHAPTER TWENTY-FOUR

behind bars

Shyne would always catch me on my cell at the weirdest times. I'd be at the mall, and my phone would ring with a private number. The first time, I don't pick up, not knowing it's him. The second time, I'm annoyed but I answer. "This is Shyne Po," he would say. I never met him, but around the time when he was about to release an album from behind bars, he started calling me to line up an interview and to tell me his side of the story.

He got my number from a mutual friend, Manny the CEO, now the manager for Keyshia Cole. Before I got to the *Source,* I knew Manny through Don Pooh, who managed Foxy Brown. Back then, Manny was a dude in the industry whom everybody knew, but no one knew exactly what he did. Still, you could find him at Mr. Chow every week, picking up the tab. Sometimes, Shyne would be there with him.

After Shyne gave me bits and pieces of his story, we talked about a potential *Source* cover, an exclusive from inside the belly of the beast. Ultimately, this story would end up in *XXL,* when he appeared on their cover instead. I pitched the Shyne cover to Ray a bunch of times way before *XXL* happened. Ray would just shake his head as if he were feeling the idea, then say, "We'll see." At the same time, Johnnie had been pitching a "prison package," where we would do mini-recaps of the cases of hip-hop's population behind bars. To me, it made sense for Shyne, who was about to announce that he had closed a deal with Def Jam while he was locked up, to be on the cover of an issue that would feature the prison package.

Shyne was sentenced to ten years for assault and reckless endangerment for a shooting that took place at Club New York back in 1999. One woman was shot in the face when Shyne opened fire in a crowded club. Back in '99, Club New York was poppin' on Sunday nights. I was at the club two weekends before the shooting occurred. Luckily, I had opted to stay home that night.

The Eminem issue got a mild response. It didn't generate the press we had thought it would, and the readers were over it by the time it came out. Ray decided that it was time for the "Behind Bars" issue, but he was opposed to giving the cover to Shyne alone. I told Shyne what we were planning to do—put the mug shots of about ten artists who were locked up on the cover, including him—and he eventually decided not to do the interview with us.

Selecting the models for photo shoots was never really my thing. The fashion department worked with the photo department to choose models for swimsuit issues, the "Dimepiece" section, the photo shoots, and whatever else they were needed for. Models selected for a hip-hop publication were generally thicker than the norm. Whereas the normal model size in a mainstream fashion magazine would be a 2 or 4, or a size away from complete starvation, the models selected for hip-hop publications and video shoots were 6 to 8. They would be considered cows in Hollywood. We always complained to the photo department that the models they were picking were too thin.

After numerous complaints from within the staff and from Ray and Dave, I asked to see comp cards and attend castings to help in the selection. Of course, a number of the male editors on staff made it their business to get involved in picking the models too. One day, a model came up to the office with her "manager." While we were sitting in a meeting, someone invited her to come into the conference room and audition. I don't know who asked her to, but she started to unbutton her shirt. "No, no, no." The women in the room started shaking our heads and waving our hands, motioning her to stop. The guys in the room were clapping and encouraging her to take it off. "You don't have to do that, just leave your number or your comp card," someone told her.

Another day, Ray came into my office when I was going through the models' comp cards.

"I like her." Ray pointed to a card that featured an Asian-and-black model named Jade. "I know her."

"You don't like her. You like her bawdy," I said jokingly.

"Call her. Call her and tell her I want to meet her." Ray's response took me by surprise. He was admiring her looks, and that was fine, but now he wanted me to call her and say what?

"I can't call her and tell her that," I said, trying to come up with a reason.

"Call her for a photo shoot. Give me her number so I'll call her after that."

"You are crazy." As politically incorrect as it may sound, I jotted the number on a piece of paper and handed it to Ray before he walked out of my office. I mean, he was going to get it regardless, so I figured, why not just give it to him now and save myself the scolding.

Tanya walked in right after Ray, and since I never gave up an opportunity to tell her how disgusting I thought he was, I told her, "Your boyfriend just left here."

"Ewww. Please don't refer to him as my boyfriend. It makes my stomach turn."

"He was just drooling over the models' comp cards." Ray was what we referred to as a thirstbucket, someone who was thirsty for any piece of pussy he could get.

"He's disgusting. I don't wanna know. Don't tell me anymore."

"Yes. He took a couple of phone numbers and said he would call them." Or I gave them to him, but what was the difference?

"Good, maybe he will stop calling me."

The office environment was changing. The tension from the Eminem drama had created such horrible morale among the staff, people had decided to move on. Despite the drama, I had always wanted to stay. Deep down, I believed that the magazine would regain its luster in a weird twist of events. To me, we were always one breaking story away from being back on top. The *Source* was the only job where I had been that I hadn't ever looked at any other job listings. When you are comfortable in your occupation, you get complacent. I hadn't entertained any offers or made any new connections. But it seems everyone else at the office had. Paul was quitting, and he was extremely happy when he sat down to tell me.

"I'm moving on," he said, smiling. I was shocked and confused. I didn't know Paul was planning on leaving, but I didn't honestly even care. When I first got promoted, I had a lot of resentment toward members of the staff. And I almost wished I hadn't known about the letter that was signed. Paul and I worked together, and up until that day, I thought that was all we needed to do. It wasn't anything personal, but because he had signed that letter, I expected him to rebel against the decision to promote me. But in an environment such as the *Source*, where so much is riding on relationships, an editor in chief needs to do much more than just work with the art department. Someone in that position needs to be your right hand. Everyone needs to be on your side, because just having one person on your staff against you can result in career sabotage.

"Where are you going?"

Paul told me he had been offered a position with Mark Ecko's clothing line, a partner company with his magazine *Complex* which had actively been recruiting *Source* employees. The two companies were under the same umbrella.

"I can't stay here anymore. I'm here all night. I'm always working. I just had a baby, and I want to be home and enjoy that with my wife." In his whole time at the *Source,* Paul had never been as open with me as he was that day. I'm not sure if he felt that he couldn't be honest with me before then, but when you're leaving a job, there's no point in trying to cover anything up.

"I've never really had a problem with you, Kim. But I just can't stay and work under these conditions. This place is nuts. I don't know how you deal with it. If you want my advice, you need to get a better managing editor. The scheduling, shipping the pages. All of that stuff that I do, that is all part of the managing editor's job, and if you had someone stronger in that position, it would free up your time to deal with some of the stuff you're dealing with."

In the last two years, Paul and Tanya had bumped heads quite a few times. When Paul had a complaint about timing and closing, he would go straight to Jeremy because they had a good relationship. Because Tanya was someone that I'd hired, he rarely complained about her to me. Nine times out of ten, what was holding us up were things that Ray had asked us to do. But Paul didn't always know this. So the few times the book was late, Jeremy and Paul blamed it on me.

"Wake up, Kim. Wake up. Splash some water on your face or something, because you need to deal with this right now." I was actually awoken by the ringing of my cell phone, set to the loudest ring for some idiotic reason. The first thing I did was look over at the clock, which read 2 a.m. *I am not dreaming*.

"Ray?" I answered in a groggy, half-sleep voice.

"Yeah, this is Ray." He sang his next sentence. "Way-akke up, Kimmmm."

I wasn't about to get out of bed to splash water on my face, but I sat up in bed to try to make sense when I spoke. "I'm up. I'm up."

"This shit is wack. This ain't it. You're gonna have to do better than this." Ray must have been looking at a mock of the May 2004 cover, because he was referring to the photos we had just gotten in earlier that week.

"Look at T.I. What the hell is he wearin' in this photo? Why is he wearing a suit? Why is this picture on a white background? Who was the photographer?" Ray's voice over the phone was like question vomit. "No, no, no. Who did this?"

"What do you mean 'Who did this?' We were all there at the shoot." I refused to take full responsibility because I knew no one would do it for me.

"You were at the shoot and you let them wear this?" he furiously questioned.

"They all have their own stylists. I didn't let them wear anything. That's the look they had in that shot. They had a number of looks, but that's the one picture that we chose." I don't know why I was trying to rationalize anything because once Ray had something in his head, there was really no changing his mind.

"They're all just standing there. Against an ugly fuckin' white background. This shit is wack. Change this. Reshoot this. Do this cover over."

Just like that I was back to square one. It took me a minute to coordinate the schedules of T.I., Lil' Flip, and the Young Gunz, who were all supposed to appear on the cover together for a "young guns" type of concept. The game was changing, and it was no longer being led by the old-ass rappers that I had came up on. I had to change with the times. I couldn't expect to keep winning with Jay-Z, Puffy, or Nas. But the magazine was too scared to take a chance on a newer artist such as T.I., so we would try them all at once and see how it worked. Unfortunately, we had this mentality back then that the *Source* cover was some crowning achievement that required you to put years in the game before you could grace it. In hindsight, we should have taken more chances. Post-Eminem, we needed something to recover from the story drought we were in.

The original shoot had taken place in New York, and they had all agreed to be there together, even Lil' Flip and T.I., who later started beefin' with each other over that very shoot. Now, Ray wanted to do it all over again. And we had to do it in Los Angeles this time.

"Yo, you up, right? You hear me? Kim, fix this, Kim. Paulie's leaving so he don't give a fuck. That's why he turned in some wack shit like this. But you, Kim, you gotta catch these things. What's wrong with you anyway? You can't see that something is wrong with this?" Ray was being a bit overly critical, especially at two in the morning. But he was right. The cover was boring. There was no connection among any of the subjects. The colors in each of their outfits were clashing. The shots were full body shots so the people were so small you couldn't tell who they were if you took three steps back. I knew when I saw it that it could have been better, but what was I going to say to Paul? He was already leaving, and the art department rarely changed things if it was coming from me.

"You think this is hot? Kim, do you think this cover is hot?"

I paused before I answered, unsure of the right one. "It's not hot, but—"

"Okay! Okay, then why would you put this out?" Ray posed the question that I already knew the answer to. I just wasn't going to tell him. I was so fed up with it all. I was tired, and after the continuous struggles with Ray and Dave all the time, I didn't want to have to struggle with the art department too. Instead, I just decided to let it go. But all that was about to change.

"We can do it over." I knew there was no time, but I had to pick and choose my battles.

The next morning I called a meeting with the staff and told them we had to shoot the cover all over again. T.I. was unavailable for the second shoot, so we replaced him with Cassidy and J-Kwon. It was our new jack cover, featuring the hottest upcoming MCs in the game, sans T.I., who happened to be the hottest upcoming M.C. in the game. We had to fly to L.A. to get it done in time, but as with most of what Ray asked me to do, it got done. Such as the time he told me to get rid of the more serious content we had planned in association with our annual sex package.

Khary Turner, a freelancer, had pitched me a story about rape in the hip-hop community. It's important to say that it was a man's idea, because of the way everything turned out, Ray made it seem as if the idea came from me. He started asking to see the issue plans ahead of schedule so he would know what pieces we were working on. But when he found out we were planning to do this story, he flipped.

"This type of story should not be rearing its ugly head in the *Source*," Ray said to me. I was in the office trying to close an issue, and Ray had called me on my cell after he had reviewed the issue plan.

"What's wrong with this story? It's already done. It's an investigative piece where the writer talked to—"

"I don't give a fuck who they talked to. This is some woman's shit. This is supposed to be the sex issue. What page are y'all on?"

"It's a good story."

"This is a good story to you because this is your point of view. *You*. You're responsible for these points of view, but niggas ain't trying to hear all that. Niggas wanna fuck. They don't want to read a story about rape."

I disagreed. "A guy pitched the story."

"You can't let some shit like this get through. You're the one running this. Dave was pissed when he saw this on the plan." Ray was yelling at me so loudly that his voice was scratching. "This is the type of shit we're talking about when we say you don't have the right perspective."

Pause. "Right perspective?" I was insulted. I knew this was turning into a gender issue and it wasn't that.

"Yeah, this is the type of shit that those black Afrocentric bitches be on. The bitches with dreads and shit. I don't want to have to micromanage every story, but c'mon, yo. Rape?! Do a story on strippers. Talk about the stripping industry and how hip-hop is making the stripping industry boom. Look at Lil Jon and Snoop."

"Huh?" Ray's story idea made sense, but I didn't understand why the two stories couldn't coexist. The *Source* was what it was because it represented a range of perspectives, including female perspectives. In the past, it had dealt with the harsh issues that existed in the hip-hop community. Rape was a reality. But with Ray controlling content, it wasn't going to be a reality that got any burn in the *Source*.

i know you got soul

These days, hip-hop has no soul. Not soul in the musical way, but soul as in inner spirit. By the middle of 2004, I lost my soul right along with it. I forgot what my purpose was. I went to work in the morning and went through the motions, but I didn't feel anything anymore. When writers called me, I made faces behind the phone and tried to make up excuses about why I couldn't have a conversation at that moment ("Can I call you right back? I'm finishing up a story"). I wasn't interested in any of their pitches. I didn't care.

My passion for hip-hop was gone. Such as when you wake up in the morning one day after five years and look over to your left and notice that you don't want to be with the person you are lying next to. Then you notice that the same person has long nose hair or something. I was over hip-hop. It was wack. It had long nose hair.

I was raised in the Catholic Church, the real strict kind where you gotta pay $1 to light a candle and say a prayer for a loved one. Right before I came to the *Source*, I started going to Mass every Sunday. "God gave his life for you. You can give him an hour every week," Tia told me every Sunday to get me to go to church with her. There, we would close our eyes and reflect on the sins we had committed during that week. Then, we'd leave and go back to being sinners.

"Come to church with me this Sunday," I said to Tia, who was in Miami living with her new husband.

"What? You coming down here?"

"No, but I'm going down to Atlanta. Come with me. I need to get away from all this." I was taking a weekend break to research a story that I knew needed to be told, the Mason Betha story, because he was coming out of retirement to rap again.

Tia entertained the conversation, meaning she was thinking about coming. "What you going to Atlanta for?"

"I am going to church. Don't laugh, but I am going to church to hear Pastor Betha. Pronounced *Bethay*, not *Betha* like they used to say up in Harlem."

"Bethay? Oh, you going to Mase's church. The irony. You better hope he doesn't see you. He might have God strike you down." Tia was with me the morning after Mase called me and threatened me for writing the review of his second album, *Double Up*. At the time, I didn't even work for the *Source*, I was a freelance writer. Yes, my byline was on the review, but I didn't rate the album. That was the responsibility of the music editor and the music staff. That's one of the misconceptions that so many artists have. They believed that because you wrote the review, you rated their album. But the truth was, as a writer who didn't work there, you were lucky if your Mic vote counted. The Mic rating was an average of votes compiled from among the staff. Mase never called the *Source* with his complaint, I was told. Instead, he called me and told me he knew where I lived, and that there could be girls waiting for me downstairs when I came out in the morning.

"No, if God was going to do that, then God would have turned him into flames the minute he walked in that church. I think God will allow me to be there," I responded.

"Are you interviewing him?"

"That's the good part. Not really. I'm doing the investigative reporter 20/20 thing. He's coming back out with an album, and I wanna put him on the cover. But I've been told that I can't go to his church. The interview is supposed to stick to the music. But who really cares about his new music?"

"I should go to protect you from him. He might slash your tires or something," she said, recounting the morning after the call when my car was mysteriously sitting on flat tires. Tia and I spent the entire day getting the four tires on my Toyota Camry replaced, convinced someone in his camp had done it.

That weekend, Tia and I met up in Atlanta and attended Mase's church, S.A.N.E. Ministries. I have to admit that I was surprised that someone who had been mimicked for his slow drawl could make so much sense in front of hundreds of people as a preacher. Mase had left the rap game a few years before because he felt that something was inherently wrong with it. After this weekend, I had that same feeling. Something was wrong with the things I was doing.

My interview with Mase actually took place in a car as we drove around Harlem the next week. I don't know what it was about that day, but I was in need of some guidance. "When artists see me or people in the industry, they always look at me like they just saw a ghost or something," he told me. "I could just look at people and see where they're headed."

"Oh, yeah. Where I am headed?" I asked sarcastically, expecting him to give an answer as if he were a palm reader.

Mase played along, "You are taking a turn for the better."

One day as I was on my way home from work, I ran into Ray down by Dave's office and he asked, "Kim, what are you doing this weekend?"

"Nothing, I'm staying home with my daughter."

"You're always home with your daughter. You need to lighten up a bit. Get out. Have fun. Why don't you come out to Atlantic City with me? We'll have a good time."

"Atlantic City? For what?" At first, I was confused. I wasn't sure why he was inviting me.

"C'mon, think about it, we can have fun. Don't you think we would make a good couple?"

"Couple?" I was shocked to hear this coming from Ray, because he had never come at me that way. "Uh . . . no. We work together." Then I used the excuse that all girls use when they don't want to outright say no. "Plus, you're like a brother to me."

"No. No. We could be good together. We would be like the king and queen of the *Source*."

"King and queen?" I laughed at Ray's royal imagination. "Uh, I don't think that's such a good idea." I was being nice about my first right to refusal, but I was running out of ways to be nice as I was making my way out of the office toward the elevator.

Ray followed me to the elevator. "I'm going downstairs too."

The elevator was already on the eleventh floor when we got to the elevator banks, so we both got on.

"C'mon, I got a room in Atlantic City, you could stay with me."

"I'm not going to Atlantic City with you." The elevator opened on the lobby, and both Ray and I stepped out. A black Suburban was waiting in front of the building.

"Where are you going now?" he asked.

"I'm going to the parking lot to get my car." The lot was less than two blocks away.

"C'mon, I'll drive you around."

I could have said no and walked to the lot, but Ray was persistent and I didn't want to make the situation seem awkward. So I climbed into the backseat of the car with him.

"Atlantic City will be fun, Kim."

"I'm not going to Atlantic City, Ray, I can't. I have my daughter at home and I can't leave her anywhere. Plus, why are you asking me to go with you? I thought you liked Tanya." I was trying everything to get Ray to stop. I didn't want to bring up Tanya but it made sense to call him out on it. I knew he'd been coming on to her for the past year and a half, and now he was coming on to me. I knew his game, and mentioning Tanya was one of the few ways I thought I could get him to stop.

Tanya be frontin', Kim, you know that. I don't like Tanya like that. I like you."

"You do not like me," I said as the car turned into my parking garage.

"Yes, I do. Go home and pack your things. You're coming to Atlantic City with me. I'm gonna call you. I'm calling you, Kim."

I stepped out of the car and gave Ray a look, then shut the door. I was nervous. Tanya had gone through it for a year and a half, and now he was on me. *How did this happen?* I thought. As Ray was pulling away, he pulled his window down halfway and yelled to me, "I'm calling you tonight, Kim."

I jumped into my car and called Tanya immediately. "Tanya, Ray just told me to come to Atlantic City with him. Talkin' about he got a room for us."

Tanya burst out into laughter. "Ahhh. Thank God, now he'll leave me alone. He's on you now."

"It's not funny. I can't have him callin' me and doing this to me."

"What did he say?"

I detailed the last couple of minutes.

"Yup. That sounds just like Ray," Tanya said, then started imitating his voice. "*Come to Atlantic City. Come on, Kim.* Ewwww. He's so gross. What are you gonna do?"

"I'm gonna go home and hope he forgets about what he just did."

Ray didn't forget. After I got home, he called me again and again, even on my home phone. I did not pick up. A message from him on my cell phone told me to call him, but I never called back. On Monday, when I went to work, Ray wasn't there. And I didn't mention it to him again, but it was bothering me, so I confided in a few friends.

"You need to talk to this guy." Michelle gave me a phone number to an attorney that she had met. He specialized in employment discrimination and had advised her on some things. "I'm telling you. What they are doing to you isn't right. Just call him."

"If I call him and word gets out that I spoke to somebody, I'm finished. They will fire me."

"They can't do that. It's against the law."

"Do you think they care about the law? Look at everything that goes on in that place. They won't care. I'll be out of a job."

"Whatever you say to him is confidential. He can't tell anyone, just talk to him."

"I'll think about it."

The next weekend, I thought about it. I thought about everything. The invitation to Atlantic City had scared me into believing that Ray might come at me again, and the next time it would be worse. There was so much history of my being mistreated. The Antoine situation, the constant references to my sex life, the accusations of me sleeping with people on the staff. It had all built up inside me, and I needed to talk to someone. I called the attorney, Ken Thompson, on his cell phone.

"Ken Thompson, please."

"Yes, this is Ken."

"Hi, Ken, I'm Michelle's friend. My name is Kim and I was wondering if I could talk to you about some things going on at my job."

"What kind of things, Kim? Where do you work?"

"Well, I really don't want to get into that type of stuff over the phone. Can we meet in person?"

Ken seemed thrown by my secret-squirrel conversation. I didn't know whom he knew, and I couldn't afford for my conversation to get back to anyone at the *Source*.

"Uh. Okay, well, I live in New Jersey, so I won't be in the city until—"

"I live in Jersey too. Can we meet here?"

"Yes, meet me at the Borders bookstore in Fort Lee at seven p.m."

That night, I met Ken Thompson and gave him the skinny on my problems at the magazine.

Ken listened, then said, "You need to file a complaint with Human Resources."

"I can't really do that. I'll be complaining about the owners, and I will get fired."

"They can't fire you for complaining about discrimination. It's against the law."

After I met with Ken, I realized that there was no way I could file a complaint with Human Resources. Human Resources was one person, Julie. I knew if I told her everything, she would be obligated to go to Dave, and I'd be fired for making the complaint. It might have been against the law for them to do, but the *Source* didn't always follow the letter of the law.

The law says that sexual harassment is a form of unlawful discrimination on the basis of sex. But the textbook definition can be interpreted in many ways. Harassment has to be unwelcome to be harassment. The unwelcome part then goes to the state of mind of the person being harassed. The difficulty comes into play when, as a woman, you are too scared to voice your state of mind because the person committing the harassment has control over your job.

Many things happened at the magazine that could be considered unwelcome, but I can't speak to anyone else's state of mind but mine. If Ray said, "You have a fat ass," and a person heard him say that to a woman, it would only be considered harassment if that woman or anyone who heard him was offended by it. If said woman says that she took it as a compliment, then she welcomed it. This was the case with one of the women who was subpoenaed to testify in the case that I later brought against the *Source*, Dave, and Ray for sexual harassment. Many of the women at the *Source* heard things like "You got a fat ass" all the time, but it didn't bother them. "I took it as a compliment," someone later said. But for me, it was a problem. I was offended.

It doesn't matter if I went to a club and heard it all night. When I'm at work, I'm not trying to hear that type of "compliment." In hip-hop though, the depiction of women has changed. The days of LL Cool J needing love were long gone and now it was all about skeet-skeeting on and making females crawl.

friends

"I hate these fucks." Ray was on another of his tirades. This time, the targets were all hip-hop journalists. Anyone who never supported his music—and that was almost everyone. "These college motherfuckers. They don't know shit about the streets."

Although it was a long shot, the media might have taken Ray's side in the Eminem/Benzino beef once the tapes were public. But the media did not crucify Eminem as Ray had wanted. In fact, much of the hip-hop media called Benzino out on his cruel intentions instead of shining the light on what Eminem had said. Therefore, Benzino thought he had an ax to grind with journalists too.

"Kim, we need to do a fuckin' story on their asses. Turn the tables around and write about them," he said to me during one of our meetings. I was listening to him carefully to make sure that I didn't misinterpret any direction he was about to give, because I knew I would have to answer later for anything that he didn't like.

"These fuckin' douche bags. They all hide behind their little computers and write all this shit, and they'd never say any of it to my face." Ray was mostly referring to a class of journalists who had, ironically, come up through the *Source*. Whether it was as an intern, a freelancer, or a full-time staffer, most journalists who wrote about hip-hop had, at some time, been a part of the *Source*.

"I wanna expose all these dudes for the suckfaces they are." Ray had a creative way of making up interesting-sounding words. Words such as *suckface* or even *slut monkey*—the famous insult that he invented out of anger during a phone call to Julia Beverly, the editor in chief of *Ozone* magazine—somehow found their way out of Ray's mouth. It made for entertaining conversation. Unfortunately, that creativity never made it onto his records.

"You want to do a story on writers?" My tone was purposely sarcastic, in hopes that he would realize how stupid it sounded to write about writers, who weren't generally known to the readers.

"Yes, I want all of them in there. Elliott Wilson, Sacha Jenkins, Selwyn Hinds. Show how all these idiots came through the *Source*."

"Uh-huh." I acknowledged his request by nodding my head in agreement and acting as if I didn't care about what he was doing. But in my head, I was focused on how I was going to squeeze a manicure into my closing schedule, and when I myself was going to stop partaking in Ray's nonsense.

"Yeah. And put Mimi in there too. Right, D?" Ray looked over at Dave, who gave the blank "Whatever you say, Ray" stare.

My relationship with Mimi Valdes, the newly appointed editor in chief of *Vibe*, was cordial, but I had never heard Ray say anything negative about her before she became EIC at *Vibe*. It spoke to Ray's pettiness. All of a sudden, Mimi was the enemy too. She hadn't really ever said anything bad about Ray or Dave, but needless to say, now that she held a position of power, Ray saw her as a threat to the *Source*. He started to include her in the conversations about journalists whom he didn't like.

"Oh, yeah, and your little friend Michelle. That ching-chong slut. Put her in there too."

I woke up from my brain sleep when he mentioned Michelle in such a derogatory way. "Why are we putting her in this story?" I asked, disturbed by his newest target, and overly disturbed by his making such a racist remark. Ray was so calculating, though. It was almost as if he was waiting for me to react. And it wasn't enough that I was ready and willing to go along with any smear campaign he planned, he wanted me to hate doing it. He needed to piss me off just so it was guaranteed that I would want to go against him, just so he could exert his power and make me do something that I didn't want to. He knew that pulling in my close friend was going to make me react. Never mind the fact that my mother is half-Chinese, so I didn't take to his comments too well.

"Why, Kim? You're asking why? Because she's a hater too. She's a haterrrrr."

"She doesn't hate you, Ray." I was trying everything I could to keep her out of the story. But her name was damn near already in print.

"Yes, she's a hater. She used to work here too, and now she's running around on the radio trying to be down. As a matter of fact, she gets her own sidebar, Kim. She needs to have her own column dedicated to her. Let everyone see what she looks like."

Maybe if I had been quiet when he mentioned her, it wouldn't have gotten worse. I knew I had to stop objecting, because the more I objected, the worse it got.

As ridiculous as Ray was, some readers of the magazine still didn't know what went on behind the scenes, and as a writer, I hated the idea of doing a story like this, especially when it involved my friend. But I had decided to stick with the job, and that meant, for the time being, that I did what they asked me to do. I didn't want to even see the page, but I had no choice. I didn't consider myself going along with it, but I guess I was. Once the story came out, it wouldn't matter whether I actually wanted to do it or not, but rather that it was printed. The story would make me look like an outsider in my own field. These are people whom I had to come into contact with more so than Dave or Ray. People who had been in my position and had, in some way, managed not to have to do something like this. They would look at me as if I had three heads the next time I saw them. Ray wanted us to make the field of journalism look corny. How was *I*, of all people, supposed to assign that to another writer? *Uh, we're doing a story about how wack journalists are. Do you want to write it? No, you're not wack, you're a special case. Everyone else is just wack.*

Journalists often get blamed for things that artists are trying to hide. When they slip during an interview and want to take back what they've said, it's much easier to just say that a journalist misinterpreted their statement, or that the media is twisting the story around, than it is to admit that they actually said it. But at the end of the day, if they would never have said it, it wouldn't be in print. At the *Source,* we got blamed for taking quotes out of context, leaving out part of someone's answers, or just printing quotes that artists claimed they didn't even say. Lucky for us, the research department always had tapes of the interviews. But with Ray's new directives, this story on writers being one, we were toeing the line of exposing ourselves.

October 22, 2004. I specifically remember that day because it was the day before Kayla's birthday party, and I swore to myself that I would not work. I decided that I was taking the entire day off to spend with her. Kayla's twin friends, Yuri and Ahri, also had a birthday party on that day, and I wanted to take her and then meet up with Tia for dinner. She was flying in from Miami for Kayla's party at American Girl the next day.

At around six thirty, when I was on my way to meet Tia, Dave called my cell phone and asked, "Where you at?"

"I took my daughter to a birthday party today. It's her birthday," I replied in a don't-even-stress-me-about-not-being-at-work kind of attitude.

"I need you to come in the office and finish up this story." I felt the weight of disappointment on my shoulders. The issue was closed, at least I thought it was, and Dave was calling me back to make one last change. It was another of their attack stories, the hip-hop journalists story.

"I can be there at seven thirty," I said, knowing that Tia was going to be furious I was canceling dinner plans to go into the office.

"All right, I'll be here when you get here. Oh, and one more thing." Dave paused. "We had to fire Tracii."

"Uh, what happened?" I said hesitantly, afraid to seem to be dissenting from their decision. But I was shocked. Tracii had worked for the company for nine years, and even though some of us may have considered her to be a little odd, she was loyal to them. If she could get fired, I knew that so could I.

"She was doing some crazy shit. She fucked up the Source Awards. A lot of shit. We made her get her shit and get out." Dave delivered his answer so fast that it felt as if he had rehearsed it. It didn't sound right to me, but I accepted it and moved on. I felt bad for Tracii, who I later heard had to sneak in at 5 a.m. to pick up her belongings, but I couldn't do anything. I headed back to the office with Kayla, where I stayed most of the evening. Tia met me there and we ended up skipping dinner and carrying a sleeping Kayla out after 11 p.m. Most of the time was spent watching Dave sit at my computer and come up with disguised insults for former journalists whom he was trying to ridicule in the magazine. That turned out to be a long day, but it was only about to get worse. We were not printing lies (at least not that we knew of at the time), but it was a new brand of reporting, where the stories were motivated by one person's agenda and the coverage was knowingly biased.

one more chance

Ray blamed the editorial department whenever an artist came to him about something that ran in the magazine. His way of handling it was not to defend us but rather to make himself seem like the good guy so he could turn around and ask the artists to be on his record or something. That's how he treated the team who worked for him. So imagine what he said about outside journalists, who didn't at least have to worry about losing their jobs.

A few months had gone by since the Eminem tapes, and despite the story on journalists we were working toward rebuilding our credibility—again. But just when you thought it was time to move on, Ray would pull you right back into his agenda. Ja Rule was preparing a comeback, and Ray had ordered us to put him on the cover of the November issue.

Ja Rule covers always did pretty well for the *Source*. But we had maxed out on his stories with little left to say after the last few, which had dealt with Murder Inc. and 50 Cent. This was his comeback, though, so we figured we could come up with something creative to help sell the magazine.

The art department had this idea of catching a photo of Ja Rule while suspended in the air, à la Kevin Garnett's old *Source* sports cover. It had nothing to do with the story, but it seemed like a really cool-looking thing to do. We all agreed that a flying Ja Rule was better than a standing-still Benzino any day—and we knew that was always a backup possibility.

We rented a trampoline and took pictures of Ja Rule jumping on it for hours. But when the photos came back, they all looked pretty bad. In every photo, Ja looked smaller than he already was, and he looked way too happy. Happy was a no-no for a rapper on the cover of the *Source*. Rappers didn't smile in most of their pictures. The better picture had the subject looking menacing or throwing up his fingers. We were afraid of what might happen to our jobs if we ran a picture of Benzino's only chance of another record deal smiling in the air. Luckily, we had some straight-up portraits from the shoot that ended up on the cover.

I assigned the story to one of my staff members, Thomas Golianopolous. Thomas was not a Ja Rule fan, but was a decent writer who knew how to get the job done. Tanya warned him to be extremely delicate with the story because Ray would be right over all our shoulders. But Ray had always called Thomas a hater behind closed doors, so I should have known that he would pick Thomas's story apart.

Once we moved to 28 West 23rd Street, which was within walking distance of 215, time seemed to fly by. I was only there for about four and a half months, but so much happened it such a short time. That office just seemed to have a bad vibe for me. I'm extra-superstitious, so maybe there was some poster I didn't hang up the right way that reversed my luck.

It was the weekend and I was finally getting my manicure when Ray called my cell phone. "Yo, Kim. I just read the Ja Rule story and your boy is finished. He's done."

"What? Ja Rule? That was a really good story."

"A good story, Kim? You think I'm stupid?" Ray's voice was coming through my cell phone so loudly that the manicurist could hear that someone was yelling at me.

"No, Ray. But I read that story and there was nothing bad said about Ja Rule." I couldn't recall anything that Thomas had written that was going to hurt my argument.

"Don't tell me there was nothing bad about Ja Rule. I just got off the phone with Rule, and he's pissed."

"Pissed at what? Thomas didn't write anything negative." Now I was second-guessing myself, because maybe I'd missed something.

"He called him the Cookie Monster."

"No, Ray. 50 called him a Cookie Monster, Thomas just put it in his story."

"Exactly! Why would he put something like that in his story?"

"It's a fact that 50 said that about Ja Rule, and Thomas was making a reference to it." As an editor, I picked up on the reference and the context of how it was being used, but Ray thought that Thomas was subliminally dissin' Ja Rule.

"Yes, why would he make a reference to it? Is this guy a Ja Rule fan, Kim?"

"I mean, he's not not a Ja Rule fan, but—"

"But nothing. Then how can he write a story if he doesn't even like Ja Rule?" Ray's rationale was that only a Ja Rule fan could write a Ja Rule story, but only a 50 Cent enemy could write one on 50.

"He doesn't like or dislike him. He's neutral. That's the point."

"He's not neutral. He's finished. He's outta here. He gotta get the fuck out." No matter what I said, it wasn't going to help Thomas's situation. Ray had his mind made up, and it was probably better that I didn't say anything else. Still, I tried to plea one last time.

"But I don't understand why we're firing him. He works hard."

"Works hard? Hmph." Ray sarcastically snickered as if I had given him the wrong answer. "I'll cut his pinkie finger off and he won't work again."

"Are you serious?"

Ray was speaking in a serious conversation, one in which he was yelling at me. Regardless of whether he would actually go and cut Thomas's pinkie off, the point was that he made a threat.

"I'm very serious. He's finished. On Monday, he's gone." Then Ray hung up.

I was appalled. We were now at a point where people would be fired for not doing something wrong, but for actually doing their job. And in Thomas's case, doing his job well. I couldn't let my career at the *Source* end in my being fired for doing a good job, and I figured that Ray could get pissed at me one day and decide my days at the magazine were over too, or that I only needed four fingers. But I enjoyed my career and I didn't want to leave. I was torn between my job and a fate I knew I would eventually have to come to terms with.

CHAPTER TWENTY-EIGHT

paper-thin

My stomach was in a knot for the rest of the weekend. I couldn't think of anything else but how to tell Thomas that we had to let him go. Thomas was a Greek kid who I hired as a research editor after he worked as my intern. He came from NYU when I was the music editor, and I told him if he did well in the research department, he would create more opportunities for himself to write. His writing was grammatically correct, researched, and always on time. But it sometimes lacked the flavor that the stories needed. Still, because I respected Tom's hustle and all the hours he put in, I made him a staff writer. Ray was always looking for an excuse to get rid of Tom, and now he had one.

When I came in on Monday, I called Tom into my office and told him what had happened. I couldn't go the day waiting for Ray to come in and turn the office upside down. "Should I leave now?" Thomas asked.

Tanya and I decided that Tom should stay to see if Ray had changed his mind or forgot about it when he got there.

He didn't get to the office until the late afternoon, and unfortunately he hadn't forgotten. Ray called a meeting with me, Tanya, Tom, Boo, and other staff members to discuss the Ja Rule story and what had gone wrong. Turns out Ray was just in a mood to fire someone. Tom did such a good job of defending his position that Ray let him stay. But someone still had to go.

"You three stay in here. We need to talk about these fashion pages. This here. This ain't hot enough," Ray said to me, Tanya, and Katie, Schad. He was flipping through a fashion spread of an office holiday party. Boo was playing Santa Claus in the spread, but Ray hadn't noticed that yet.

"What is this shit? What is this dude wearing here?" Ray was pointing to another model who was dressed up.

"Ray, that guy is dressed up because the concept is an office party," Katie explained.

I relied so heavily on my photo department to get the fashion pages ready when the book was in production that I left it up to Katie to answer Ray's questions about the fashion pages.

"This ain't how our office looks. This shit looks gay," he replied.

"It's not supposed to be our office, though," Tanya added, trying to help out.

"Who put this shit together?" Ray asked. And that "Who did it?" question was usually how it started. Someone was getting chopped, and we could feel it. Once again, he was looking for someone to be held accountable for something he didn't like.

Katie said, "Michelle Ten put it together." She had already expressed concern to Tanya and me after we brought Michelle Ten on board. Katie didn't feel that Michelle had the experience. A few months before we moved into the new offices, Misa had decided to leave the magazine because of some drama that had taken place between her assistant and the photo department. That left a void, and I hired a former fashion assistant, Michelle Ten. It was a junior position, but it gave her the freedom to work with the photo department and get the experience she needed.

"She did this? Then she's wack. She gotta go," Ray said bluntly. Michelle had been back for a minute now, and working her into the staff had been easy since she had already known everyone. She knew the routine and was willing to come back as an associate editor. Phat Farm, Eckō, all that stuff just wasn't really me, so I let the fashion department run with their plans or tell me what was working. Then there was the advertising factor, where we had to include certain clothing in the fashion pages to give the advertisers a little plug. Unfortunately, Ray was extremely dissatisfied with this particular fashion spread in the December issue, and he was looking at it on a day when he was looking to fire someone.

"The fashion spread looks good, Ray," said Tanya. "What's wrong with it?"

"What's wrong with it? It's wack. Y'all just can't understand it. Uhhh." Ray let out a big sigh. "I know why you don't understand. Y'all can't see that there's something wrong with this fashion spread. You're women."

The three of us sat quietly in our chairs, waiting for Ray to finish his tirade, but it kept going. "Ugk. I feel like I'm surrounded by the witches of Eastwick."

Tanya looked over to me with her eyes opened wide, and I just shook my head in disgust. We were all sitting there in disbelief that Ray was stereotyping our professional opinions.

"I can't take it in here. There's too much estrogen in the room." Ray then peeked into the hallway, where Boo was standing, conversing. "Boo, come in here, yo. I need a man's opinion."

Boo came in the office, looking clueless, trying to figure out what was going on.

"Yo, look at this fashion spread. Is this shit hot? What you think?" Ray asked.

Boo looked through the pages and saw himself, dressed as Santa Claus, staring back at him. When fashion needed someone to play Santa, they asked Boo, so of course he was going to support himself. "Yeah, it's hot," he said.

"Aaah, you just saying that 'cause you in it. Look at the clothes, though." Ray started pointing at the models in the magazine. "This is wack." Flipped the page. "This is wack." Flipped the page. "This is definitely wack. I'm sorry, but your fashion girl, she gotta go. Get rid of her."

I didn't know whether Ray was downsizing the staff because he just hated everybody, or if he had a specific reason for firing people at random, on the spur of the moment, on any given day. But considering how poorly the magazine was doing, I knew that firing people freed up money for him to continue doing what he wanted to do. In essence, I guess it wasn't bad business for his career. If I were a rapper, I'd probably figure out a way to squeeze everyone else's budget instead of tapping into my own, especially since he didn't have one. But there is no excuse, however, for a businessman who neglects to take care of business. If I didn't check up on my writers' contracts and checks, they wouldn't get paid. We operated on a pay-on-request type of system. You wouldn't get paid unless you asked more than once. My cell phone was paid directly through the *Source*, and the *Source* would sometimes neglect to pay it.

Back at 215, the accounting department was located on the seventh floor. I guess someone was smart enough to keep the checks as far away from the staff as possible. But when we moved to 23rd Street, we were all conveniently bunched together. So whenever there was a problem with the checks, we were close enough to the finance department to just swing by. That made it much easier for us to find out information about the company's financial troubles.

"We don't have any money," Tanya said to me when she came in my office. "Writers haven't been paid in months. They're calling me and I don't know how to lie to them anymore."

"Yeah, I know. My cell phone is shut off and Ron Lefkon says there is no money to pay it."

"Haha, your cell phone is off? Ghetto," Tanya joked.

"It's not funny. I'm waiting on important calls." Just as I said that, my office phone rang as if on cue. It was Dave, and he had some more evilness for me to take part in.

"I've been trying to call you."

Before he could go on, I offered up my excuse: "My phone is off."

"What do you mean your phone is off?"

"The bill isn't paid. It's off."

"Uh. The bill isn't paid?" he repeated, as if he didn't know his company's bills were behind, but he pretended that wasn't an issue. "Well, go to Ron Lefkon and tell him to pay your cell phone bill."

To get Ron Lefkon or Jeremy Miller to do anything, especially to cut a check, it had to come from Dave or Ray. When I mentioned financial things like this to Dave, he made excuses for why things were the way they were, but I knew that it wasn't the case if someone on the business side was owed a debt or needed something. Dave always felt that it was a privilege to write for the *Source*, and for some writers it was. But I didn't feel as though that made it okay to not pay them. Come on, now. On the outside, I appeared to have some sort of power. But inside the office, it didn't matter much what I said. So I became a master at using the "Dave said . . ." thing with the executives at the *Source* who were responsible for its finances. That day, when I went to Ron and told him, "Dave said to pay my cell phone bill," well, all of a sudden, the company had the money. This would explain the unexplainable. The bills would be behind and yet they would still find money to support a Benzino album, photo shoot, and trip. During our financial crisis, I heard that Ray had put a down payment on a car for Trina, who Ray claimed was his girl.

During a phone conversation with Ray one day, he pressured me to talk about my own sex life by using his as an example.

"C'mon, Kim. Why don't you tell me who you slept with? I already know."

"Okay, I thought we were talking about the Power 30 issue, Ray."

"Yeah, we talking about it, but why you act like that? I know who you did it with."

I felt that Ray's questions were totally inappropriate in the context of our business conversation. I understand the difference between a personal conversation and a business conversation. For one, we weren't in a personal setting. Many times we were all just hanging out, but when I'm having a phone conversation about what's going in the magazine, I don't want to be pressured to talk about my personal life.

"C'mon, Kim. Just tell me. Admit it."

"Admit what? Why? For what?" It's not that I was ashamed to tell Ray whom I had been with. It's that I knew exactly what he wanted to know, and more important, I knew that he would use it against me.

"We all do it. You know I've been with Trina right?"

"Really, that's nice."

"Yeah. Even Dave did it. Back in the day, he was with Yo-Yo and Nikki D." As much as I didn't want to encourage this kind of conversation with Ray, I have to admit that the tidbits of information about Dave were comical. The magazine had been around since 1988, and knowing just how incestuous the music industry was, I could only imagine what relationships Dave had had. Still, I had to resist.

"Ray, that's hilarious, but it's too much information. I don't want to know about Dave's personal life." Lie. I did want to know, especially because I knew they'd be throwing my own relationships back in my face. So if Ray or Dave ever said anything about me publicly, it was good to know that I could throw out the image of Dave and Nikki D.

"Yeah, so c'mon. Admit it. Admit that you were with Nas. You know Steve Stoute already blew your spot up." I didn't know what Steve had said to Ray and Dave about me, and I honestly believe that he probably didn't even know how much harm he was doing at the time. It was probably just locker-room talk, but knowing that whatever he had said had put my job on the line upset me so much that I was still somewhat happy that story on him did come out.

"Steve Stoute wasn't there. He doesn't know."

"Ah, he wasn't there. So you did do it!" It didn't matter what answer I gave Ray. He always heard what he wanted to hear.

"I'm not having this conversation with you. Can we get back to the magazine?"

"No. No. Let's talk about this." Ray was playful over the phone. He was using his brotherly persona to try to pull information out of me. At times, I almost fell for it. It wasn't that he was always evil and destructive. Sometimes, Ray was cool. It's just that when he flipped, his evilness canceled out the good. By this time, I had learned everything I needed to know about his tactics. I never wanted to lie to him, but I knew that if something went wrong tomorrow, any information that I gave him today would be turned around and used against me. So I had to cover it up.

"Bye, Ray. I'm not telling you anything."

TWENTY-NINE

toy soldiers

I have a theory. When artists foreshadow their own death in their music or music videos, they are creating a dangerous situation. It always spooked me out that Biggie called his only two albums *Ready to Die* and *Life After Death*. Even when Tupac did that Makaveli album, it seemed as if something was off. Death is not something that should be mocked or used as a theme or concept in hip-hop. In too many instances, it has come true.

Eminem had a song called "Like Toy Soldiers," and in the video, Proof plays his friend who is killed. The song dealt with Eminem's beef with Benzino and the *Source*, but it wasn't a dis record. The song predicted what would happen if he allowed the beef with Benzino to continue. In the video, Proof is shot and dies in the hospital. Years later,

Proof would be murdered outside a club in Detroit after an argument with a bodyguard escalated.

When we all heard the song, we were nervous that it would revive the beef. And for a minute, it definitely opened up some opportunities for the *Source* to revisit it. Dave went out to Detroit to do an interview with the radio station WDTJ and promote the *Source*. After the interview, he called me from Detroit, amped up, telling me that he had just gotten into an altercation with Eminem in person while he was on the air. Apparently, while Dave was being interviewed, they asked him about Em, and within ten minutes Eminem had showed up at the station with about ten of his people. When Dave described it to me, he said Eminem was threatening him, but left out the part about Eminem spitting in his face. But everyone talked about it in the office behind closed doors.

The Eminem situation riled up Dave and Ray again, and even though they'd never really let it go, it had been left alone for a time. They still had that vindictive spirit that had set things like the journalism story in motion. Now, Eminem's new video had awoken the evil spirits in Ray and Dave again, and as always, they started to look for things to pick apart.

One evening, my phone buzzed with the caller ID that always made my head hurt. "You're confirmed to participate in this 'Feminism in Hip-Hop' conference in Chicago." Dave was talking in that ol' condescending tone, and I didn't know why this was the topic of choice, but I was about to find out.

"Uh. Yes. I think I know what that is. It's in April, though. I have to find all the emails because I don't know too much about it," I told him. The University of Chicago was hosting a "Feminism in Hip-Hop" conference, which they had invited me to speak at. News of the conference had spread on the internet and found its way into Dave's reading material for the day.

"This is extremely dangerous. We should bash these people, not participate in things like this," he continued.

I hadn't given too much thought to the conference when I agreed to do it in Chicago. I read the initial emails from the organizers, and it seemed to be for a good cause. It never crossed my mind that I would be doing something that would be a problem.

"We need to be attacking them in the magazine. You should be on the phone right now canceling. This is not what the *Source* stands for."

After we got off the phone, I thought about what Dave had said and how ridiculous it sounded. I was too embarrassed to call and cancel because it was three months in advance, and a cancellation that early would seem fabricated. But more important, doing everything Dave told me to do was starting to bother me, especially when it related to my career outside the *Source*. My mind started racing. *Why can't I participate if I feel it is for a good cause? Who is he to tell me I can't go?* I had never been a textbook feminist, but damn it, if being feminist meant you didn't let a man tell you what to do, then it was my new identity.

Just as I thought, before long Ray joined Dave in telling me what to do. A few days later, I was in my car when I got a call from Ray.

"Yo, where you at?"

"I'm leaving Irv Gotti's office. I was meeting him about a story he's going to do."

"Yo, this 'Dimepiece' is wack. That's it. You can't be involved in this anymore."

"Dimepiece" was a few pages where the *Source* would get its *King* magazine on, keeping the magazine skewed toward male readers. I understood the rationale, but thought if there was a way to uplift the women in these features, then we should do so. We could show the skin and show that they had a head on their shoulders as well. We had featured Kimora Lee Simmons, and Serena Williams in some of the first few columns, but after that Ray had regulated so that we just went along with what the other magazines were doing and showcased the hottest video girls. By the time he called me that day to vent about it, I was no longer involved in picking the girls.

After Ray attacked the "Dimepiece," implying that I was responsible for making it "wack," I asked, "What do you mean?" playing dumb to hear him say what I actually thought he was getting at.

"It's wack. Let me tell you what you're gonna do." Ray was upset. I could hear it through the phone. He was raising his voice and I could hear the growl in it.

"I don't pick the Dimepieces."

"See, that's the problem. You can't even take any accountability. 'I don't pick the Dimepieces,'" Ray mocked. "You're the editor. Everything in this book that isn't decided by myself or Dave is you. Take some fucking responsibility, Kim. You did this. You fucked up. Now, you're gonna fix it."

At that point, I couldn't do anything else but listen. I wasn't a dictator boss, so I let the majority vote choose things such as the Dimepieces. But everybody was so paranoid about his or her job, whenever people were asked, "Who did it?" they usually pointed to me. "Okay, so what do you want to do?" I asked Ray, knowing that no matter what I said, he wasn't going to believe that I wasn't responsible.

"I want you to arrange a meeting. A closed-door meeting. Of men only. No women. No you, no Katie, no Tanya. Just men. Get Bum. Get EB. Get Dale. This is the 'Dimepiece' meeting. No fucking angry, hating-ass women . . . especially none wearing headwraps and shit."

I knew how crazy what he was saying was. And I couldn't believe it.

"So you want me to have a meeting with men only?" I didn't have any paper to write down what Ray was saying, but my BlackBerry was handy so I started to type it.

"Yes. No women. All men. 'Cause this shit gotta be right it don't make no sense."

"It has nothing to do with women picking the models, though, Ray. Men are involved in picking them too."

"Men? What men? Who, Miguel? No, Kim. Get some real mu'fuckas to pick these chicks. Do this shit today."

Closed-door. No women. Men only. These words stuck out in my head and were typed out in my BlackBerry. At times, management at your job may do some questionable things, but to me this wasn't questionable at all. In my mind, it was outright employment discrimination. I was the editor of the magazine, and part of my job responsibilities had been stripped because I was a woman.

CHAPTER THIRTY

it's tricky

As a manager, I have learned a lot by understanding just how crazy management can be. These days, bosses feel free to call you and talk about work over the weekends, and lunch hours dissipate. My weekends are reserved for my family, and so are my evenings, although I do occasionally get sucked into working during these times. But back when I was at the *Source*, I never had time for anything or anyone else. I mean, I was at the *Source* for over five years, and I had never taken a vacation. I had taken days off around the holidays, maternity leave, and had even had some relaxing business trips. But as far as having my own time, separate from the *Source*, it wasn't an option. Even when I was off from work, I was always available, always either a cell-phone call or a BlackBerry text message away. When September of 2004 strolled around, I decided to go to Portland to see my sister. I hated leaving because I knew that I would miss something.

And the minute I disappeared for a few days, something happened. My sister and I were at Target when I got a phone call from Bum telling me that Ray was firing Johnnie because of a huge argument at the office the night before. Johnnie worked with Saigon, and apparently they had all been up at the office drinking together. Not surprisingly, Eminem's name came up, and Saigon made a comment about the Eminem situation that was not in Ray's favor. According to Bum, Ray felt disrespected by Saigon and wanted Johnnie out because he was responsible for having Saigon up at the office in the first place. "You don't let no one come up and be disrespectful. Johnnie has to go." And then sounding like a nicer version of Ray, Bum said, "'He gotta get the fuck out of here.'"

I had just about had it when I heard this. My job was becoming unbearable with these ups and downs. Johnnie had been working at the magazine longer than me and had started as an intern. When it came to his loyalty to the *Source*, there was no question. The Eminem shit was going too far. Ray wanted to fire someone over an argument with someone who was *with* Johnnie. *What was this, the fifth grade?* He came with you, so you can't be here. What a stupid reason for someone to get fired.

When I got back to the office, Johnnie came into my office and quit before he could get fired. I was shocked. He looked really sad, but I guess he figured, why wait around for what he knew was about to happen. It was inevitable. Everyone's time was numbered, including mine.

Shortly after Johnnie left, another significant staff change occurred in the department. Boo was serving as the sole music editor, and a couple of important album releases were coming down the pike. Responsible for the reviews section, Boo showed me his plan to review both the Game and Fat Joe's albums for the March '05 issue.

The first time that I heard the rapper the Game, it was on a mixtape, and the "Fuck Dave Mays" shout-out garnered my attention. Before 50 Cent and the Game turned on each other, Game was reppin' G-Unit hard, pledging his alliance by coming out of the box dissing Dave Mays and the *Source*. We knew that he was going to be successful because he was the first talented thing to come out of the West Coast since Snoop Dogg. Plus, he had the gangster persona that rap fans couldn't help but love, especially with the I-killed-somebody-and-I-want-everyone-to-know-tear tattooed under his eye (though it was later changed to a butterfly). By the time his debut album dropped in January of '05, most of us at the office were trying to downplay his affiliation with 50 so that we could cover him in the magazine. We'd gotten an early copy of the album, and from what we could tell, it was really good. We voted to give it a 4 Mic rating. Boo assigned the review to a freelancer, writing under an alias. Innocently, a positive review of the Game's album ran with a mention of Eminem in it. It was so insignificant that I didn't even notice it. After going back and reading the review, I still don't understand why Ray flipped out, but he decided to fire Boo because of it. He used that coupled with the excuse that Fat Joe's album had been reviewed too early. To have albums reviewed timely, we'd have to get a copy of them early enough to send out to a writer. Sometimes we'd review the albums and they would end up getting pushed back. We tried to have other reviews banked so if we had to switch one out at the last minute, that could get done. In the case of Joe's album, we found out too late that it was getting pushed back, so the review still ran in the magazine. The released album wasn't much different from the one we heard, but Dave said the review wasn't to Fat Joe's liking and he called to complain about it. I never had a problem with Fat Joe, but Dave and Ray said he went off on me—all this stuff about how I never liked him and was purposely trying to give him a bad review. I'm not sure that I believe this, because Dave and Ray have been known to make stuff up just to create issues. Plus, I don't know what on earth Joe could have against me since we always seemed cool in public. Interestingly, he was on their list to testify against me in the case I filed against the *Source*. They never called him to the stand, though, so I'm guessing he either changed his mind or had said, "Hell no," in the first place.

As a result of Ray's unhappiness with the "Record Report" section, he decided that Boo was no longer a loyal supporter and fired him, since the "Record Report" was technically his section. Now, with Boo and Johnnie gone, the editorial staff was left with just a few top editors, with myself and Fahiym at the top.

"You need to start looking for a job," Fahiym said to me in late February of 2005. Then, he scribbled a name and phone number on an orange sticky note before handing it to me. "Here's a name of someone at MTV. I interviewed with her and she's looking for people to help start a new website venture they have coming. I think you would be good for that."

Confused, I took the paper and stuck it to the bottom corner of my computer monitor. I didn't originally intend on calling because I was always embarrassed about approaching people for a job. I felt as if every move I made was being watched. I couldn't do anything without Dave and Ray getting in my business. *Apply for a job?* Yeah, right.

"What, are you tryin' to tell me that I'm about to get fired or something?" I was halfway joking, but job security was always a seious issue at the *Source*.

"Yo, I spoke to Bum the other day, and you're not gonna like what you're about to hear."

I usually trusted Fahiym. I had hired him full-time when I got promoted. "Oh, boy. What are they saying now?" By "they" I meant Dave and Ray, because Bum had been serving as their messenger while they were down in the Dominican Republic shooting a Benzino video.

"He said that Ray and Dave said you can't be the editor in chief because you're out there"—Fahiym paused, seeming embarrassed to continue his sentence—"'out there sleeping with rappers.'" The emphasis was on the word *rappers*.

"Eeh." I spit the Cinnamon Dolce Latte back into my Starbucks cup and immediately let out an annoyed, loud laugh. "Ha. That I sleep with *rappers*?"

"They said that to you?" said Tanya, who was sitting on my couch reading pages.

"Yeah, they said that. I know, I know. It's crazy."

I wasn't surprised that both Ray and Dave had been talking about me behind my back. They felt that since I worked for them, they had the right to know whatever they wanted about me. They couldn't afford me the same respect they did for the male editors that came before me. I have spoken to former male editors of the magazine who were never asked the same questions. So why was my situation so different?

After Fahiym left the office, Tanya and I dissected the conversation that had just taken place. One of our collective talents was to take pieces of information that we gathered from everyone around the office, cut off the fat that came with that information—which usually resulted from the messenger's self-serving agenda—and put it all together so we could decipher the truth.

"It sounds like it came from Ray," Tanya offered.

"I'm heated."

"I know you are. I would be too."

"Why the fuck are they so obsessed with my sex life?" I asked, not expecting a reasonable answer, especially after countless accusations by Ray that I had been sleeping with artists that I had never even met.

"Okay, you know they're not gonna fire you. You do know this. Who else are they gonna get to do your job?"

"That's not the point. How many times is he going to bring this shit up? And now he's telling people on the staff. He's still asking me about rappers all the time. It has nothing to do with anything."

Tanya and I continued our conversation until my aggravation forced me to get back to proofreading the hundred or so pages that were due at the printer. I was exhausted from trying to close up an issue of the magazine, overdosed on Starbucks, and about $40 deep in overtime with the babysitter. By 11:30 p.m., it was time for me to go home.

If I was ever going to make a formal complaint, this was the time to do it. All the inappropriate things were marked down on my mental chalkboard. The estrogen and witches of Eastwick comment, the "Dimepiece" models and the closed-door men's meeting Ray ordered me to put together, the invitation to get with him and go to Atlantic City, the accusations that I was "fucking" people on the staff, the vulgar and racist comments in the office. All of it. Now, this "sleeping with rappers" thing was more than annoying. It was insulting, and it sent me into bold mode.

Later that day, I stopped by Julie's office to get a copy of the "Employee Handbook." In my days at the *Source*, I had never received one. While I was in her office, I sat down and started to confide in her. I told Julie that I needed a copy of the handbook because I needed to do something, and I wanted to make sure I went about it the right way. A lot of words were exchanged between us. She even told me that she had "one foot out the door" herself. At the end of our conversation, she handed me pages from the company handbook, which was not bound. She told me that she needed it back, but I could photocopy it. She said she hadn't given it to employees because she was revising it. Julie seemed sympathetic to the things I was telling her. I took the handbook, photocopied it, and returned it to her. "I'm going to send you an email," I said before I left her office.

As I started to craft my complaint the next morning, a lot of details ran across my mind. I was tempted to file one of my three-page memos and lay it all out. But when I couldn't decide how to say what I needed to say, I made a phone call.

"Listen to this email I'm about to send," I said to Tia, who had the same legal background as me. Tia had a few months earlier suggested that I file a complaint.

"Go ahead. Read it."

Staring at my computer screen, I started to read her what I had already typed. "'As the head of Human Resources . . .'" I paused. "I'm sending it to Julie 'cause that's what—"

"Just read the email."

"'As the head of Human Resources, I am notifying you that I have been discriminated against on the basis of my gender. This unlawful discrimination must come to an end.' That's it. That's all it says."

"That's enough," Tia said. "They're crazy. They can't keep going on and saying things like that about you when they're out there doing worse. So what, if you slept with a couple of guys? What does that have to do with how you do your job? It's completely wrong and they're crazy for accusing you of that. It's none of their business."

Tia always had a way of making a big situation seem minor.

"But what if they fire me for it?"

"If they fire you, they fire you. So what?"

"Okay, cool, so when I can't pay my mortgage because I don't have a job, then I'll just move in with you."

"The email is fine. Send it."

Believing that what I had heard from Fahiym the day before just added to years of unfair treatment, I convinced myself that I was doing the right thing. "You're right. Why do I constantly feel like I'm seventeen and I'm keeping my sex life from my parents or something. I'm a grown-ass woman. They can't do this."

I clicked on send twice and the message box disappeared. It was gone. And there was no taking it back.

"I sent it," I told Tia. "Damn, I sent it."

CHAPTER THIRTY-ONE

rebel without a pause

Two weeks went by before anyone responded to my email. I was nervous. I didn't know whether they had been talking to lawyers or what.

On the Friday before Dave and Ray returned from the Dominican Republic, everyone in the office woke up to a bit of a surprise. Emails were going around via BlackBerry: "The money isn't there." Employees who had direct deposit usually had their bank accounts credited with their paychecks early in the a.m. But on this particular day, no one got paid.

For months, rumors had circulated that the *Source* was closing its doors, and I had been bombarded with calls and messages asking whether this was true. Staff members who were secretly worried about the company folding would come to me and ask. I usually just dismissed it as rumor. At least that's what Dave had told me to do. This time, however, with the paychecks not being in, I became worried myself.

"Fahiym said he ain't coming in," Tanya told me over the phone early that morning.

"Well, I'm on my way to the office, so I'll see you when I get in. I'm sure they'll have our hard checks for us in the office. Why don't you page Julie or Ron Lefkon and see what's going on?"

When I got to the office, an email from Julie said that the *Source* had switched banks, thus delaying the direct deposits. It sounded like a good reason, only Ron Lefkon, the CFO, told us a completely different story.

"I don't know why Julie sent that email, because it's not true," he said to Tanya and me when we bum-rushed his office.

"So what is going on with our checks?! We need our money. We can't get in touch with Dave because he's out of the country, and no one seems to have any answers," I said.

Ron looked bothered. He wasn't saying what we all believed, that our checks weren't in because our money was in the Dominican Republic.

That Friday, most of the staff walked out, not wanting to work as charity. The money showed up in employees' accounts Monday, but that didn't change that the company had somehow missed payroll. It was some ghetto shit. As much as I loved my job, I knew that I couldn't work there for free. I started to reach out to some friends to see if they knew of any job openings. We had all done some crazy things working at the *Source,* printing stories that we didn't stand behind. But when there's no check at the end of the week, that's when following orders has to stop. I was doing what Ray and Dave said because I had to get paid. When they stopped paying me, I had to rethink my loyalty to them.

By the middle of the next week, an email popped up in my in-box, a response to my complaint from Julie. She said that she had mistakenly placed my email in the trash folder and that she wanted to meet when she returned to the office. *Seems a little fishy that she would mistakenly throw away such an important email,* I thought. "In order to bring clarity to your concerns, we will need to discuss the issue in detail," her email read. *Sounds like somebody spoke to a lawyer.* By the time I had seen her response, I had already heard that Dave was looking for me.

Later that day, an attorney for the company asked to have lunch with me as well. "You never want to get to a point at a job when you're sending emails like this," he said to me over lunch at Mangia's, right next door to the office. "You should be able to talk about this first."

But I couldn't talk about it. I told him over lunch that I was even concerned about having a conversation with him about it, because he was the attorney for the company. Although our relationship was cordial, I knew enough to know that lawyers talk to lawyers. And I realized that I wasn't going to be able to talk without my own.

I didn't hear from Ray until I got home that evening.

"What the fuck is this? You don't send no email like this." Ray was yelling at me through Bum's phone, which was the only contact to him in the DR.

"You know we do things loosely around here." *Loose? Is that the word they're using now?* Saying "we do things loosely around here" was Ray's way of acknowledging his disrespectful behavior.

Ray continued his rampage, obviously upset that I had dared to even put it down on paper. "As much as everybody has done for you, Kim, how could you send an email like this! You make the most. Fucking. Money."

The problem with working at the *Source* was that you could never get any credit for doing a good job. Ray looked at it as if he were doing you a favor. "I just needed to send this email so you would take my complaint seriously."

My response really pissed him off. "Fuck these emails. I could send an email too. I could hang up this phone and you would never have to hear or see me again. You need to do another email. Yeah, we got issues, but you take it and you move on. You don't send no fuckin' email like this. You're opening up these cans of worms. Take it back, Kim," he said. "If you don't like the way we do shit over here, then you can step down." It didn't matter that I couldn't get a word in, because Ray seemed like he didn't want to hear what I had to say. So I took a big gulp to push my fear from my throat to my stomach.

"I'm not taking it back, Ray. We should sit down and talk about this." I was trying to remain calm, but I was focused on writing down everything he said.

"I'm not sitting down with you about that. I don't got to sit down with you." Ray continued to yell, but the more quiet I was, the more he went on. I wasn't saying what he wanted to hear, and I wasn't telling him I would take the email back, so he started to try another approach instead of yelling.

"You know what, Kim? I look at you like someone that we've grown into a certain kind of relationship. Don't do this shit, disregard that shit. You're raising red flags that don't need to be raised. We got a lot of good shit. Email Julie back and disregard it. Send that email back."

Ray's intimidation tactics weren't working. I couldn't take the email back now, because if they were going to fire me for it, they were going to do it regardless.

A few hours later, Dave called, asking, referring to the retraction, "Did you send the email?"

"I never said I was sending an email."

"My understanding was that you were going to do that right away."

They were trying to pressure me into sending a retraction, but I wouldn't send it because what I was saying was true.

Dave was a little more diplomatic in his response to my email. "This is a form of assault on my company. You have every opportunity to talk to me. Julie works for me. You have something that you want to talk about, then you talk to me. You don't go to Julie."

In a normal company, a complaint with Human Resources would be the right move to make, but at the *Source*, there was no concept of employment law. It was all about Dave and Ray. As an employee, you did what they said or you bit the dust.

Although he was telling me to send a retraction, I figured he must have been acting under orders from Ray, because Dave had to have talked to his lawyer before speaking to me. Even though ordering me to send another email did not sound like good legal advice that he would have gotten from any lawyer, he continued, and I knew the only person who could influence him to do that was Ray.

"This is a very aggressive step on your part. This is what you're going to do," Dave instructed. "If you don't send the email, then you're going to turn in your resignation."

Frustrated at my lack of control over the situation, I remained quiet. "I'm not going to take it back. This is something that we can talk about in person," I responded, holding the tear ducts from bursting in my eyes.

"I'm not sitting down and talking to you about any of this. I don't have to. This is my magazine. I can run it the way I want." Dave sounded like a tape-recorded, cleaner version of Ray. For years, every time I had had an idea that went against their agenda, I was reminded of their ownership interest. This time, they clearly believed their interest gave them the power to be above the law, no matter what the cost. "We can finish this conversation when we get back from the Dominican Republic."

In my five years at the company, they had done a long list of things that had made me uncomfortable. In my desire to get ahead at the company, I had let it all go and sometimes even complied. From the inappropriate comments to the harassment to the physical threats I'd received from coworkers, I was willing to deal with all of it to maintain my job at the magazine. I had complained about all of it many times before, whether it be to coworkers or to the Human Resources department. Everyone knew that was just the way things went at the *Source*. But now that I had made a formal complaint in writing, it was about to get ugly, and from their reaction I could tell that my end at the company was near.

The next Tuesday, I was at a meeting at J Records when I saw my phone light up with Dave's name. *They must be back in the States,* I thought. So I stepped out of my meeting at about 8 p.m. and took the phone call. I stood outside the door, listening to Dave.

"Um, uhhhh. Did you send an email taking it back?" Dave was stuttering, so I knew Ray was around him.

"No. I told you I wasn't going to send an email." My voice cracked a little when I answered him because I felt that something bad was about to happen. After a silence, I heard some shuffling in the background. It sounded as if someone had grabbed the phone.

Ray's extremely loud voice took over. "Oh, you not gonna send an email? Okay, okay, well, then you need to be outta here then."

"Are you firing me?" As vague and ambiguous as they could be, this was my job and I needed clarity. It was so easy for him to throw his power around, and it made me furious to know that he didn't really give two shits about me or my job after everything I had put into it.

"Yeah, that's right, you're fired." Ray hung up, and just like that, my conversation was over, and so was my career at the *Source*. I was worried about my next step and how I would make my next mortgage payment, but in a weird sort of way, I felt as if the weight of the world had been lifted off my shoulders. No more bullshit from Dave and Ray! I never said I would take the email back because I couldn't. I had to stand for something, and I didn't know where I was going to take it from there.

In the days following, I had a lot of time to think about my next move. Obviously. (It's not as if I had any job possibilities.) Because I believed that everything that had happened was against the law, I met with Ken Thompson again and decided to retain him as my attorney. He told me quite frankly, "You have a strong case for discrimination and retaliation, but before you go forward, think about it. Is this really something that you want to do?" Think. I had no choice. I wasn't like the other women who felt that the climate at the *Source* was discriminatory but weren't going to do anything about it but complain. I complained, and they retaliated. It was simple math to me. A lawsuit was my next step. I knew it wouldn't be easy, but in the end it was a step I had to take. Not for any monetary recovery, but because of the principle. *Who were they for me to let them back me down?* Firing me was the same as daring me to sue them. That's how much power they thought they had. Someone had to do something.

"This is something I have to do," I told Ken at our meeting. "But they are going to come after me. They are going to say horrible things. They'll call me all types of hos and bitches, in public, and make me look like I was incompetent. I know these guys. I've spent years watching how they think."

Ken was shocked. I don't think he believed that the case would have to go to trial. But I always knew it would. "Trust me, Ken, this case is going to go all the way," I said. "But I'm up for it."

I had dedicated years to the magazine, and I couldn't let it end with my just being fired. I had spent years writing about the beefs in hip-hop, and now I was about to make history by becoming one.

epilogue

I have heard people in the music industry say that you are only as good
as your last big hit, or in the case of people like me behind the scenes,
you are only as good as your last big gig. To those people, I say, "Get a
clue." A job could never make me, I make the job.

In April of 2005, I filed a complaint with the EEOC, the Equal
Employment Opportunity Commission, against the *Source* and Dave
Mays and Raymond Scott as individual defendants. Without getting
into the legal mumbo jumbo of it all, filing with the EEOC was a
formality to bring my case in federal court. My trial began in October of
2006 and lasted a little over two weeks. In the end, I won on retaliation
and defamation, with the jury awarding me $7.5 million in damages
(although it was originally reported at $15.5 million, which is what we
all believed to be the right amount when we left the courtroom).

The defamation claim stemmed from remarks that Ray made about
me in the months following my termination. He said that I was trying to
extort the company by sending my email. He also said that I was having

sex with artists, a remark that made me seem promiscuous. Although he had his suspicions about Nas and 50 and accused me of being involved with other artists, he never named any of them by name, because he didn't know anything for sure. My assumption about that has always been—as much as he thought he was bold by trying to put me on blast in his interviews—he wasn't brave enough to say anything to or about the men that could have been involved, which further proves my point that he is chauvinistic. The *Source* did, though, name them in my case. Imagine the humiliation of having to relive the Sway/Hot 97 interview all over again.

Despite being successful on those two claims, I will never be able to recover my reputation as a woman. And although the girls and I in the network can, as one of my friends jokes, walk up to so many men in the industry and embarrass them by holding our hands up in front of them as a measure of how big or small we know they are, the truth is that I will never be able to shake my image in the eyes of some people as the girl who slept with a bunch of rappers. I don't regret anything—or anyone—I've done (okay, well, maybe there is one, but that's another book), but I wouldn't change any of it. Some moments in the courtroom were humiliating, but in the end I knew it was all done for the right reasons.

I love talking to women about my case because so many of them understand what I went through. When I went back to work after the trial, women were applauding and shouting in the hallways when they saw me. It reinforces my belief that I did the right thing. Still, some men, for the most part, just don't get it. I will sit for hours trying to convince them that they are wrong for judging a professional woman by what she does in private. The difference between how men and women view my situation is crazy to me.

Sometimes I think the hip-hop industry is a bit antiquated in its thinking. As if it's 1920 or something. When I look at other industries, what's on television, and what we consume as Americans, I wonder why the hip-hop circle is so damn judgmental. From the conversations I've had with many people, most of them believe that Dave and Ray were stone-cold lunatics in how they ran the magazine. But throughout it all, the industry supported them, then quietly cheered as they were fired from their posts a year after they fired me. And there were even some women that may have supported the *Source*'s cause just because they had their own issues with me.

I learned a big lesson from working at the *Source*. I try to tell people now that the work you do speaks louder than the place where you work. One day in my office I had a meeting with someone who asked me what I would do once I left the *Source*. I said that I didn't know how to continue my career if I left. I felt that I would be like an intern again because there was nowhere that I could go from there. "You may not always have this place, but you will always have those," he said, pointing to a stack of magazines on my desk.

"The work you do will always speak for you, no matter where you work at," I was told. I could see the faces pictured on the magazines staring back at me. All whose stories I had documented from my own point of view, sometimes great and sometimes not so great. But in the end, stories that I knew others could relate to.